THE CLARETIANS

Their Mission and Spirit in the Church

The Claretians

Their Mission and Spirit in the Church

JOHN M. LOZANO, C.M.F.

Translated by
JOSEPH DARIES, C.M.F.
from the original manuscript in Spanish

Claret Center for Resources in Spirituality

RELIGIOUS LIFE SERIES

Volume One

Chicago, 1980

© 1980 by Claretian Publications
221 West Madison Street, Chicago, Illinois 60606, U.S.A.

Printed in the United States of America
Library of Congress Catalog Card Number: 80-65044

This is a translation by Joseph Daries, C.M.F.
from the original manuscript in Spanish.

Contents

Chapter III

A Congregation of Missionaries

Chapter IV

The Ministry of the Word

Chapter V

Apostolic Life

Chapter IX

The Cofounders: Fathers Xifré and Clotet

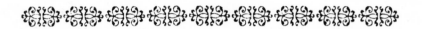

Foreword

In the summer of 1967 the book *Misión y Espíritu del Claretiano en la Iglesia* was published in Rome. It was a rather full study dealing in its first part with the founder, the cofounders, and basic documents for a study of the Claretian Congregation. From this it went on to investigate the mission, ministries, and nature of the Congregation, as well as the type of community that characterizes it. The third part analyzed the fundamental traits of the Claretian spirit, ending with an overall projection within an ecclesial framework.

The book appeared in the clearly defined context of preparations for the Special Chapter to be held in September 1967, when the Claretians, in keeping with the mandate of Vatican II, would attempt to search out their original inspiration. During this period before the Chapter there was agreement in essentials, although there were a number of conflicting interpretations of what Claretian life and vocation should mean, many of which would surface at the Chapter itself. The author of the book, as a member of the central preparatory commission for the Chapter, wished to offer his colleagues a generous selection of texts and data relating to what the founder, cofounders, and successive

General Chapters and superiors have had to say concerning Claretian identity. In fact, he himself used these data as the basis for his own incipient theological reflections. The context in which it was written left its mark upon the book, although it still contains much that is valid today.

The situation of the Congregation has greatly changed since then. Many of the ideas that were fought for at the General Chapters of 1967 and 1973 have since become an integral part of the prevailing self-image of the Claretians.

In 1968 the author answered the first invitation to give a series of conferences to the Claretians of both United States Provinces. It was his first contact with an area of the Congregation that had contributed effectively to pre-Chapter dialogue and had carried some weight at the Chapter itself. In the years that followed the invitation was repeated a number of times until, in 1974, a position as Visiting Professor of Spirituality, first at St. Louis University and then at Loyola University of Chicago, brought him to live with the novices and scholastics of the Eastern Province. Incardinated into the Province in 1975, the author is presently a member of Claretian House of Studies in Chicago.

By this move, the author brought his rather weary bones to rest in this America, this "young vineyard" where St. Anthony Claret, as an old and broken man, would have liked to have spent his last days working for the Kingdom of God. This American experience has been an incisive one for the author in many ways. His contacts with novices and students have forced him to attempt a reformulation of the Claretian vocation in terms not necessarily tied to his own cultural origins, terms that must take into account the different ecclesial and theological context in which this new generation lives and moves.

The present book, although it picks up some of the themes treated in its predecessor and even reproduces some formerly published materials, is really a new study. Chapters I and VIII are totally new. Chapter II reproduces the introduction to "Documents of the Apostolic Fraternity," in the author's edition of *Constituciones y Textos sobre la Congregación de Misioneros,* with a few additional pages. Chapters III through VII reproduce chapters from the author's earlier work, *Misión y Espíritu del Claretiano en la Iglesia,* with additions, deletions, and changes in format. The additions lengthen and deepen the reflections begun in 1967. The deletions mainly involve texts from the tradition that came after the founder's time, preserving only the more important statements of two of the cofounders—Fathers Xifré and Clotet—and a few isolated texts from some of the later superiors general. The reason for this is that we no longer feel the same need as in 1967 to insist on demonstrating the continuity of an idea throughout the history of our General Chapters and superiors. It is more than sufficient for us to affirm, by way of precise dates and unequivocal texts, the idea which the founder had of his institute. This has led to the discarding of many secondary elements, with a resultant gain in simplicity and clarity.

Apart from this, a number of important studies have appeared since the Special Chapter of 1967. In 1970, Fr. José M. Gil published his two-volume edition of the correspondence of St. Anthony Claret, the *Epistolario Claretiano.* In 1972 the author of the present work published the critical edition of the *Constitutions* and other texts by the founder, relating to the Congregation. Somewhat earlier, he had brought out a study on the spirituality of Fr. James Clotet, a cofounder, followed by another on the religious experience of Mother Antonia Paris, the foundress of the Claretian Sisters. This last-mentioned work occasioned the discovery of a number of secondary but significant data that affected the evolution of the Claretian Congregation before its founding. The present book uses all of these investigations, but it is also the fruit of the author's personal reflection during these past years.

In this edition, Fr. Joseph Daries offers us his English translation of the original, unpublished Spanish text. Whoever has read his translations of Claret's *Autobiography,* the author's *Mystic and Man of Action,* and Bishop Casaldaliga's *I Believe in Justice and Hope* will already be familiar with his abilities. The author of this book is most grateful to Fr. Daries for his friendly and patient collaboration.

It only remains for us to offer our work and that of Fr. Daries to the English-speaking Claretians, especially the novices and students.

J. M. L.

Preface

The church, in recent years, has encouraged religious communities to initiate new studies to rediscover and to live more accurately the charism of their founders. The grace that the Lord has given to His people in the life and genius of these outstanding men and women is too precious to be misdirected or lost in time.

Claretian Publications is pleased to present this history and study of the Claretians by John M. Lozano, C.M.F. Through his careful research and analysis of the manner in which the Claretians have nurtured the spirit of their founder, St. Anthony Mary Claret, the Claretians today have been given new impetus to keep alive the graceful life of St. Anthony Mary Claret. In this time when we, the church, will never return to the former great numbers of men and women in religious life, it becomes even more essential for those in religious communities to bring forward the particular grace and richness of variety represented in their founders.

Claretian Publications hopes this will be the first in a series of studies on religious communities and their living out the charism of their founders.

James F. Maloney, C.M.F.

I

A Founder's Vocation

The history of nearly all religious institutes begins chronologically with the vocation of one person. Fr. Jerome Nadal perceived this clearly at the outset of his reflections on the origins of the Company of Jesus.[1] Even the most cursory review of the history of the religious life would soon lead us to the conclusion that there is more involved in the founding of a religious institute than its mere material beginning. Take a sample listing: Basil, Augustine, Benedict and Scholastica, Norbert, Dominic, Francis and Clare, Philip Neri, Ignatius, Teresa, Vincent de Paul and Louise de Marillac, Francis de Sales and Jane Frances de Chantal, Madeline Sophie Barat, Anthony Claret and Mother Antonia Paris, Don Bosco, Isaac Hecker, Mother Seton and Mother Cabrini. What a wealth of personality and religious experience these names (and countless others we could list) evoke! However, it is enough to give us some inkling of the extent to which the lives of a number of religious families have depended on these initial outbursts of grace. This is doubtless why St. John of the Cross, in his commentary on the second stanza of *The Living Flame of Love*,[2] states that God has reserved the

1

highest graces for founders. A founder's grace is essentially a grace of spiritual fecundity or fruitfulness.

We have dealt with this theme at some length elsewhere.[3] In this study we will restrict our considerations to the relationship between the charism of a religious family and the charism of its founder. By *charisms* we mean the different gifts of the Spirit granted to various Christians for the common building up of the church. This seems to be St. Paul's basic concept of a charism, but we would like to narrow the concept somewhat for our present purposes. What we obviously do not mean are those *gratiae gratis datae* that are transient manifestations of the Spirit—which could be received both by founders and some of their spiritual sons or daughters—but, rather, we mean permanent gifts that define the vocation of various different Christians in the church. This is, we might add, the precise sense that Paul tends to attribute to the category of charism: the gift given to some makes them apostles, while the gift given to others makes them prophets or teachers (1 Cor. 12:8-11, 28-30; Rom. 12:6-8; Eph. 4:11-13). Some have a gift for celibacy; others, for matrimony (1 Cor. 7:7). These are vocational charisms. In this sense, Vatican II applies the concept of gift to the typical traits of the religious life, the "counsels,"[4] and then goes on to apply the concept of gift, within the religious life, to various forms of that life.[5] Paul VI referred frequently to the founder's charism[6] and to the fidelity of religious institutes to that charism, in several allocutions.

Charism, in this context, is the gift of the Spirit that calls and moves a founder to a particular mission in the church and prepares him for it. Initially, the founder or foundress discovers this gift as a personal calling to a kind of life or ministry in the church. Later, he or she discovers the vocation to establish a religious family that will follow the same rule of life or be dedicated to the same ministry. Either spontaneously or at the invitation of the founder, a group of disciples or companions realize that they have received the same call from God as the founder has, and they join forces with him. The founder's gift then appears as the gift of a whole religious family.

Since this charism gives a religious institute its origin (in the theological, not necessarily the canonical, sense), it involves some elements that are common to all forms of the religious life (such as exclusive commitment to the service of God and the following of Christ, with celibacy and common life, poverty and sharing of goods, and obedience), as well as specific elements that refer to the particular spirit, rule of life, and ministries of those who receive it. In the case of institutes founded for apostolic or charitable ministries, the call to these works is usually the first element to appear in the founder and the group. In such cases, the religious life arises as a form of existence oriented toward this special service of God in His church. The ministry of evangelization, Christian education, or care of the sick first appears as a personal vocation of founders or foundresses, and this vocation becomes more precisely crystallized and pressing, until they are convinced that God is calling them to establish a new, permanent institution in the church.

The popes have frequently ascribed the idea for founding an institute to an inspiration, light, and movement of the Spirit received by its founder.[7] Vatican II has stressed the need to remain faithful to this "original inspiration."[8] What is the basis of this need? Simply the fact that it concerns a charism of the Spirit granted for the good of the whole church. The church is embellished and strengthened by the variety of religious institutes, by the multiplicity of schools and spheres of spirituality, and by the diversity of ministries. These are simply different modes of being and building church. Fidelity to one's own identity is nothing less than fidelity to the Spirit of the Lord who calls, and an expression of love towards His Spouse. Fidelity to one's original inspiration does not mean a material repetition of what the founder did in another age or milieu but, rather, fidelity to his spirit and intention; since what the founder did materially is not necessarily the only possible expression of his vocation but simply the best he could do under the circumstances in which he received his calling. We must never forget that a charism is a gift of the Holy Spirit; and, as we know, the Holy Spirit is God, who gives life, renews the face of the earth, and restores dry bones to life. A charism is, hence, a creative energy, which throughout history impels communities to undertake new initiatives for the good of the church.

Anthony Claret

The history of the Claretians, like that of nearly all religious institutes, begins with the vocation of one person, their founder. St. Anthony Mary Claret was born in Sallent, Catalonia, Spain, on December 23, 1807, and died in the Cistercian Monastery of Fontfroide, Aude, France, on October 24, 1870. He was first a textile worker and designer; then a priest (1835); a missionary in Catalonia and the Canary Islands (1841-1850); Archbishop of Santiago, Cuba (1851-1857); Confessor of Isabel II of Spain (1857-1868); and a member of the First Vatican Council (1869-1870). He founded two Congregations, one for men and the other for women; established the basis for a secular institute for women; founded the Religious Library publishing company, the Spiritual Fraternity of Good Books, the first licensed credit unions in Latin America, and the Academy of St. Michael for Catholic intellectuals and artists. Finally, he promoted popular lending libraries, wrote more than ninety books and short works, and edited some thirty more.

Personally, Anthony Claret was a very active man, of a practical bent and a passionate temperament. Although he had an above-average intelligence, circumstances prevented him from obtaining any deep intellectual formation; but he made up for this by assiduous reading. He read a great deal, with an eye to those productive ideas that could help his apostolate or enrich his interior life. Although he was much inclined to activity, he was a man of few words. He was a strange mixture of volitional tenacity and sentiment. His spiritual life bore all of the earmarks of 19th-century religiosity: predominance of private forms of prayer, an ascetic methodology, and austerity, all of them seasoned with devotional piety. The action of the Spirit continually drew him toward the essential. He felt the powerful effect of the Word of God in his Bible readings and savored the action of Christ in the liturgy and, above all, His presence in the Eucharist. The main thrust of his asceticism focused on the imitation of Christ. He always felt a vibrant filial love toward the Mother of the Lord and closely associated her with his apostolate. But he was, before all else, an apostle. Even his interior experience was oriented toward apostolic service. He was keenly aware of the presence and movement of the Spirit within him.

Anthony Claret happened to live in a period of transition and, for that very reason, a period of crisis. His homeland, Catalonia, was being transformed into an industrialized country. This brought a great wave of migrants from the agrarian and conservative interior to the industrial and liberal coastal zones, with their great cities and towns. Spain was locked in a struggle to free itself of the monarchical *ancien regime,* which meant both the throne and the altar. There was an alternation of constitutional and royalist governments, popular outcries and military manifestos. Until 1848 a good part of the bishops and lesser clergy were royalists, and the church possessed a considerable part of the land. To create a modern state, the liberals would have to clash with the church. The church had reasons enough to distrust the liberals, with their Encyclopedist ideas and their anticlericalism. Religious and political motives were closely intertwined in the contest. All religious institutes were suppressed in 1835, the year of Claret's ordination to the priesthood. By 1841 only five of the sixty Spanish dioceses were actually governed by bishops. The rest of the bishops had either died off and not been replaced or had been forced into exile. The vacancies created by the fall of old institutions began to be filled up, especially after 1848, by new religious congregations, especially congregations of women dedicated to welfare and education. The church began to recover its life, and in 1851 a new Concordat was signed between the Holy See and the Queen of Spain. It was in this historic and social context that Anthony Claret had to live and work.

Discovery of His Vocation

Claret began to have a clear awareness of his vocation when he was twenty-three years old. We could say, then, that he was an adult vocation. As usually happens, he had gone through some experiences that had marked him deeply. When he was only five, the thought of eternity kept him awake at night worrying about people being condemned to hell forever. As an adolescent of twelve his piety quickened intensely, and he felt a desire to become a priest. He had to abandon his studies, however, because his clerical tutors died. Then, when he was eighteen, like so many young men of his age, he felt the urge to build a career in business and went to the big city—Barcelona—where he experienced great success at work but also had a number of close brushes with evil, which led him to rethink his life. He had been offered the directorship of a good-sized textile factory, but decided to run away from it all to enter the Carthusians. Meanwhile, he enrolled in the Seminary of Vic, to take a few prerequisite studies before going to the Carthusians. He soon perceived that this was not his real calling, so he continued in the seminary to prepare himself for the diocesan priesthood.

During a period that began with a powerful temptation against chastity from which he was freed by a vision of the Blessed Virgin, he began to discern his future with greater precision, thanks to his reading of the Bible. Following the recommendation of his bishop, Don Pablo Corcuera, Anthony had begun the practice of reading three or four chapters of the Bible daily. This was the first time that he had read it all the way through. He found some passages hard to understand, while others delighted him with their simplicity, and still others attracted him because of the vividness of their Semitic imagery. There was a long series of texts, however, that moved him deeply. He has left us a record of these experiences: ". . . what moved and stimulated me most was reading the Holy Bible, to which I have always been very strongly attracted."[9] St. Athanasius wrote that the great hermit, St. Anthony, felt "as though God had inspired his thought of the saints and the passage had been read aloud on his account."[10] In fact, young Claret experienced something very similar: "There were passages that impressed me so deeply that I seemed to hear a voice telling me the message I was reading. . . . He [the Lord] said to me. . . ."[11] The young man felt called, illumined on his mission and impelled to give himself over to it. Note that this phenomenon went on repeatedly over the course of seven or eight years, that is, until he had finished his studies in 1839 and was thus free to dedicate himself to his task. This means, in effect, that the Bible presided over his formation during the last years of his youth and the first years of his adulthood.

The Crucial Biblical Texts

Obviously, if we examine the texts which struck him most deeply during this period in which he was discovering his vocation, we will be able to form an idea of the type of life and ecclesial ministry to which he was being called. Claret has left us three successive lists of these texts. The first was written on a separate sheet of paper, dating from about the time he had his original experiences. Later, after he had been made archbishop, he added a heading to this list: "I understood this when I was a young student [*estudiantito*]." The second list was written in 1856 in Cuba, a period when he was undecided about his future and when he and Mother Antonia Paris received some illuminations that led him to reflect on the ways along which the Lord had been leading him. Finally, the third list forms Chapter I of Part II of his *Autobiography,* which is dedicated to narrating the story of his vocation.

The texts in question are from Isaiah, Ezekiel, and Luke. In the table that follows on pages 8-10, the reader can graphically see which texts appear, respectively, in List I (Ms. Claret), List II (Resume) and List III (*Autobiography*). If a verse extends across the entire page, it indicates that it appears in all three lists; otherwise, it appears only under the list(s) to which it is peculiar.

Since Claret himself has told us that there were many biblical passages through which he kept hearing the call of God, we should not be surprised that one list contains texts that the others do not. It was not his intention in any of these lists to give us a complete enumeration. It is clear that in his *Autobiography* he only wished to offer a representative sampling of those texts that best expressed the central aspects of his vocation: Isaiah 41:9-17 and Luke 4:18 (the vocation of the Servant-Prophet), Ezekiel 3:17-19 (solidarity with the sinner). The most impressive text for Claret was Luke 4:18, in which Christ applies Isaiah 61:1 to Himself. Following this in importance comes a series of texts relating to the prophetic vocation: Isaiah 41:9-17 was important enough to figure in all three lists; Isaiah 48:10 was particularly applicable to a man who was destined for great persecution in his ministry; Isaiah 49:3 was indicative of his

	Ms. Claret	Resume	Autobiography

Isaiah 41:8   But you, Israel, my servant,
                Jacob, whom I have chosen, the
                offspring of Abraham, my friend;

41:9   you whom I took from the ends of the earth, and called
       from its farthest corners, saying to you, "You are my
       servant, I have chosen you and not cast you off";

41:10 fear not, for I am with you, be not dismayed, for I am
       your God; I will strengthen you, I will help you, I will
       uphold you with my victorious right hand.

41:11 Behold, all who are incensed against you shall be put to
       shame and confounded; those who strive against you shall
       be as nothing and shall perish.

41:12 You shall seek those who contend
       with you, but you shall not find
       them; those who war against you
       shall be as nothing at all.

41:13 For I, the Lord your God, hold your right hand; it is I
       who say to you, "Fear not, I will help you."

41:14 Fear not, you worm Jacob, you
       men of Israel! I will help you,
       says the Lord; your Redeemer
       is the Holy One of Israel.

41:15 Behold, I will make of you a threshing sled, new, sharp,
       and having teeth; you shall thresh the mountains and
       crush them, and you shall make the hills like chaff;

41:16 you shall winnow them and the wind shall carry them
       away, and the tempest shall scatter them. And you shall
       rejoice in the Lord; in the Holy One of Israel you shall
       glory.

41:17 When the poor and the needy seek water, and there is
       none, and their tongue is parched with thirst, I the Lord
       will answer them. I the God of Israel will not forsake
       them.

		Ms. Claret	Resume	Autobiography
Isaiah	41:18			I will open rivers on the bare heights, and fountains in the midst of valleys; I will make the wilderness a pool of water, and the dry land springs of water.
	48:10	Behold, I have refined you, but not like silver; I have tried you in the furnace of affliction.		
	48:11	For my own sake, for my own sake, I do it, for how should my name be profaned? My glory I will not give to another.		
	49:3		And he said to me "You are my servant, Israel, in whom I will be glorified."	
	61:1			The Spirit of the Lord God is upon me, because the Lord has anointed me to bring good tidings to the poor; he has sent me to heal the broken-hearted. (Cf. Lk. 4:18)
Ezekiel	3:17			Son of man, I have made you a watchman for the house of Israel; whenever you hear a word from my mouth, you shall give them warning from me.
	3:18			If I say to the wicked, "You shall surely die," and you give him no warning, nor speak to warn the wicked from his wicked way, in order to save his life, that wicked man shall die in his iniquity; but his blood I will require at your hand.

	Ms. Claret	*Resume*	*Autobiography*
Ezekiel 3:19			But if you warn the wicked, and he does not turn from his wickedness, or from his wicked way, he shall die in his iniquity; but you will have saved your life.
Luke 2:48	And his mother said to him, "Son, why have you treated us so? Behold, your father and I have been looking for you anxiously."		
2:49	And he said to them, "How is it that you sought me? Did you not know that I must be in my Father's house?"		
9:58	And Jesus said to him, "Foxes have holes, and birds of the air have nests; but the Son of man has nowhere to lay his head."		

awareness of being a servant; Ezekiel 3:17-19 was both an expression of his sense of solidarity with the sinner (as noted above) and a further motive for his deep sense of the urgency in the apostolate. We must also note the Lukan texts (2:48-49 and 9:58) which appear in the first two lists.

We have mentioned these texts here to call attention to the biblical passages that lighted his way during his young manhood. Later, when he was archbishop, he would receive some further illuminations concerning his mission and these, in turn, would recall to his mind the memory of further texts. We would like to include a consideration of this later series of texts in our commentary on the series we have just enumerated.

Content of the Texts

In these extraordinary experiences, which left an indelible mark on the personality of Anthony Claret, there were obviously some elements that were strictly personal, with reference to the manner in which they were produced or the impression they caused in the subject. For example, the repetition of the "I am" in Isaiah 41 seems to have produced in Claret both the sensation of ineffable and majestic presence and a sense of contact with the protective power of God. Years later, in 1859, he was to feel the power of this "I am" in Jesus' words to the Samaritan woman, to the Apostles, and to Saul; and, in the Old Testament, in the words of the Lord to Moses.[12] All of those to whom these words were addressed were converted into prophets and evangelizers, as Claret noted in his comment on these passages. *why not?* This aspect of his vocational experiences is strictly personal and, hence, nontransferable to others. For this very reason we need not be concerned about it here, since we are interested in Claret precisely inasmuch as he was the receiver of a charism transmitted to other men and women who have been able to identify with him in this charism as their founder. But these texts that we have been dealing with do have certain constants or, if you will, certain points of convergence that manifest the sort of vocation the Saint had—a vocation that was to become mission for his sons and daughters in the church.

There seem, in fact, to be three points of convergence in these texts:

1. *Some of these texts—among them the ones that moved Claret most deeply—relate to Christ.* We have noted that Claret felt moved and illumined above all by Isaiah 61:1, but precisely in the rereading it receives in Luke 4:18. This is highly noteworthy, not only because the suppression of Isaiah's "year of vengeance" bathes Luke's text in the light of pure grace and mercy but, more profoundly, because it represents an oracle that Jesus uses to explain his mission to others and probably, too, to formulate that mission verbally within his own psyche. The words of Isaiah were quoted in Jesus' first sermon in the synagogue of Nazareth (Luke 4:18) and in His response to the disciples of John the Baptizer (Matt. 11:5; Luke 7:22). This

oracle also seems to be related to the Lukan form of the Beatitudes (Luke 6:20-23) and, in combination with Isaiah 41:1, seems to shine through in the Baptismal theophany, which is pervaded by the theology of the Servant-Prophet.[13] The influence of this text was central in Claret's life, and seems to have continued throughout his life. During some enlightenments he received while at prayer in 1859, the same oracle with some added verses came to his consciousness.[14] When he transcribed these lights in his *Autobiography,* he applied them to his missionaries: "The Lord told me, both for myself and for all these Missionary companions of mine...."[15] We are dealing here, then, with a biblical text that in the mind of the founder defines the vocation of his Congregation in the church.

The remaining two Christological texts are Luke 2:48, where Jesus says that He is consecrated to His Father's business, and Luke 9:58, where Jesus tells a would-be follower about His own rootless and itinerant lifestyle.

We can conclude, then, that in Claret's vocational experiences Christ appears basically as the Servant-Prophet, anointed by the Spirit to preach the Good News to the poor and, for that very reason, leading a difficult and unstable way of life. For Claret, this was the meaning of being consecrated "to the Father's business."

2. *All of these texts refer to the prophetic vocation.* We have just seen how the Christological texts point in this direction. In Isaiah 41:8-18 Israel appears collectively as the Servant of Yahweh, an image that in the saint's interpretation is invested with distinctly prophetic traits. The "threshing sled" is for him (although he does not expressly say so) the "two-edged sword" of God's Word. He also interprets the water that refreshes the parched tongues of the poor in the new Exodus as the living water of the Gospel.[16] Isaiah 49:3 is in the second Song of the Servant of Yahweh, and here the imagery is prophetic, even in the literal sense. Later, we will reflect at some length on this fact. Some of the prophetic texts in which Anthony Claret gradually discerned his vocation refer to the mission of the Suffering Servant. As we will see, the image of Christ Himself appears in his vocational experiences with the traits of the Servant of Yahweh.

Years later, in September 1859, Archbishop Claret received
some new enlightenments in prayer concerning his vocation.
These illuminations also called to his mind a series of biblical
texts, all of them relating to the prophetic vocation, both in the
Old and the New Testaments: "My word is not my own" (John
14:24); "See! I am putting my words into your mouth" (Jer.
1:9); "The Spirit of your Father will be speaking in you" (Matt.
10:20); "The Spirit of the Lord is upon me, because the Lord
has anointed me to bring good tidings to the poor; he has sent
me to heal the brokenhearted" (Luke 4:18 = Isa. 61:1). These
texts are cited in *Escritos Espirituales,* in the section entitled
"Luces y Gracias," for the year 1859, p. 636 f. Almost thirty
years after his youthful vocational experiences, then, we find
him reliving this prophetic call in two biblical texts relating to
the call of two of the greatest prophets (Isa. 61 and Jer. 1), together with a third text taken from the missionary discourse
(Matt. 10). But note that even in these cases the prophetic mission of Jesus constitutes the real core of Claret's experience.
The series of texts opens and closes with accompanying Christological texts. The first, taken from the discourse at the Last
Supper, presents Christ as the prophet of the Father. The last
(Isa. 61) is cited by way of Luke 4, where it forms the basis for
the first sermon of Jesus in the synagogue at Nazareth.

The idea of a prophetic mission accompanied him all his life.
In founding the Congregation he proposed this idea to his first
companions as a source of inspiration. In the second talk for the
founding retreat, concerning vocation and mission, he cites the
call of the Apostles and Paul, but also adds the missions of Jeremiah (Jer. 1:4-10), Isaiah (Isa. 6:8-9), and Moses (Exod. 3:1-12).
Furthermore, as a point of departure for the whole talk he chose
a text in which Paul describes his own mission (Gal. 1:16) in
clearly prophetic terms that echo Jeremiah 1:5 and Isaiah 49:1.[17]
In his *Autobiography,* Claret presents the prophets and apostles—
especially St. Paul—as examples and incentives to help his missionaries understand their own vocation.[18]

Among the prophetic texts that shaped his youthful personality, one—Ezekiel 3:17-19—stresses the prophet's responsibility
for the salvation or loss of his brethren. We know that when
Claret was only five years old, he shuddered at the thought of

those who were eternally lost and that the salvation or perdition of his neighbors was always a powerful incentive for him.[19] Now this text from Ezekiel brought home to him the notion that his own salvation was linked with his efforts at cooperating with God for the salvation of others. In the chapter on incentives and examples that moved him to preach, Claret portrays Jeremiah as the "lover of the brethren and of the people of Israel," and states that "the principal trait of this great prophet was his tender-hearted love for his neighbor, a charity full of compassion for both their temporal and spiritual need, a charity that never let him rest."[20]

The prophetic vocation, then, involves a twofold relationship: with God and with our fellow humans. In this connection, the notion of "mediation"—in the service of God and in favor of humanity—enters into the overall picture of Claret's vocation. The Saint was to develop this notion more explicitly at a later period in his life. In a series of biblical texts that he found particularly helpful for his prayer and reflection, Claret cites two from Ezekiel, on the prophet's responsibility and his mediative function: "You did not step into the breach, nor did you build a wall of prayer about the house of Israel. . . . I have searched among them for someone who would build a wall or stand in the breach to keep me by his prayers from destroying the land; but I found no one" (Ezek. 13:5; 22:30). And Claret goes on to say: "I am nothing, Lord, yet like Moses I want to pray: 'Pardon, then, the wickedness of this people. . . .'" (Num. 14:19).[21] The image of Moses with hands upheld on behalf of his people was always very dear to him,[22] and it flashed through his mind when his duties at the court of Madrid prevented him from launching out on missionary campaigns.

3. Finally, there are three texts that speak of the poor and of poverty. Isaiah 41:17 refers to the sufferings of the poor, and promises a new Exodus in which the desert will be transformed into a garden. Claret understood by this that his prophetic ministry was willed by God as a means of supplying living water to the poor who thirst for grace.[23] In Luke 4:18, Christ, citing Isaiah 61:1, says that He is called to proclaim the good news to the poor. Lastly, there is the text of Isaiah 48:10, which in the Vulgate reads: *"elegi te in camino paupertatis." Poverty,* then, is the "furnace of affliction" in which the prophet is purified. This is a theme that will require more lengthy reflection on our part: the relationship between evangelization and poverty.

A Prophet's Vocation

The foregoing analysis of the biblical texts in which Anthony Claret heard the call of God provides us with sufficient data to help us understand precisely in what this vocation consisted.

The dominant element in them is that of *prophecy.* These texts either expressly relate to the call of a prophet (Isa. 49:3, 61:1; Jer. 1:9; Luke 4:18); or express some typically prophetic trait, such as guidance by the Holy Spirit (Matt. 10:20) or the fact that the prophet's word is not his own but the word of God (John 14:24); or else they are understood by their reader in a prophetic manner (Isa. 41).

This element presents some problems. It presented even more problems some years ago when, within a one-sidedly hierarchic view of the church, it was taken for granted that the New Testament charism of prophecy had made way for ecclesiastical offices. But even in the broader perspective of the church proposed at Vatican II, which recognized the charism of prophecy as distinct from those charisms linked to offices, there are still a number of open questions. In what sense, for example, did Anthony Claret feel called by God to be His prophet? Before answering this question, we should first briefly recall what we know about prophets in the Bible. The prophet (*nabi*) is etymologically one who is "called" by God to speak in His name. The prophet is God's messenger. This implies a number of fundamental concepts. Above all, the prophet is a person chosen by God to transmit His Word. This presupposes a possession by the Holy Spirit, who enlightens and moves the prophet. But it would be far too narrow a view of the biblical notion of prophecy to limit it exclusively and necessarily to those charismatic moments in which the prophet is "inspired" to speak, let alone write. The great prophet Elijah, for example, was not an inspired author; nor was the ministry of the great "writing" prophets in any way confined to their hagiographical activities. The important thing is that they felt that the message they transmitted came not from themselves, but from God.

Another characteristic of the prophet is that he is an instrument through which God intervenes in real, human history. God searches out man in his concrete situation. Through His messengers, the God of Israel begins to be a God-with-us. The prophet confronts his historical situation with God's will and tries to orient that situation in the direction that God wills. This involves moral judgments, threats, promises—and hence, although not necessarily—predictions of the future. The essential element here is a special "spiritual" understanding of history.

One further aspect of biblical prophetism remains to be considered: the prophetic message is always, in the long run, a message of salvation. Even when the prophet utters a warning, it is a saving warning. Our God is a God who saves. The prophet appears, then, as a concrete manifestation of the love of God toward His people.

Both the formal and the accessory aspects of the phenomenon of prophecy occur in the case we are considering. Claret describes his youthful experiences in terms that are typically charismatic. He writes that he felt "moved and stimulated"[24] and "impressed so deeply" by his biblical readings that he "seemed to hear a voice telling [him] the message [he] was reading."[25] "I felt the voice of God," he adds.[26] We might note here that in these descriptions the Saint used terms such as "I understood . . . , The Lord made me understand," etc., which clearly belong to the vocabulary he customarily employs when he is describing his mystical experiences. This is confirmed, moreover, by the fact that years later he wrote a superscription to the list of biblical texts he drew up in his youth: "I *understood* this when I was a young student." The experiences in question include enlightenments concerning his own future: persecutions and the effects his preaching would produce.[27] Later, during his ministry in Catalonia and Cuba, he would occasionally let fall a number of prognostications: a storm, earthquakes and plague in Cuba, the future independence of Cuba. But the essential point is that he felt chosen by God in a special way, precisely to proclaim His Word. Consciousness of a special vocation is evident in this chapter of the *Autobiography,* but it is equally clear in many other experiences and events.[28] That he was called to proclaim the Word of God is even more obvious. His exegesis of Isaiah 41 refers exclusively to preaching, and the other texts he cites refer to evangelizing or bringing the message of salvation to others.

Equally important is the fact that he was fully aware that the message he bore came not from himself but from God, above all, because he knew that he was an instrument of God, sent by Him. His own person and activity disappear in the light of divine grace. Secondly, he was aware that his mission consisted in transmitting the Divine Word par excellence—the Gospel of Jesus Christ. This places him squarely in the line of New Testament prophecy. The Word he preaches is nothing new: it has already been fulfilled in Christ and proclaimed in the New Testament. Hence, the prophet's mission is to go back to this already manifest Word and bring it to man in his concrete historical situation.

This presupposes, on the part of the prophet, a keen awareness of the flow of history. Anthony Claret was distinguished particularly by his acute sensibility to the implications of the concrete situations that surrounded him. "Studying and gaining a thorough knowledge of the maladies of the social body," he discovered in his own day, when Catalonia was becoming a heavily industrialized region, that the desire for wealth was developing into a consuming obsession, and he responded to this situation by adopting a life of heroic poverty.[29] He was quick to perceive the great influence that the press was beginning to exert on a recently literate population, and so founded, first, the Spiritual Brotherhood for Good Books and then the Religious Library and other printing enterprises.[30] In Cuba he wrote for farmers and founded both a school and licensed credit unions for them. In Catalonia he launched a campaign against blasphemous language, and in Cuba he attacked racism, as well as the common-law liaisons that gave rise to it. In Madrid he fostered the spiritual formation of the court and promoted an apostolate to the intellectual and artistic elite.

Christ and Prophecy

For Anthony Claret, prophecy was centered and summed up in Christ. He felt his own vocation to be an extension and prolongation of the prophetic mission of the Lord. This helps us form a more precise appreciation of the thrust that Claret's life took.

He was above all keenly aware that there is no other name

under heaven whereby we may be saved (Acts 4:12). He felt that he, like the Apostles, was sent by Christ as a sharer in His mission.[31] More than this, he understood that those experiences of the Spirit that moved him charismatically on certain occasions were none other than impulses of the redeeming love of Christ, communicated to his heart.[32] In this connection, we should remember that the motto he chose for his episcopal shield was *"Caritas Christi Urget Nos—*The love of Christ impels us" (2 Cor. 5:14). While he sometimes interprets this expression as the love he feels for Christ, he most frequently interprets it as Christ's own love for the human race, communicated to him (Claret) through grace. In this sense, he identifies "love" with the "uncreated love" of the Holy Spirit.[33] In *The Well-Instructed Seminarian,* speaking of the priestly spirit, he defines the latter as a participation in the Spirit that was poured forth invisibly on Christ in His Incarnation and visibly at His Baptism.[34] Christ, he tells us, was anointed with the Holy Spirit Himself, while all other saints are anointed by grace and the gifts of the Spirit. The apostolic spirit that enlivened St. Anthony M. Claret was, then, a sharing in the prophetic Spirit that anointed the Lord at the beginning of His ministry. By means of His anointed Saint, the Lord was continuing His own mission.

This helps us understand why Claret had such a lively sense of the need for being in communion of love and life with the Word made flesh, as the prime precondition enabling him to accomplish his mission. If one is to preach the Gospel of Christ, one must live in Christ. First there is a personal and communal experience of the Resurrection; then, the proclamation of this experience wells up spontaneously and irrepressibly from the depths of the soul. In his *Autobiography,* Claret dedicated a series of chapters to the various traits of spirit and life that should be the driving force of the missionary, in other words, the evangelical virtues he should possess: humility and meekness, modesty, mortification, and, above all, love for God and his neighbor.[35] He did the same in the retreats he preached to his missionaries[36] and in the *Constitutions* he wrote for them.[37] In the *Autobiography,* he devoted a whole chapter to the out-and-out material imitation of the lifestyle of Jesus.[38] Remember, too, that one of the texts that awakened his vocation was Luke 9:58, where Christ recommends His own uprooted lifestyle to anyone who would like to be His disciple. Vocation, proclaiming the Good News, and discipleship all go together. We co-work with Christ the Prophet, to the extent that we follow Him. The following of Christ was translated by Claret into celibacy, total poverty, and obedience to his church leaders—the traits that have traditionally come to be thought of as distinctive of the religious life. The Saint was theologically and spiritually a religious—one totally consecrated to the service of God—although he was not so, canonically. But for him, the following of Christ and hence the service of God were translated into an apostolic vocation.

In reality, this was not a question of simply sharing in Christ's mission and living in communion with Him or even following His own rule of life. Anthony Claret felt called to preach Christ and His Gospel. The Good News of Salvation is incarnate in Jesus. The saving God appears once and for all with us, in our midst, in His Son. In the founding retreat for the Congregation, after the preparatory talk, he devoted one whole talk to the vocation and mission of himself and his missionary companions. The talk was based on the text of Galatians 1:16, where Paul defines his vocation as follows: "God who had set me apart while I was still in my mother's womb, called me through His grace and chose to reveal His Son in me, so that I might preach the Good News about Him to the Gentiles. I did not stop to discuss this with any mere human being. . . ."

The vocation of Paul, then, is the ideal that Claret proposed to his first companions at the founding of the Congregation, citing precisely a text in which the Apostle refers to both Isaiah 49:1 and Jeremiah 1:5, namely, to the vocation of the Servant of Yahweh in the second Servant Song, and to that of the prophet Jeremiah. The novelty of the citation is that salvation is revealed in the Son of God. The prophecy was converted into the New Testament proclamation of salvation as already put into effect in the life and death of the Lord.

The Servant of Yahweh

We have just seen, in the text where Paul alludes to his vocation, how the theme of the mission of the Servant of Yahweh serves as the source of inspiration for the mission that the Saint and his missionaries must carry out in the church. This was not the only occasion in which this theme played a role in the Saint's vocation. It had already appeared in the biblical passages that had awakened his vocation.

Two of these texts, from the "Book of Consolation" of Isaiah (ch. 40-55), refer explicitly to the "Servant of Yahweh," a title and image that came to acquire an ever-richer content of meaning throughout the Old Testament and eventually became one of the main titles applied to Jesus in the New Testament to explain the meaning of His ministry and death. Claret singled out Isaiah 41:8, in which God calls Israel "my Servant," and 49:3, which is taken from the second "Servant Poem." To these we must add Isaiah 61:1, which Claret read via Luke 4:18 if, as it seems certain, the account of the baptism of Jesus combines references to this text (the Spirit descending upon Jesus) with references to Isaiah 42:1 and 49:3 (the first and second "Servant Poems").

In the Old Testament, "Servant of Yahweh" designates someone chosen by God to work with Him in the salvation of His people. Occasionally applied to the patriarchs as a title of honor (Gen. 24:14, 26:24; Exod. 32:13; Ezek. 37:25), it is more frequently applied to Moses (Exod. 14:31; Num. 12:7; Deut. 34:5), to Elijah (1 Kings 18:36), and to the prophets generally (Amos 3:7; Jer. 7:25; 2 Kings 17:23). In another strain of thought, it is applied to David (2 Sam. 7:8; 1 Kings 8:24) and to Zerubbabel, as prototypes of the Messiah King. The Servant of Yahweh speaks of a prophetic figure who reunites Israel (Isa. 49:5-6) and who, through his ministry (Isa. 50:4-10), his sufferings, and the offering up of his very life (Isa. 53:4-10), brings salvation to all peoples. In the New Testament, Jesus says that He is called to proclaim the Good News of Salvation (Luke 4:18), declares that He is the servant of His disciples (Luke 22:27), and gives His life for the redemption of all (Mark 10:43 ff.; Matt. 20:26 ff.). The preaching of the apostolic church uses the title of Servant to express the redeeming sense of Jesus' ministry and especially of His death (Acts 3:13-18; 4:27-28; Phil. 2:5-11). We might add, however, that in following Jesus and sharing in His mission, others in the New Testament receive the title of Servants of God or Christ. Mary proclaims that she is the Servant of the Lord, prepared to fulfill His Word (Luke 2:38, 43, 48). Paul, referring to his own mission as an Apostle, calls himself the servant of Christ (Rom. 1:1; Phil. 1:1; Gal. 1:1). Throughout Acts, the figure of Paul is modeled on that of the Servant of Yahweh. Mary and Paul, then, represent two different ways of cooperating with Jesus in the salvation of the human race.[39]

In this discovery of his vocation in some biblical texts relating to the Servant of the Lord—especially in one text relating to the mission of Christ, the Servant-Son of the Lord—St. Anthony Claret simply understood that God had chosen him to participate in the mission of Jesus and to cooperate with Him to save mankind, through the ministry of the Word, through suffering, and through the sacrificial dedication of his life even to the point of death. This is the sort of vocation that is described in Isaiah 41:8-18. In Isaiah 49:3, Claret understood that God had chosen to manifest His glory through him, His servant. And the glory of God *is* the salvation of men. God manifests His transcendence in the closeness of His love for His creatures. Feeling called as he did through reading certain biblical texts that describe the mission of the Servant of Yahweh—which was definitively realized in Christ—Claret saw himself as associated with those whom God had chosen to share in an eminent way in the saving work of Christ: Mary, the Mother of the Lord, and Paul, His Apostle.

The image of the Servant of Yahweh, as embodied in Christ, served to focus the prophetic vocation of Anthony Claret. He felt called to cooperate with Christ in the work of saving his brothers by bringing them the Gospel message, by preaching and suffering, by living and dying for them.

Apostolate

Anyone who is even passingly acquainted with the life of Anthony Claret must be keenly aware of the fact that the central focus of his vocation was the preaching of the Gospel. Claret himself affirms this in his account of the way in which he discovered his vocation: "In many passages of the Bible I felt the voice of God calling me to go forth and preach. The same thing

happened to me while I was at prayer."[40] "The Spirit of the
Lord is upon me, for He has anointed me. He has sent me to
bring good news to the poor," as the text that moved him most
deeply reads.[41] Indeed, the proclamation of the Gospel, the
ministry of the Word, was the grand obsession of his life, as it
was with St. Paul. Throughout it he was in constant search for
the most pressing and effective means for evangelization: preaching missions and retreats, publications, associations dedicated to
spreading the Word of God, and the training of priests and laity
for apostolic ministry. His personal mission was to be the instrument of Christ in founding and refounding His church by means
of Gospel proclamation.

It is a significant fact that in listing the biblical figures who
moved him, he should have chosen a combination of prophets
and apostles. This phenomenon was not simply confined to his
young manhood, when his vocation gradually emerged in contact with texts relating to the prophetic vocation; in the illuminations he received much later in his mission, these same prophetic texts are interwoven in passages relating to the mission of
the Apostles. Moreover, what struck him most in these passages
about the mission of the Apostles was precisely the prophetic
aspect of that mission. In referring to his vocation, he never
cites those New Testament texts where the theology of his day
sought support for its notion of the teaching authority of the
hierarchy, such as "Go and teach" or "Whoever will not listen
to you. . . ." On the contrary, he was impressed by the mission
charge, the apostolic rule of life, and the affirmation of the
power from on high of the Spirit: "The Spirit of your Father
will be speaking in you" (Matt. 10:20).[42] We would not like
to be misunderstood. He had the greatest esteem for episcopal
authority, especially for that of the bishop of Rome. He professed the deepest obedience toward his own bishop and toward
the pope, and believed that ecclesial communion with and obedience to those whom the Spirit has appointed as shepherds of
the church is an essential trait for any ministry. He stated this
explicitly in the second number of his *Second Constitutions,*
where he defines the object of the Congregation.[43] He devoted
an entire chapter of his *Autobiography* to "the care I took to
see that the Superior sent me to preach, since I was well convinced that to be effective, a missionary must be sent."[44] It will

be noted that he speaks of "the Superior" (Sp. *el Prelado*), and not the bishop because until 1848, for most of the period of his Catalonian ministry, his diocese (Vic) was not governed by a bishop, but only by a vicar. But the fact that his vocation was awakened and nourished on texts referring to the prophetic vocation—and on those texts on the apostolic vocation that refer to the prophetic aspects of that vocation—reveals that, in his calling, personal elements prevail over institutional elements. For him, proclaiming the Gospel meant unleashing a pent-up, irrepressible inner force; it meant putting into act a charism he had received from the Spirit. Then came his sacramental, priestly, and episcopal ordination to channel his vocation.

Prophets and apostles have in common the mission of proclaiming the Word of God, hence Claret felt equally drawn and impelled by his reflections on both. And yet it is clear that in the church of Christ, the apostolate adds a further dimension to prophetism. We are not referring here to the possible distinctions between the ministries of prophets and apostles as the New Testament sometimes speaks of them. In any case—aside from the fact that such distinctions are beset by a host of obscurities— both ministries, in their more substantial and permanent aspects, came to be subsumed into the episcopate. In the later church the apostolate consists in that preaching of the Gospel by means of which Christ founds and refounds His church. Prophetism, in contrast, is a supplementary power granted by the Spirit to help the church find its way throughout history. The judgment of prophecy concerning the concrete situation is of its essence. Anthony Claret shared in both. He was an apostle who, in proclaiming the death and resurrection of the Lord, collaborated with Christ in the establishment of His church; and he was a prophet, raised up by the Spirit to help His church in its mission.

To Proclaim the Good News to the Poor

The biblical texts in which Anthony Claret discovered his vocation spoke to him of proclaiming the Good News to the poor. "The poor and needy ask for water, and there is none; their tongue is parched with thirst" (Isa. 41:17). Above all, the central passage in Luke 4:18 spoke to him of the poor: "He has sent me to bring good news to the poor, to proclaim liberty to captives" (Cf. Isa. 61:1).

The numerous studies that have been appearing on the theme of poverty in the Bible have familiarized us with the meaning of the term "poor" in the Sacred Scriptures. We know that it does not refer simply to an economic class, although it is not merely a spiritualistic term, either. In a society such as Israel after its establishment in Canaan, where there was no middle class but only a great number of very poor people and a concentration of wealth in the hands of a select few—especially the king and his courtiers—there was a tendency to regard poverty almost as an inescapable law of nature. In such a situation, it was crucial that the rich should not be allowed to suborn judges into even greater oppression of the poor. In the Bible, then, the antonym for "poor" is not so much "rich" as it is "oppressing." When Christ proclaimed that He had been anointed to preach the Good News to the poor, He was doubtless thinking of the great mass of simple folk who were looked down on by the Jerusalem "establishment" as being ignorant of the Law. Jesus Himself belonged to this class of outsiders. If we want to form a still clearer notion of what Jesus meant by "poor," we should consider the preferential treatment He accorded other groups of outsiders in His ministry: eating with (rich) tax collectors, asking a Samaritan woman for a drink of water, allowing Himself to be touched by a sinful woman. All of these cases involved not only spiritual misery and need, but also a situation of social stigma and excommunication. And it is on the side of these outcasts that Jesus ranks God! He says, in effect: "Blessed are you poor," because God is with you (Luke 6:20-23).

In his book *The Well-Instructed Seminarian* (1860-1861), commenting on the *evangelizare pauperibus* of Luke 4:18, Claret remarks that Christ's mission was to proclaim the Good News both to sinners, "poor people without grace," and to "those who were poor in the goods of fortune."[45] About a year later, near the beginning of 1862, he commented on the same text in his autobiography and included both groups—sinners and the economically poor—in his own evangelizing mission. "The Lord made me understand that I would not only have to preach to sinners but that I would also have to preach to and catechize simple farmers and villagers. . . . God our Lord gave me a very special understanding of those words, 'The Spirit of the Lord is upon me; therefore he has anointed me. He has sent me to preach the good news to the poor and to heal the brokenhearted.'"[46] Claret clearly understood, then, that by God's will he was to direct his ministry toward reviving the Christian life of his neighbors, especially of the humblest social classes of his day. Note that he speaks of "farmers and villagers." To grasp the point of this expression, one must realize that the inhabitants of small farms and villages were at that time the most abandoned from a religious point of view, especially after the civil government had suppressed religious orders and closed their centers of evangelization. In the society in which Claret lived, "farmers and villagers" were clearly the most abandoned classes.

Nevertheless, it would be a great mistake to tie the mission of Anthony Claret to a single economic class. Christian and apostolic charity should preferentially minister to those who suffer most, and these are, ordinarily, the poor. But a vocation to evangelize cannot be limited to the socioeconomically poor. The redemption of Christ is not simply or mainly a form of economic liberation, although in certain social situations the fraternal love that the Lord instills in us demands that we work and strive for economic liberation. The liberation which the Gospel proclaims and effects goes beyond this, reminding us of the powerful misery and alienation that wealth can entail. We are *all* in need of the liberation proclaimed by the Gospel. Anthony Claret, who devoted the greater part of his ministry to farmers and villagers in Catalonia and the Canary Islands and to the very poor in Cuba, spent most of his time in Madrid evangelizing the rich and the aristocracy. To the rich he preached the same uncompromising Gospel of the Beatitudes and fraternal service, and he preached it not only by his words but also by the example of his extremely poor and austere way of life.

Since Claret discovered his vocation through reading the biblical prophets, one might readily expect a certain amount of interpretation and exegesis in any attempt at explaining it. On the other hand, in examining the concrete way in which he lived out that vocation, one might suspect that a simple narration of the events would suffice. We must state in advance, however, that this is not the case. The things a founder does to carry out his vocation can never be regarded *simply* as the outcome of his charism; they are also conditioned by the society and times in which the founder lives. In fact, initiatives undertaken by founders or foundresses are attempts to respond to the concrete needs of the church in a particular historical setting. From their point of view, these initiatives are the best way they feel they can put their charisms into practice, within determinate circumstances. This is why, if one is going to understand the charism of a religious institute in the church, one cannot rest content with simply enumerating the decisions its founder took; he must also place these decisions within their historical context—and this, too, involves interpretation.

Claret felt called to preach the Gospel. He set to work fulfilling this task—briefly in 1841 and continuously from 1843 onward—by adopting the techniques and methods of "parish missions," a form of evangelization which began in Europe in the 17th century, reached its zenith in the 18th, was revived in the 19th, and lasted until about the middle of the 20th. Some of the most famous itinerant preachers of this movement were, in Spain, St. John of Avila (d. 1569) and, in France, St. Vincent de Paul (d. 1660) and his confreres in the Congregation of the Mission. In the 17th century, the themes commonly used in missions were based on the first week of the Spiritual Exercises and the treatise on the Last Things. There were also catechetical talks on the Commandments and on how to make a good confession. Missions were, then, a sort of retreat for the whole parish and a period set aside for renewing the people's knowledge of Christian doctrine.

People were drawn to the mission by an opening procession, to the accompaniment of church bells and children singing, which served to welcome the missioners. Everyone gathered at church several times a day. In those times before movies or television, the presence and oratorical abilities of the missionaries made the mission a real event for the whole town, and many came to witness it all, if only out of curiosity. Naturally, missions could only be held at times when farmers would not have to be working in the fields. They began after the fall and continued until spring.

Anthony Claret learned his mission techniques and methods from the works of St. Alphonsus Liguori, especially from the latter's *Selva di materie predicabili.*[47] But he also learned a great deal during the months he spent as a young priest at the Jesuit novitiate in Rome. The coadjutor of the master of novices gave regular talks on pastoral theory and practice to the priest-novices.[48] Claret's library included, besides the works of St. Alphonsus, those of St. John of Avila and St. Francis de Sales,[49] as well as the lives and sermonaries of the two Segneris,[50] Siniscalchi, Cuniliati, Santander, and Valsecchi.[51] According to St. Alphonsus, the entire apparatus of parish missions was geared toward bringing the faithful to the confessional.[52] In fact, the success of a mission was gauged by the number of confessions heard, communions received, marriages validated, and enemies reconciled during the services. This presupposed a solid Christian environment, where the main problem was not so much one of faith as it was of fidelity to Christian morals.

St. Anthony Mary Claret was intensely involved in the mission apostolate from 1843 until his episcopal ordination in October 1850. When he went to Cuba he organized a team of missionaries to evangelize his archdiocese. After the advance work of this team, the archbishop would follow through, confirming those who had been instructed and legalizing marriages. He had special cause to devote himself so tenaciously to this task. During the period of 1820-1823, and especially in 1835 (the year of his priestly ordination), the liberal government strove for the suppression of all religious orders. At a single stroke of the pen, thousands of religious houses were closed in Spain, and with them, the numerous Jesuit, Capuchin, and Franciscan centers dedicated exclusively to missionary preaching. Moreover, civil authorities did all they could to hamper the preaching of parish missions, since they feared they might be used to turn the people against the government. The fault was not entirely on the side of the politicians. Until 1848, a good number of the Spanish clergy were avowed partisans of the *ancien regime* and enemies of the new liberal state. Many missionaries from northern Spain were notorious for their stand against the new politics, while civil authorities only sharpened the clergy's distrust by their ceaseless attacks on church institutions. One had to be brave indeed to preach missions at this time, and few were, in fact, disposed to do so.

The people, then, were being deprived of this powerful means for moral and spiritual renewal. Naturally, the ones who felt most abandoned in all this were the inhabitants of small rural towns and farms. This helps us understand why St. Anthony Claret, in commenting on the biblical texts that awakened his vocation, should speak of those "parched tongues" that needed the refreshment of the living water of the Word, and why he should identify the biblical "poor" with "simple farmers and villagers."[53]

New Apostolates

Since Claret felt called to evangelize, he adopted the most effective method available in his day—parish missions—and dedicated himself to the most abandoned sectors of the church, the rural population. In this sense, he was the last great representative of a tradition and, so to speak, the last ray of a school whose sun had set. He certainly introduced some changes of his own into this method. He devoted his first sermon, for example, to the theme of salvation, thus confronting his audience with the supreme choice of accepting or rejecting redemption in Christ. Among his "obligatory" mission sermons he included one on eternity, doubtless because he felt that this theme would have the same effect on his hearers as it had had on him in his childhood,[54] and another on the glory of heaven, so as to give all of his preaching a positive thrust. But none of these changes could entitle him to be called an innovator in pastoral practice.

In contrast, where Anthony Claret shone as an innovator of creative ministries was in his promotion of the Christian press and the lay apostolate. Both of these approaches seemed to open up to Claret during the first phase of his ministry, when he began to write and publish summaries of the advice and counsel he was currently offering others. St. Alphonsus, too, had been both a missionary and writer, but St. Anthony Claret concentrated on publishing a large number of booklets and pamphlets aimed at the masses. This was possible because, especially in Catalonia, broad sections of the lower classes had learned to read and write and had become avid readers of anything in print.[55] Claret realized that printed preaching could reach a vaster public and have a more lasting effect than oral preaching could.[56] Later, during his first pastoral visitation of the parishes in the arch-diocese of Santiago, Cuba, he distributed 98,217 books and booklets and 89,500 leaflets.[57] But these individual efforts could not satisfy his deep commitment to the ministry of the Christian press. Hence, around 1846, he began planning a Spiritual Fraternity of Good Books and, in 1848, founded the Religious Library Press, which issued its first book in December of that year. The Religious Library was very influential in Spain. Through it Claret published not only popular pamphlets, but also works on apologetics, homiletics and church history, as well as spiritual classics for the clergy and cultured laity. Publications of the Religious Library were abundantly represented in the libraries of seminaries and convents and in the private collections of priests, until well into the 20th century. One of the main activities of the Academy of St. Michael was the promotion of the Catholic press. Claret launched public lending libraries for Catholic books in 1864.

The second initiative for which Claret is justly renowned is his promotion of the apostolate of the laity. Most mid-19th century lay associations were devoted to fostering some religious devotion, although a few (the Pious Unions) aimed at the spiritual growth and development of their members. In the 1840s there was a considerable development of associations dedicated to apostolic prayer. One of the most outstanding of these was the Archconfraternity of Our Lady of Victories, founded by Father Desgenettes in Paris. The Saint worked for the advancement of this archconfraternity in Catalonia, the Canary Islands, and Cuba, thus associating himself with a movement initiated by others.

Where his own innovative talent shows most clearly is in his founding and organizing of associations of apostolic action by the laity. The Spiritual Fraternity of Good Books included lay members. In 1847 Claret launched his Apostolic Society of the Most Holy and Immaculate Heart of Mary, whose membership was to include priests and laity, men and women, to work in whatever field of apostolate was open to them. Unfortunately, the Saint had not reckoned on the prejudices of the archbishop of Tarragona, who was mightily displeased at the thought of involving women in apostolic work. And so Claret had to abandon this truly prophetic initiative. Later, in Madrid, as archbishop, he returned to his original idea when he founded the Academy of St. Michael, an association of Catholic intellectuals, artists, professors, priests, and lay men and women, working together for the apostolate. Finally, in the promotional statement for Catholic lending libraries in Spain, Claret expressly recommends that pastors entrust them to the care of the laity. The Saint's reasons in support of this procedure are significant. On the one hand, priests have ministries enough of their own to attend to, and by restricting themselves to these ministries, they would be opening the way for the laity to broaden their proper ministries; on the other, it seemed clear to the Saint that God wills to entrust to the laity a great role in the work of saving souls.[58]

These two initiatives of the lay apostolate and the Catholic press place Anthony Claret in the vanguard of forward-looking thinkers in his day, and merit for him the title Pius IX gave him: "The Modern Apostle." They also define more clearly his role as an apostle (preacher, writer, pressman, founder of missionary institutes, promoter of the lay apostolate and of the apostolic mission of women in the church). If we wished an even sharper-focused apostolic profile of Claret, we would have to add a number of other traits. In Cuba (1851-1857) he had to face the almost overwhelming problems of an archdiocese that had been left without a bishop for decades and a people who suffered from all the ills of colonialism. His personal mission as archbishop was to evangelize his chaotic diocese, but he also had to reorganize the seminary (which was turning out more lawyers than priests) and reform the parishes (where there were grave abuses of all sorts). He was deeply concerned with the problems of farmworkers, on whose behalf he not only wrote two short, influential works on agrarian reform, but also established a model farm and trade school. For the poor in general, he founded and funded the first licensed credit unions in Latin America. He fought against the discriminatory laws that prohibited interracial marriages (laws that had led to mass concubinage on the island), and made public pronouncements against the practice of slavery. On his return to Spain in 1857, he founded an interdiocesan seminary and a boys' school at the Escorial, and did all he could by writing and example to promote the good formation of priests. Since his duties as royal confessor obliged him to live at court, he spent a great deal of his time writing, hearing confessions, and giving spiritual direction. Whenever the court traveled, he used it as an occasion to launch apostolic preaching campaigns throughout the regions of Spain. Expelled from Spain by the revolution of 1868, he gained some valuable insights in France and Italy into the educational work being carried out by various groups of teaching brothers, and asked his own missionaries to open schools, without prejudice to their itinerant preaching ministry. His apostolic work, which was accomplished in ever-widening circles (parish evangelization, the rebuilding of a whole archdiocese, the reform of the entire country of Spain), eventually reached the level of the whole church with his participation in the First Vatican Council.

Conclusion

If we study the biblical texts that awakened the vocation of St. Anthony Claret in the church, we begin to see him as a man chosen by God and moved by the Spirit (prophetism) to dedicate himself totally to His service by cooperating with Christ for the salvation of the human race (servant of the Lord) through the proclamation of the Good News (aspostolate). Evangelization, then, radically defines his historic mission and was, in fact, the all-encompassing ideal of his entire adult life. For it he prayed, worked, suffered, lived, and died.

He put his vocation into practice by listening to the most urgent needs of the church in the wide variety of circumstances and environments in which Providence placed him and by responding to those needs with the apostolates and means that he judged there and then to be most effective. This explains the great diversity of apostolic activities that he adopted, renewed, or initiated.

II

Gathering Companions

In 1839 St. Anthony M. Claret finished his seminary studies and was thus free to set about realizing his plans.[1] In the summer of this year he decided to put these plans into practice. According to the testimony of a friend and classmate of his seminary days, Luis Sauquer, the Saint confided to him at that time that he intended to consult his spiritual director, Father Bach, about founding a center for missionaries in Catalonia.[2] This sort of project was by no means a novelty. In the 18th century and in the first half of the 19th, similar centers had been managed by the Franciscans, Capuchins, Vincentians, and—during those periods when they were not disbanded—the Jesuits. But all of these had been brought to an abrupt halt in 1835, with the suppression of religious orders in Spain. What St. Anthony Mary Claret wanted to do—doubtless, in collaboration with a team of priests—was to continue a work that religious could no longer carry out. His object, then, was to keep a missionary tradition alive. Father Bach, who had retired to his family home after the Oratory in Vic had been suppressed, seems to have dissuaded the Saint from following through on his project. His reasons would have been sound enough: circumstances were extremely unfavorable, because of the prevailing civil unrest and governmental opposition to all ecclesiastical institutions.

Since his plans had been blocked in this direction, young Father Claret set out for Rome, to offer his services to the *Propaganda Fide*. It should be noted that in those days the *Propaganda* was not only in charge of foreign missions, but could also confer the title of Apostolic Missionary, with faculties to conduct popular missions among the faithful. He brought with him a letter of recommendation for the Very Reverend Francis Vilardell, a missionary bishop in Lebanon,[3] and we may surmise that the Saint would have gone on to Lebanon, if Bishop Vilardell had not left Rome before Claret's arrival. Accepting the invitation of a Jesuit, the Saint entered the Roman novitiate of the Company of Jesus on October 20, 1839. Here he attended the courses in pastoral theology given by the father minister and assistant novicemaster.[4] Afflicted by a mysterious leg ailment, he left the novitiate and returned to Catalonia in March 1840.

He had come back with the intention of dedicating himself to preaching missions in his native land. With this in mind he consulted the Capuchin, Fr. Fermín de Alcaraz, the representative of the Pretender, Don Carlos, to the Holy See. De Alcaraz advised him to establish himself at Berga, a stronghold of the Royalist Party, where missions were being preached.[5] But the ecclesiastical governor of Vic decided otherwise, and sent him as administrator to Viladrau, on May 13, 1840. Here he began the first of his missionary forays in August of the same year. In mid-January 1841, he left the parish to dedicate himself full time to preaching missions, returning from time to time to his home base in Vic.[6] A few months later, during the spring of 1841, he received an order from the alcalde, bringing his preaching ministry to a halt, and he retired for a time to the village of San Andrés del Pruit. Perhaps during his preaching in Vic he had written to the Holy See requesting the title of Apostolic Missionary. At any rate, he received this title on July 9, 1841. From that date, and until May 1842, he resumed his missionary preaching.

The Search for Apprentice Missionaries

In May 1842, Claret took charge of the vicarage of San Juan de Oló. He had been sent there to restore peace to a parish that had been upset by the eccentricities of an aging pastor and, perhaps, to extricate Claret himself from some potential imbroglio. From his base at San Juan he still managed to engage in a few missionary excursions. But the idea that was uppermost in his mind at this time was to take advantage of his enforced stay in the parish by gathering together some priests interested in learning the art of preaching. They were to make a retreat with him and afterwards attend some conferences at which he would explain the basic pastoral rules of missionary work.

Toward the beginning of November 1842, he had already outlined these plans to his friend, Canon Jaime Soler, and had received responses from Soler on November 15 and 19. On November 25, the Saint wrote him again. This is the only remaining letter we possess of the Soler-Claret correspondence of 1842, but it is invaluable for the light it sheds on the matter at hand. Soler had pointed out the difficulties that would be entailed in Claret's leaving his post as vicar, thus depriving himself of all upkeep. The Saint replied that this was no problem for him, since he was not asking that the vicarage support him, but only that he be provided with a suitable place in which to carry out his plans for missionary formation. Come what might, he felt that if need be, he could achieve what he wanted to in San Juan de Oló. There was no need for the pastor's residence to be allotted him, as Soler had suggested. The priests who came could be lodged there, as long as they paid the caretaker something. Claret's wish was that Soler would send these priests two at a time, that they would make a ten-day retreat with him, followed by his lectures on the pastoral aspects of giving missions. He would take advantage of the occasion to expose them to some ideas on missionary preaching, based on Segneri, Liguori's *Selva,* and the lectures he himself had attended at the Jesuit novitiate in Rome.[7]

A comparison of this letter with Document I of the Apostolic Fraternity reveals that the latter had already been sketched out in November 1842 to serve as notes for the lectures Claret was planning to give his "novice" missionaries. We do not know whether he was able to put these plans into effect during the following months. The first set of retreats for which we have any documentation were preached in July and August of the following year, 1843. Both of these bore the initiatory stamp that the Saint wanted to give them.

In the light of the letter to Soler and Document I of the Apostolic Fraternity, we can conclude that in the autumn of

1842, St. Anthony Mary Claret aimed at preparing a group of priests for preaching missions, by grouping them in a purely apostolic and spiritual association—without any organization, strictly speaking—called the *Germandat de Maria del Roser* (The Fraternity of St. Mary of the Rosary). One of the members of this fraternity was Canon Soler, vice-rector and professor at the Seminary of Vic, who was in charge of recruiting priests for the group. We do not know whether any of those who attended the first session with Soler in July 1843, at Campdevanol, ever decided to follow the Saint. But at the one held at Gombreny around the beginning of August, Claret won over to his ideals young Mosén Stephen Sala, the same Fr. Sala who was later to become a cofounder of the Congregation of Missionaries.[8]

By the end of 1844, the Saint had already formed a group of disciples and collaborators. We know this from a letter Soler sent to Fr. Joaquín Masmitjá on December 14, 1844: "He (Claret) continues to work with his sermons and apprentices in Calecha."[9] Unfortunately, we lack any further information on these collaborators until August 1845. At this time the Saint sent Brother Francis Bosch, S.J., a letter addressed to the Holy See, petitioning the title of Apostolic Missionary for ten priests. In it he writes:

> "Our Heavenly Father, out of His great mercy, has deigned to call other Apostolic Workers, filled with zeal and disposed and resolved to follow the same style of life and apostolic labors as those of the present applicant, and thus they will be able to spread throughout other Provinces of Spain, there to sow the Seed of God's Word."[10]

These words clearly disclose Claret's conviction that he was called by God to be an effective spiritual guide for a group of missionaries. In this letter he speaks first of his own personal vocation and of the apostolic rule of life he has been following. Then he affirms that God has called others to follow his own style of life and ministry. At the same time the text reveals his intention of extending his work and that of his collaborators to other areas in Spain.

The letter includes the names of ten of his missionary associates: (1) his friend and supporter, Dr. Jaime Soler, then rector of the Seminary of Vic; (2) Canon Passarell; (3) Mariano Puigllat; (4) Mariano Aguilar; (5) Fr. Peter Bach; (6) Francis Gonfaus;

(7) Stephen Sala; (8) Manuel Subirana; (9) Manuel Batlle; and (10) Raymond Vicens. Of these, the first four could have worked with the Saint only occasionally, if indeed they ever collaborated with him in preaching, since the offices they held in the chancery and in 'the seminary would have greatly curtailed their freedom to do so. None of these four appears in later lists of collaborators. It is certain, however, that Soler's prestige and influence were a great help in recruiting members for the group, and that he followed the Saint's progress with considerable satisfaction, as can be seen from his letters to Fr. Joaquín Masmitjá. Later, Claret and Soler were to collaborate in spreading the Archconfraternity of the Heart of Mary. Puigllat, too, appears in later transactions with Claret. It was in Puigllat's library that Document II of the Apostolic Fraternity[11] was discovered. Mariano Aguilar later cooperated in the apostolate of the printed word.[12] The first fraternity member to appear in later lists was Fr. Bach. This leads us to believe that he took part in some missionary campaigns, although his post as superior of the Oratory and his chief ministry as a confessor and spiritual director could not have allowed him much time for giving missions. Sala, Gonfaus, and Subirana, on the contrary, were assiduous co-workers. Batlle, too, was later associated with the Saint. Vicens, however, was one of those whose names do not appear in later lists. Possibly, Claret was thinking only of his regular co-workers when he drew up this list and then, because of the prestige and faculties attached to the title in question, was moved to include those friends of his who held important posts in the Chancery of Vic and who had been helping him in one way or another.

First Organization of the Apostolic Fraternity: 1846

In the summer of 1846 St. Anthony Claret took a further step toward the realization of his plans. Up to that time, in the most important places where he had preached missions he had also preached retreats to the clergy. These retreats began winning him some priests for his missionary enterprises. As his biographer, Francis Aguilar, tells us: "Some of the more courageous of these priests gave up their positions and small comforts to dedicate themselves to preaching missions, under the orders of their Prelate and under the direction of Father Claret."[13]

But during the summer of 1846, with the approval of Dr.

Casadevall, administrator of the Diocese of Vic, the Saint organized a series of conferences for priests, which were held, apparently, in the diocesan seminary. He refers to these conferences a few months later in a letter to Dr. Casadevall, dated February 4, 1847. Unfortunately, we know the identity of only one of those who took part in them, Fr. Ignatius Carbó, an exclaustrated Cistercian, whose name is mentioned in the aforesaid letter. He, at least, must have been won over to the cause of preaching missions since during a trip to Rome near the end of 1846 he obtained the title of Apostolic Missionary and later, toward the beginning of 1850, was received by the Saint into his Congregation of Missionaries, and died as a member on December 3, 1852.[14]

We do not know the exact date on which these first conferences were held. The above-mentioned letter to Casadevall says only, "in the Summer." St. Anthony Mary Claret was in Vic from June 19 until mid-September 1846. In all likelihood, then, the conferences were held in July or August. One further detail we know of, thanks to the testimony of Fr. Carbó, is that during these conferences certain resolutions were drawn up, and that Dr. Casadevall communicated them to Cardinal Pietro Orsini, Prefect of the Congregation of Bishops and Regulars who, in turn, informed the pope of them. In his *Diary of a Voyage to Rome,* Fr. Carbó writes:

> He [the Cardinal] told me that the aforesaid Administrator [Casadevall] had sent him the resolutions from the conferences given at the seminary by Mosén Claret and others, and that he had shown them to His Holiness, Pius IX, and that both had been pleased with them.[15]

We have not been able to locate Casadevall's letter to Cardinal Orsini (if, indeed, it was preserved) in the records of the Congregation of Bishops and Regulars, now in the Vatican Archives. Nor is there any mention of this matter in the *Regesta Episcoporum* of this congregation for 1846-1847, although the Diocese of Vic is mentioned in them several times. This is understandable enough, in view of the fact that the letter in question was a simple report and not a request for faculties. But this is not particularly important. It was Casadevall who took the initiative, while the Saint was not especially concerned about it. In the above-mentioned letter of February 4, 1847, he wrote to Casadevall without referring to the matter of sending the resolutions to Rome.

Rev. Ignatius Carbó (the Monk who attended our Summer conferences)
has arrived here from the journey he made to Rome, etc., etc., and
after many other interesting things he says that His Eminence, Cardinal
Orsini, asked him to convey his good wishes to me and to the
Ecclesiastical Governor of Vich [*sic*].[16]

On the other hand, although we do not have Casadevall's report, we do know the Saint's intentions during the days when
he was giving these conferences. We know them (1) from letters
he sent to various persons during the following autumn, requesting their collaboration in expanding the Catholic press, and (2)
above all, from the document entitled: "Points on Which We
Have to Talk,"[17] which was drawn up in August 1846. These
letters and the "Points" probably formed the basis for Claret's
conversation with Caixal in the following month.

Canon Caixal, on his return from exile in 1845, first met the
famous missionary in February 1846. It would seem that both
men hit it off well from the start, and the Saint thus gained an
extremely effective collaborator.[18]

In the "Points" referred to above, St. Anthony Mary Claret
drew up a sketch for an organization. There would be two teams
of priests: one, directed by him, would be dedicated to preaching missions; the other, led by Fr. Coll, would preach retreats.
Both groups would be part of a single organization, carrying out
a joint venture based on the same fundamental principles.

The Saint offered Dr. Caixal the coordinating directorship of
this enterprise, but he also needed someone to take charge of
printing the various booklets and leaflets needed for the missions and retreats, and of sending them out to the missionaries
involved. Caixal declined the offer of acting as coordinator for
the activities of both groups, but accepted instead the job of
printing and sending out the required materials. This venture
amounted, in effect, to a genuine apostolic organization that
aimed at simultaneously fulfilling three roles: missions, retreats,
and the Catholic press. As originator of this enterprise, Claret
was concerned with many of its details, including the problem
of where he could send some of the exhausted or aging missionaries who had offered their services. The fact is that while the
apostolic activities of the group were well thought out and struc-

tured, the internal bonds that held the associates together were
as yet very weak. The founder wrote that it would be better if
the missionaries were united—i.e., living in community—but,
doubtless because he realized that this was impossible in practice, he attached only one condition to membership: that they
be united in spirit. In succeeding documents and in his correspondence, Claret refers to this association by the generic designation of "Apostolic Fraternity," without adding any further
designation of a specifically devotional character. Of the 1842
"Fraternity of St. Mary of the Rosary," there remains not even
a trace. Only in one later document does he use the title of
"Brothers of Jesus and Mary."

Who were St. Anthony Mary Claret's companions in this enterprise? We have seen that in his "Points on Which We Have to
Talk," he names Coll and Caixal as directors. In the "List of
Brothers,"[19] which dates from about this time, he mentions
fourteen companions, not counting Caixal, since the list was
sent to Caixal as an informative report. Stephen Sala appears
in second place after the Saint, as his most staunch and long-
standing supporter. Of those already included in the petition of
1845, the following are listed: Fr. Bach (3rd), Fr. Francis Gonfaus (4th), and Fr. Manuel Subirana (7th). Some new names also
appear: Fr. Coll, the young priests Manuel Vilaró and Dominic
Fábregas (both of whom would later become members of the
Congregation of Missionaries), and Fr. Joseph Benet (who must
be identified with the Augustinian who, together with the Saint
and Fr. Coll, formed a team at the time).[20] Benet had already
made a retreat under the Saint's direction during the summer
of 1844.[21] Also listed we find the Franciscan, Michael Febrer,
preceded by Francis Gonfaus and a Raymond Gonfaus, possibly
a brother of the former. After Fr. Fábregas there appear six
names, but the only one we know anything about is that of
Fr. Benet.

A new petition for faculties[22] for "companions of the Reverend Claret," which the Saint sent, it would seem, toward the
close of 1847, includes Frs. Coll, Benet, Vilaró, Raymond Gonfaus (all mentioned in the preceding list), and the Carmelite,
Francis Solá. These must have been the Saint's most active helpers toward the end of 1846 and during the following year.

In fact, of all those mentioned, only a few seem to have collaborated directly with the Saint. Fr. Coll preached a number of missions with him. In a letter to Caixal in May of 1847, he refers to Coll as "one of our companions."[23] Vilaró accompanied him on his campaign through Tarragona around the end of 1846 and the beginning of 1847.[24] He is mentioned expressly in two letters to Casadevall, dated February 4 and 22, respectively.[25] A letter of December 26, 1846, alluding to the companion who is assisting him, must also refer to Vilaró.[26] We have already noted that Fr. Benet was most likely the Augustinian who worked with the Saint and Fr. Coll on a mission team. In 1848, when St. Anthony Mary Claret was in the Canary Islands, Benet preached the course of Lenten sermons in Solsona.[27]

The foregoing applies to the companions the Saint gained during his retreats and pastoral conferences. It is evident, however, that his group of disciples was far more extensive than that of his close collaborators. Somewhat later, in July 1848, his friend, Anthony Palau, wrote as follows in the *Revista Católica* of Barcelona:

> Besides Father Codina, there is the Catalan Apostle, Mosén Claret, whose tact in dealing with the formation of young missionaries is much admired in the Diocese of Vich [*sic*], where numerous young men have been formed in his shadow, in order to confront the hazards of the apostolate.[28]

These labors as a trainer of missionaries were to continue in 1847, as we shall presently see.

The Apostolic Fraternity in 1847

In 1847 St. Anthony Mary Claret took yet another forward step in shaping his organizational plans for the missionary ministry. This is the year in which he speaks most frequently about his companions. A number of factors prevented him from engaging in his customary missionary journeys: the uprising of the "Early Risers" guerrilla band; an order from the governor forbidding him to preach; and a painful and apparently dangerous illness he contracted during the spring. Hence it was that he spent most of his time in writing and in forming a few new missionaries. From June through July he was almost fully occupied in the last-mentioned task.

Besides other tasks, I am occupied in preparing some young priests who have not as yet left the nest, but are showing signs of emerging in due time as accomplished fliers and warblers. Next month, with God's help, we will make a retreat, as is our yearly custom.[29]

Right now I am, among other things, occupied with some young priests who are being prepared to preach and hear confessions, and they will swell the ranks of those [prepared] last year.[30]

I am extremely occupied with the conferences, although I'm thinking of ending them soon, both because of the warm weather and because the group is already *au courant.* Some of these boys show great promise.[31]

At the same time, he took great satisfaction in following the comings and goings of his companions of the previous year. Sala was with him in Vic and assisted him in the ministry of the press.[32] He wrote enthusiastically to Caixal, concerning the feats Fr. Coll was accomplishing in Gerona.[33] From another letter to Caixal we learn that the Saint was in communication with twenty priests from his conferences, who were giving missions in and beyond the Diocese of Vic. He had just finished sending them packets of booklets and leaflets to distribute in their work.[34] Since these priests had attended his pastoral conferences, they were, so to speak, his disciples.

This relative state of calm, together with the good results deriving from his work of missionary formation, continued until midsummer of 1847, and gave him a chance to outline his plans more clearly. But soon enough, his inability to engage personally in missionary journeys through Catalonia—which was then locked in civil war—led him to consider either traveling to the interior of Spain or crossing over into French Catalonia. He consulted Caixal about this on May 28, 1847, and again on August 12.[35] On September 6 he asked Caixal to get the archbishop of Tarragona's opinion on the matter.[36] If he did go, he planned to make a retreat before leaving, with two or three of his companions, at Montserrat or some other monastery.[37] We can see that the Saint was once more preoccupied with the idea of expanding his efforts into the interior of Spain, a project that he had already been thinking of in 1845.[38]

At the same time, St. Anthony Mary Claret was coming to a clearer notion of what the structure of the Apostolic Fraternity would have to be like, if it were not limited to the evangelization of Catalonia alone. Perhaps it was this desire for geographic

expansion that made the Saint think more seriously about giving
the fraternity a better-defined organization. He roughly outlined
this organization in Document VIII of the Apostolic Fraternity
(the Brothers of Jesus and Mary). Because this document is written in Castilian, and because it marks an advance over his plans
in mid-1846, we would tend to date it in the closing months of
1847. Here he speaks of a priestly fraternity dedicated to preaching missions and retreats and living in community. From his letter of December 11, 1848, to Caixal, we know that even before
he left Catalonia at the beginning of that year, the Saint had
been promised a house for this purpose in Vic, Manresa, and
Gracia, and that he had some followers ready to join him in this
work.[39]

But this time, too, he was unable to carry out his plans to establish the Apostolic Fraternity in a more stable form. When he
was on the verge of doing so, he was invited to follow the newly
consecrated Bishop Codina to the Canary Islands, and since he
was unable to work in Catalonia, the Saint accepted the offer.[40]
Everything was left hanging in midair until his return to Spain.

In the summer of this year, 1847, our missionary had been
working out his ideas for one of his most original and inspired
projects: the Apostolic Society of the Most Holy and Immaculate Heart of Mary. Although this new society had no direct relationship with the Apostolic Fraternity, it does show how Claret's
apostolic plans were broadening and maturing. The new society
was to be an apostolic association that would admit clerical and
lay members, men and women, fraternally united. This was not
just one more project of the Apostolic Fraternity, since the
priests involved did not have to be missionaries. But there is no
doubt that if both projects for 1847 had been carried out, the
Apostolic Fraternity would have been able to count on some
very effective collaboration from the ranks of the Apostolic Society of the Most Holy and Immaculate Heart of Mary. As things
turned out, however, Archbishop Echanove of Tarragona disap-
proved of the new society—mainly because it included members
of both sexes—and so the Saint disbanded it that same year.

From Apostolic Fraternity to Congregation

The apostolic campaign in the Canary Islands, with all its
astounding results, seems to have demanded all of St. Anthony

Mary Claret's attention for several months, beginning in mid-March 1848. He did not resume his correspondence with Caixal until August[41] and with his bishop, Casadevall, until September 27.[42] On that day or the day following, he received a letter from Caixal, in which the latter informed him that he had written to Casadevall asking him to order him back to Catalonia. Claret wrote Casadevall that since Caixal was "one of the principal members of the Apostolic Fraternity," he would like to mollify him.[43]

In a letter that he began toward the beginning of September but did not finish until October 17, Caixal had written to Claret on the urgency of establishing a new missionary community in Catalonia. What was behind this initiative by Caixal? Why, at this very moment, when his friend Claret was so intensely busy evangelizing the Canary Islands, did the canon of Tarragona insist on his prompt return to Spain, in order to take the necessary steps for the foundation of a missionary institute?

Some writings of Caixal, preserved in the Departmental Archives of Perpignan, show that during the years he had spent in exile (1835-1845) he had dedicated himself to missionary preaching in the northern territories of Spain occupied by the army of Don Carlos de Borbon, brother of the deceased King Ferdinand VII and pretender to the throne against the latter's daughter, Isabel II.[44] More than this: Canon Caixal had planned at that time to organize a missionary team who should be prepared by the time that he might be able to return and set things right in Spain.

But it was not these memories of his past initiatives that led Caixal to write to the Saint. Upon his return to Tarragona in 1845, he had fully applied himself to the duties imposed on him as cathedral canon, without looking back on his earlier projects. Perhaps he did so because he soon established communications with Claret and preferred to leave the matters of initiative and direction to the latter, while he himself could restrict his efforts to collaborating closely with the Saint in managing the printing of books and short works. The querulous canon was moved to ask the celebrated missionary to return to Spain to found an institute dedicated to evangelization by a series of messages, purportedly from God, that a novice of the Company of Mary, Sor Antonia Paris, kept sending to Caixal. In 1842 Sor Antonia had begun to receive certain divine lights on the situation of the church in Spain and on the means that should be applied as a remedy for its ills. Two or three years later, in 1844 or 1845, she believed that the Lord had shown her in a vision that Anthony Claret was the apostolic man whom He was giving to the church for its renewal. In a series of illuminations she had come to understand that God was destining him to found two apostolic institutes for men and women, in the founding of which she herself was to be involved. One day her confessor—Caixal— who had either not completely forgotten his projects or was reflecting on the slow progress of Claret's proposed missionary brotherhood, asked the good sister for her opinion concerning a way to give life to a brotherhood of missionaries. Sor Antonia answered that as she saw it, it was the will of God that Anthony Claret gather with some companions in community. Caixal then wrote to the Saint, asking him to return and undertake this project (without informing him, however, of the lights received by Sor Antonia), to which Caixal pledged his own unconditional collaboration.[45] Later, Sor Antonia was called to Cuba by the Saint. In 1855 she founded, together with him, the Congregation of Claretian Missionary Sisters, the Sisters of the Immaculate Conception.

St. Anthony Claret gladly accepted Caixal's offer. In reference to the projected foundation, Claret answered that he was not only in agreement with it, but that he himself had been cherishing just such a plan for a number of years.

> I see your plan and I tell you that it is of God, and that it will come about in due time. Some years ago, I conceived much the same plan, but the time for its delivery has not yet arrived. To console you I may tell you that a house has already been set aside for this; there are personnel, etc., etc., but this birth should not be forced.... Meanwhile, all of you should do what you can by the spoken and written word.[46]

In a postscript to this letter, he recommends that Dr. Palau should not give up his idea of founding a college for missionaries destined to serve in Fernando Poo,[47] because in getting approval for it, he might be able to put it to further purposes. But the group, he insisted, should be stationed in Catalonia and not, as Palau had wished, in the Canary Islands. The Saint had received a promise of a house in Vic, Manresa, and Gracia.

Can we conclude from these data that Claret had already been thinking of founding his Congregation of Missionaries even before he left Catalonia for the Canary Islands? True, it is somewhat hard to distinguish between the Congregation and the Apostolic Fraternity, especially as Claret had rethought the latter in 1847 as a stable community—all the more so, when we reflect that the early Congregation was little more than a simple association of priests dedicated full time to preaching missions and retreats. But if it is hard to distinguish both groups from a juridical point of view, they were quite distinct from the point of view of their respective apostolic horizons. When Claret founded the Congregation, he was fully conscious that he was creating something stable and important for the whole church—something destined to spread throughout the world. The fraternity, on the other hand, consisted of nothing but a team of priests gathered in a center. Even granting that the Congregation was formed as a further development of the fraternity, their distinctness is confirmed by the fact that the greater part of the members of the fraternity remained outside the Congregation after its founding. Of all the Saint's companions, only Stephen Sala and Manuel Vilaró, together with Dominic Fábregas (who had perhaps collaborated with him only sporadically), went on to join the Congregation of Missionaries. And the reason for this was that belonging to the Congregation called for a much deeper commitment than belonging to a simple mission center.

The idea of founding the Congregation of Missionaries came to him while he was working in the Canary Islands. As soon as he returned to Vic in mid-May 1849, St. Anthony Mary Claret consulted his friends, Canons Soler and Passarell, concerning his "plan to form a congregation of priests who would both be, and be called, Sons of the Immaculate Heart of Mary."[48] This testimony of the founder shows that he thought of the Congregation as something new and distinct from the other, earlier projects he had discussed at great length with his friends before leaving for the Canary Islands in early 1848. This confirms our thesis, that the idea of the Apostolic Fraternity was transformed into the idea of the Congregation during the Saint's stay in the Canary Islands.

Years later, testifying at the Apostolic Process for Claret's

Beatification, Fr. Clement Serrat shows that he held the same conviction, namely, that the Saint conceived the idea of founding his Congregation:

> ...as report has it, after the Missions he preached in Catalonia before going to the Canary Islands and, above all, in those very Islands, when he saw the abundant fruits that were being garnered and the few priests who were dedicated to preaching.[49]

According to this witness, the Saint had already formed some idea of what he was going to do after preaching his missions in Catalonia, that is, sometime between the spring of 1847 and the early months of 1848; but his ideas took shape "above all" while he was preaching in the Canary Islands. We have seen that it was in 1847 that he formed the idea of a *community* of missionary priests. But it was only upon his return from the Canary Islands that he had a clear and precise notion of the *Congregation.* Even as late as December 7, 1848, in a letter to Casadevall, the Saint was still speaking only of the Apostolic Fraternity.[50]

What had happened to bring about the great change? Certainly the Saint's apostolic experiences in the Canary Islands had made him feel the need to establish something more lasting, something that could serve to spread his apostolate to many lands. As early as 1845, he had felt a desire to evangelize other regions of Spain beyond Catalonia,[51] but here he had put his own hand into the wound of need, and the experience forced him to deepen his insights. Another factor that must have pressured him into evolving his plans was the constant urging of his friends to return to Catalonia to give life to another project, which was itself not too precisely defined. Since the Saint writes Caixal that he had already had the latter's idea in Catalonia, we must identify Caixal's plan with that of a simple association of priests, only somewhat more organized than the Apostolic Fraternity of 1846. All of these elements must have given Claret much food for thought.

But the crowning touch to these gradually maturing plans of the Saint was an idea that came to him as an inspiration from heaven. He even set this down in a set of notes. Unfortunately, these notes were eventually lost, but Fr. Xifré had them and cited from them in the second edition of his *Spirit of the Congregation.*

In proof of this, we present the affections and resolutions which he
[Claret] made at prayer on the day when the Giver of all good gifts
inspired him with this idea: "Aided by your grace," he said to God
and the Blessed Virgin, "and by the companions you have destined
for me, I shall found this Congregation—of which I shall be the last
of all and the servant of all. Hence, I shall kiss their feet and wait on
them at table, and count myself most fortunate in rendering them
these services."[52]

The style in which this note is written leads us to suspect that
Fr. Xifré was quoting the Saint's words literally. The phrase,
"aided by your grace, and by the companions . . ." (*ayudado* de
vuestra gracia, y de *los compañeros* . . .), reveals one of the oddi-
ties of St. Claret's Castilian style: the use of the preposition *de,*
instead of *por,* to indicate personal agency. Another of his typical thought-patterns was to jump from a general idea to a concrete proposal or detail. Thus we see him moving abruptly from
the general statement: "I shall found this Congregation," to the
humble detail: "Hence, I shall kiss their feet."

In fact, Fr. Xifré practically affirms that he was citing the
founder here, by a footnote referring to this passage:

All that we have related is clear from the notes he made on the day
when God communicated the aforesaid plan to him, in which he wrote
down the affections, lights and resolutions he formed while at prayer
that day, and which, by a special coincidence, we were able to get
hold of.[53]

Fr. Clotet, for his part, affirms that the Saint attributed the
idea of founding the Congregation to an inspiration he received
from the Blessed Virgin.[54]

Fr. Cristobál Fernández—and rightly, to our way of thinking—
suspects that the idea of founding the Congregation came to the
Saint during the retreat he made in the Canary Islands, early in
April 1849, prior to returning to Catalonia. He points out that
this was not the Saint's accustomed time for making a retreat,
especially since he could have done so in greater tranquility at
his accustomed time, after returning to Catalonia.[55] And, we
would add, this is the only retreat for which we possess no notes
by the Saint. Could it not be that the notes Fr. Xifré had, but
which were later lost, were this missing set of retreat notes?

III

A Congregation of Missionaries

On May 11, 1849, after returning from his missionary campaign in the Canary Islands, Fr. Claret arrived in Tarragona, the ecclesiastical capital of Catalonia, where his good friend and collaborator, Canon Joseph Caixal, lived. Although Claret does not expressly mention Caixal in his *Autobiography* among the list of priests he consulted about founding the Congregation, it is nonetheless clear that he did so on this occasion. We have already seen how in September and October of the previous year, Caixal had written Claret to suggest the advisability of founding a missionary institution, offering to collaborate in the endeavor and urging Claret to return to Catalonia. The Saint had replied that he concurred in the idea, but that the time was not ripe yet. By May 1849, however, Claret felt that the time had indeed come and, in the normal course of events, he must have talked the matter over with his old friend. In fact, just two weeks later Claret wrote Caixal that he had already received an offer from "a number of persons who will, in time prove most helpful for the idea we have proposed."[1]

Confirmed in his ideas by Caixal, the Saint immediately proceeded to Vic, where he revealed his plans to two priests of the chancery. One of them, James Soler, rector of the Seminary of Vic, generously offered Claret the use of the seminary as a gathering place for his companions. Finally, he spoke with Bishop Casadevall, who not only praised the idea but promised to refurbish the abandoned priory of La Merced for their use. The founder then set about recruiting followers and soon managed to attract five. Fr. Stephen Sala, a well-educated and well-mannered priest, had made the Spiritual Exercises under Claret's direction in 1843 and had belonged to his mission team since 1844. He was destined to become the Congregation's director general when Claret left Spain to assume his duties as archbishop of Santiago, Cuba. Sala's election was fully to Claret's liking, since he thought of him as having "one and the same spirit as I do."[2] Sala died prematurely in 1858. A second cofounder, Fr. Joseph Xifré, was a zealous and energetic man. He succeeded Sala as director general in 1858 and served in that capacity until 1899. Xifré oversaw the expansion of the Congregation into Africa and Latin America. At time of the founding, he was thirty-two years old and, although he had never worked with Claret, he had already spent some years in preaching missions. Fr. Dominic Fábregas, who was also thirty-two at the time, was a timid and reserved man, but he had worked with Claret since 1846.[3] Fr. Manuel Vilaró, who was thirty-three, was a small-town pastor who had joined the Saint's mission team in 1847.[4] He accompanied Claret to Cuba but became ill there and had to return to Spain, where he died in 1852. Fr. James Clotet, twenty-seven years old, had done parish work in two small towns. A man of intense spirituality, he was entrusted with the formation of the first Claretian Brothers and served as subdirector general of the Congregation from 1858 to 1888. As subdirector he governed the Congregation during Fr. Xifré's long absences for visits to the Claretian Communities in Africa and Latin America. Fr. Clotet died in 1898. The Cause of Fr. Clotet's Beatification is under discussion in Rome.

Although these five priests, who lived with the Saint, are the only ones he lists in his *Autobiography* as forming the original nucleus of the Congregation, we know that at the beginning the Saint considered one more man to be a "brother," i.e., a member of the community: Canon Caixal, although—by agreement with the founder—he did not live with the rest. Caixal, who had, moreover, to reside in Tarragona where he was a canon of the cathedral, was director of the Religious Library and served as Claret's righthand man in Catholic publications. In May 1850 the Saint informed him that in the assignment of Apostle-patrons to the various members of the community he, Caixal, had been given no less a patron than the great St. Paul.[5] Some months later, however, the Saint left Spain for Cuba and Caixal's bonds with the Congregation ceased de facto. The separation only increased when Caixal was elected bishop of Urgel in 1852.

St. Anthony Claret was pleased with his first companions. Recalling his first conversations with them, he later wrote in his *Autobiography*: "I talked with a number of priests whom the Lord had given the same spirit that motivated me."[6] This communion of spirits must have made a profound impression on him since he refers to it again in the first two petitions he wrote on behalf of his Congregation in 1859, one addressed to Pope Pius IX and the other to the papal nuncio in Madrid. In the former he states that his companions are "driven by the same spirit"[7] and in the latter that they are "animated by one and the same spirit."[8] It would not be out of place to mention here that shortly before Claret expressed the assessment alluded to in his *Autobiography,* he wrote a definition of the word "spirit" in his clerical handbook, *The Well-Instructed Seminarian*: "an impulse, movement or inclination of our inner being toward some thing"[9] and he goes on to speak of the ecclesiastical spirit as a sharing, through grace and the gifts, in the same Spirit which anointed Christ.[10] It was not, then, simply or even mainly a question of certain shared ideas or similar qualities and temperaments; after all, the cofounders were a very diverse lot. What they shared was a permanent inclination toward certain ideals, an inclination that, in the long run, came from the Holy Spirit. It was this coincidence of vocations that ultimately produced their communion of minds and hearts.

On July 16, 1849, at three o'clock in the afternoon, these five young priests joined St. Anthony Claret in a small room of the Seminary of Vic. The Saint prophetically announced to them that on that day they were beginning "a great work" and then went on to deliver the opening talk for the nine-day retreat in which he would lead them. We have no direct data on the manner in which this first retreat was conducted, but we do know that Claret invariably followed the Ignatian method as commonly practiced in his day, namely, a series of meditations preached to a group. We also know that from their earliest days the Claretians invariably held to the practice of four hour-long meditations each day, and we may reasonably assume that this tradition began with their founding retreat. Besides these meditations, the Saint customarily added a special talk each day. Fortunately, we still possess the outlines he composed for these talks.

After a brief introduction, the first talk deals with the theme of vocation and mission and is based on a text from St. Paul: "God, who had specially chosen me while I was still in my mother's womb, called me through his grace and chose to reveal his Son to me, so that I might preach the Good News about him to the pagans" (Gal. 1:15-16). In this passage, St. Paul refers to his vocation in terms drawn from Isaiah 49:1 and Jeremiah 1:5. Claret then goes on to recall that the Apostles and St. Paul were called to follow Christ and that Moses, Isaiah, and Jeremiah had likewise received a divine call. In doing this, the Saint was actually projecting on his companions the same biblical texts and figures of Apostles and Prophets through which he had discovered his own vocation to evangelize. In the remaining talks, dealing with the following of Christ and various evangelical virtues, Claret constantly refers to the calling and duties of the preacher,[11] although he derives his ascetical commonplaces from Alphonsus Rodriguez. The retreat ended on the feast of St. James the Apostle, patron of Spain. On that day, the five companions unanimously elected Claret as their superior and began a particularly intense period of preparation for the ministry under his guidance. On October 9, 1849, they moved to the abandoned priory of Our Lady of Mercy (La Merced), which became the motherhouse of the Claretian Congregation.

The Basic End of the Congregation as Revealed in Its Constitutions

All of the data adduced thus far clearly indicate the type of congregation that St. Anthony Claret founded on July 16, 1849. The founder had felt called to preach the Gospel and for nine years had done so in Spain and the Canary Islands. During this period he had repeatedly organized teams of priests dedicated to this same ministry. Three of the cofounders of the Congregation had belonged to these teams, while a fourth, Fr. Xifré, had decided on his own to leave parish work for a life of itinerant preaching. Thus it came as no surprise that when the Saint took the decisive step of establishing the Congregation, he spoke to his companions, during the founding retreat, of the mission of the Apostles and Prophets, as well as of the conditions required for carrying out an evangelizing mission. What he was proposing was, evidently, a "Congregation of Missionaries." And it was precisely as a missionary institute that the Congregation was classified from its inception.

Between 1849 and 1850 St. Anthony Mary Claret wrote the first Claretian *Constitutions*, although they were not printed until 1857, when they appeared with a few additions. As St. Thomas Aquinas rightly taught, the end of any society is an essential element that determines and conditions its whole being. Thus the ends chosen by a founder in creating a religious family become one of its constitutive elements and, as the Second Vatican Council has insisted, religious institutes must remain faithful to these ends throughout their history.[12] It behooves us, then, to pay special attention to those texts in which a founder defines the ends of his work.

Following a custom that began as early as the thirteenth century, when specialized forms of the religious life appeared, St. Anthony Mary Claret defines the mission of his institute in the church toward the beginning of the *Constitutions.* The second article of the *Constitutions,* which determines the ends of the Congregation, has remained essentially unchanged since its first draft: "Its object will be to seek in all things the glory of God, the sanctification of its own members and the salvation of all the inhabitants of the world, subject to the following regulations."[13] The definitive *Constitutions* of 1865 add to this only the prescription of love and reverence for the Holy See and of collaboration with the episcopate: "Its object will be to seek in all things the glory of God, the sanctification of its members and the salvation of souls throughout the world; hence, they shall show great reverence, love and obedience toward the Supreme Pontiff and the Holy Apostolic See, and shall be the steadfast helpers of Prelates in the ministry of the word, subject, however, to the following regulations."[14]

Indeed, we might even say that the formulation of this second article of the *Constitutions,* at least in essence, antedates the founding of the Congregation. In Document IV of the Apostolic Fraternity, "Points on Which We Have to Talk," written in August 1946, Claret defined the ends of an apostolic association he was then thinking of founding.

> Its material object will be a union of understanding and will, with everyone teaching the same thing... (for this, they will use the book that is being printed).
>
> Its formal object will be the greater glory of God, the sanctification of our own souls and those of our neighbors; to declare ourselves against the enemies of the soul, which are the world, the flesh and the devil; to uproot vices and plant virtues; to foster perfection and the practice of devotion to Mary and Jesus Christ, and the frequent reception of the sacraments.[15]

In Document VIII of the Apostolic Fraternity, drafted between 1847 and 1848 for the "Brothers of Jesus and Mary" (a provisional title for a future missionary association), Claret described its end.

> The principal object and occupation of the Brothers of Jesus and Mary is to go on missions and to give retreats in their house.[16]

Finally, in Document IX, written shortly before the founding of the congregation, the ends of the unnamed group of priests are formulated.

> The object of... is the glory of God, the salvation of their own souls and the salvation of the souls of their neighbors.[17]

What is lacking here is the title of the group and the extension of their mission to the "whole world." For the rest, with a few stylistic changes, we have here the text of Article 2 of the primitive *Constitutions.* We could say, then, that in this case we are dealing with the only text of the *Constitutions* composed before the founding of the Congregation.

Comparing the various draftings of the "object" of these early associations of priests, we begin to notice that Claret seems to pass easily back and forth between two distinct formulations, which we may call "Text A" and "Text B," respectively. Text A relates to the *threefold end* of the group: the glory of God, the sanctification of its members, and the salvation of their neighbors. Text B stresses the *ministries* of preaching missions and giving retreats as the exclusive pursuits of the group. Document IV (1846) follows the Text A format; Document VIII (1847-1848) follows the Text B format; Document IX (1848-1849) returns to the Text A format, with its stress on the threefold end.

Significantly, we see the same trend continuing even after the founding of the Congregation. The 1849 *Constitutions* (revised and published in 1857) and the 1865 *Constitutions* both follow the Text A format. The same is true of the prologue to the *Rules for Secular Clergy Living in Community,* written in 1864.[18] On the other hand, in a letter to the papal nuncio that same year (1864), petitioning the approval of the *Constitutions,* Claret includes a "Brief Notice," which states that the "object of the Congregation" is to give parish missions and preach retreats.[19] Again, in a letter he wrote to Fr. Xifré in 1869—twenty years after the founding of the Congregation—asking that the Congregation also become involved in the ministry of Christian education, Claret refers to missions and retreats as the *primary object* of the Congregation.[20]

The ease with which Claret passes from one formulation to the other shows us that for the founder, both formulations were equivalent. The end of the institute might be defined either by citing Article 2 of the *Constitutions* (threefold end) or by referring to the later paragraphs in which certain ministries are assigned to the Congregation. This provides us with a valuable clue in deciphering the true meaning of this second article of the *Constitutions.*

The Threefold End

Having distinguished in the *Constitutions* between the object and the ministries of the Congregation, St. Anthony Mary Claret assigns it a threefold finality, namely, to seek in all things the glory of God, the sanctification of its members, and the salvation of their neighbors throughout the world. In his enumeration of this threefold end, he was consciously following a rigorously theological order: the one established by St. Thomas in the *Summa Theologica.*[21] In this theological framework the glory of God is infinitely superior to the other two ends and in some way includes them, since God is given glory by grace, which is a sharing in His glory, and by collaborating with Him as instruments in the sharing of grace with the neighbor. Seen in this light, the glory of God is the primary and general end, which is achieved by carrying out the other two proximate and secondary ends of sanctification and the apostolate. We should note that in the primitive *Constitutions,* after a statement of the title, end,[22] and organization[23] of the Congregation, the following, longer chapters deal, respectively, with the means of individual sanctification[24] and the means for saving the souls of others.[25] By following this procedure, the Saint was simply commenting on the second article of the *Constitutions,* dealing with the threefold end of the institute.

What is the significance of this threefold end and to what extent does the second article of the *Constitutions* specify the object for which the Congregation was founded? The question is by no means idle, since stating that an institute is founded to give glory to God, to sanctify its members, and to save others is tantamount to saying everything or almost nothing: everything—because the highest ends for which any Christian should live are expressed in the statement; almost nothing—because, practically speaking, it does nothing to determine the spirit of the institute. In fact, with a few basic changes of meaning, the entire article could be made to fit the needs of institutes with the most diverse spirit and rules.

In the church there are communities of evangelical life that reject classification by the criterion of apostolate, i.e., on the basis of the presence or absence of an apostolate in their life. They are communities *of life.* Although some of them have developed an intense ministerial activity, others exclude such activities altogether and still others adopt them only occasionally.

On the other hand, there are communities that were formed above all to serve Christ and His church through ministerial activities. But even among these, we may distinguish two general types. In the first type, the concrete form of life appears as a synthesis of internal observances and external activities. Their rule of life is not derived solely from the exigencies of community life with its observances and rituals nor solely from the exigencies of apostolic ministry, but rather from both at once. This is the *conventual* type of religious life. In this second type, which has developed from the 16th century on, the concrete form of life derives from the community's orientation toward ministerial activity. Even though such groups highly value the grace of fraternal community as something substantive and not merely functional, this communion is expressed within the context of an apostolic vocation and, for that reason, community observances are either done away with entirely or reduced to a minimum. This is the *apostolic* form of life, taking the expression in the sense it has acquired in modern times.

Returning to the formulation of the ends of the Claretian Congregation as expressed by its founder in the *Constitutions,* it is quite clear that the very letter of the second article, in stating that the salvation of the neighbor is an essential part of the end of the institute, does not permit us to consider apostolic ministry as something merely marginal or tacked on as an afterthought. The Claretian family was born to work for the salvation of others. Even so, two interpretations of this fact are theoretically possible, depending on whether one follows the line of conventual life or that of the modern type of apostolic life.

One might argue the first interpretation on the basis that the second article of the *Constitutions* speaks of the sanctification of the members and of the salvation of souls, thus, on the surface of things, presenting them as two diverse finalities. Some years back (and erroneously, one might add), it was the custom to relate the religious life with one's own sanctification, while relating ministry with the salvation of one's neighbor. And it is well known that in monastic and conventual theology, the religious life is expressed through community observances. In this interpretation, where religious life and ministry are proposed as two parallel and to some extent independent ends, ministry tends to appear as something added to the religious life. In contrast, we find that the *Constitutions* of the Society of Jesus, a strictly apostolic institute, establish as its end "not only to aim at the salvation and perfection of their own souls with the aid of divine grace, but also, with the same aid, to strive to help bring about the salvation and perfection of their neighbors."[26] It is obvious that in the teaching of the Society of Jesus, religious life is not related exclusively to one's own sanctification nor is it expressed through community observances. Religious life and ministry-oriented life are identified. The theology underlying this position had already been formulated, as is well known, by St. Thomas Aquinas: what makes a life religious is the total gift of self to the service of God, and this can be done in those ministerial works whereby one serves the neighbor for the sake of God,[27] or serves Christ in His members.[28] St. Ignatius Loyola understood that the religious life could be fully realized in a type of existence centered in apostolic ministry.

Since, as we stated above, the literal wording of this second article of the Claretian *Constitutions* could be taken ambiguously and thus lend itself to conflicting interpretations, it is very important that we try to establish the founder's meaning on this cardinal point.

The Ends That Claret Proposed for His Various Institutions

A helpful starting point for discerning Claret's meaning is to examine the ends he proposed for the various institutions he successively founded. The first Claretian association of which we possess a copy of the bylaws—the Spiritual Guild Against Blasphemy—had as its end the concrete goal expressed in its title. However, when its members came to enroll in it, they had to affirm that they were doing so because they were desirous of the greater honor and glory of God, the Blessed Virgin, and the Saints, as well as of the spiritual well-being of their neighbors.[29] The introduction to the rules of the Apostolic Society of the Most Holy and Immaculate Heart of Mary (1847) states that its object is the "greater glory of God and the spiritual and corporeal good of our neighbors" and repeats, in the second article of the rules themselves, that its object is "the greater glory of God, the good of their own souls and the spiritual and corporeal good of their neighbors."[30] Even here, in this seemingly devotional brotherhood, we see that it was really a fully apostolic association, born of a desire to bring about the good of the neighbor. The same is true of the St. Vincent de Paul Conferences which, as Claret formulates their statutes, have the same threefold end.

These Conferences, under the patronage of the glorious St. Vincent de Paul and St. Michael, have as their object the greater honor and glory of God and of the Most Sacred Hearts of Jesus and Mary, the perfection and salvation of the associates of the Conferences, and the salvation of their neighbors.[31]

In the *Plan for the Academy of St. Michael,* we are told that the object of the academy is to promote and spread good books, and through them, good doctrine. But two paragraphs later we are told more precisely that the aim of the academy is to praise God in this life by means of truth and to journey toward Him by means of virtue.[32] What we really have here, then, in a somewhat different formulation (the final form of this short work was not worked out by Claret) is the same threefold end of giving glory to God (praise God), the sanctification of its members (journeying toward Him), and the salvation of their neighbors (promoting and spreading good books and doctrine).

In an appendix to *Notes of a Plan for Preserving the Beauty of the Church,* the Saint establishes the following ends for the clerical community he founded at El Escorial.

> To praise, love and serve God. To pray for the souls of the kings [buried there], and perform the suffrages prescribed for them. To strive for their own perfection and devote themselves to the formation of the seminarians.[33]

All of the above instances bring us to a single basic conclusion: For all of the institutions he founded, however they differed in nature, St. Anthony Claret customarily set the same threefold end, namely, the glory of God, the sanctification of the members, and the salvation of their neighbors. He did this for associations that were planned and centered in the apostolate, such as the Apostolic Society of the Most Holy and Immaculate Heart of Mary. In two of the cases mentioned above, the Academy of St. Michael and the Escorial Community, the concrete end that moved the Saint to found them is cited in third place: the apostolate of culture to the cultured (Academy) and the apostolate of seminary formation (Escorial). We know that the clerical community at the Escorial was not founded to pray for the kings buried there (that end had been assigned centuries earlier by Philip II of Spain) nor primarily to provide a means of perfection for the teaching staff. The main purpose of the foundation was obviously to provide a group of priests to care for the students attending the seminary and high school that Claret had established in the ancient monastery. The same can be said for the Academy of St. Michael. The real motive that led the Saint to found it was the apostolate of Christian culture. In both cases, the end that immediately and really impelled Claret to found these institutions was the one he stated in third place. He realized, of course, that anyone who really dedicated himself to the apostolate of the Christian press or to the education of seminarians would do so only for the glory of God and would, in the process, find a most effective means for his own sanctification. But when the Saint came to express himself doctrinally and in writing, he chose to spell out explicitly the three ends for which he founded a work.

This excursus on the rules Claret drew up for many of his institutions shows that the Saint constantly assigned them the same ends as those he gave to his Congregation, even in the case of associations dedicated to the most diverse concrete aims. Frequently, he expressed their proper end in third place. It would be tempting at this point to apply these findings to the second number of the *Constitutions* as follows: the Saint expressly stated the threefold end of the Congregation out of a concern for a complete and correct doctrinal formulation, but what he really had in mind as the specific element in the Congregation was the end of saving souls by means of certain missionary ministries. But is this really the case? In a word, yes. The many texts in which the founder and the first members of the Congregation explain the end for which it was founded all bolster this hypothesis, as we shall presently see.

The Testimony of the Founder

Fortunately, the Saint himself has left us some clear testimonies on the motives that led him to found the institute. These testimonies are particularly cogent, not only because they are nearly contemporary with the events of the founding, but also because they appear in official documents addressed to the pope and the papal nuncio.

Less than a month after the founding of the Congregation, Claret wrote to Nuncio Brunelli, informing him of the initiative he had taken.

> In view of the great dearth of evangelical and apostolic preachers in
> the land of Spain; in view also of the people's great desire to hear the

word of God, and of the many urgent requests for such preachers to come and proclaim the Gospel in many cities and towns, I determined to gather together and instruct a number of zealous companions, so that I might thus be able to do with the help of others, what I could not do by myself alone.[34]

Ten years later, he made a similar statement in a letter to Pius IX, petitioning the approval of the Congregation and its *Constitutions.* Upon his return from Rome, Claret wrote (referring to himself in the third person) as follows:

At that time he began preaching missions with the approval of the Bishop of Vic. Other priests with the same spirit joined him. They constantly devoted themselves to the same apostolic labors and, so that all might proceed in orderly fashion, he [Claret] wrote the present Constitutions.[35]

The first Claretian Missionaries had come, then, simply to collaborate with the Saint in the ministry of preaching missions. He had already explained this in a petition he sent to the Holy See in August 1845, regarding the priestly fraternity collaborating with him then, in what was to be a stage in the development of his future foundation, the Congregation of Missionary Sons of the Immaculate Heart of Mary. In this early letter he states:

Anthony Claret... humbly represents: that, considering the injuries suffered by the Catholic Religion, he resolved to oppose them effectively, and has spent five continuous years in the sacred ministry of missions, of preaching retreats to clergy and laity, of patiently hearing confessions—sometimes even at night, since the day was not sufficient—and of traveling in the manner of the apostles throughout the diocese of Catalonia. His endeavors were blessed by God and quite soon he saw a great number of scattered sheep return to the bosom of the Father who, in His divine mercy, has now deigned to call other truly zealous evangelical workers, ready and resolved to follow the same tenor of life and apostolic labors as that of the petitioner, so that they will now be able to spread throughout the other provinces of Spain, sowing in them the Word of God.[36]

In both of these letters, St. Anthony Claret is clearly consistent in describing how the idea of the Congregation took gradual shape in his mind. Sensing his inability to cope with the ills of the church by himself alone, he called on a group of priests to form a missionary association with him, an association dedicated to preaching the Word of God. It was this preoccupation which really moved him to found his institute.

Thus we see that years later, in 1864, in a petition to the papal nuncio for approval of the *Constitutions,* Claret still states the end of the Congregation as follows:

> The object of the aforesaid missionaries consists in giving missions throughout the world and preaching retreats to all classes of persons, especially priests, students and nuns.[37]

As anyone can see, in specifying the object of the Congregation the Saint has combined Article 2 of the first part of the *Constitutions* with Article 63 of the second part, which treats of the preferred means of apostolate.

The Cofounders

Fr. Joseph Xifré, cofounder and later general of the Claretians, presents the same picture of the institute. According to him, the primitive Congregation was no more than a "pious association whose end was evangelical preaching."[38] In *The Spirit of the Congregation,* Xifré wrote that the institute had "the same object which, with admirable results, moved him (the founder) to proclaim the divine word to all men."[39] In a letter to the *Revista Católica,* dated June 5, 1862, he stated that the object of the Congregation was preaching missions.[40] Toward the end of his life he repeatedly stated that the founder had affirmed that "our primary object is preaching missions."[41] But he had previously said the same, much more expressively, in his manuscript, *Chronicle of the Congregation,* where he narrates the origins of the institute.

> Our Venerable Founder shone, as we have said, in all the virtues. But his admirable zeal commanded everyone's attention.... We repeat: his zeal was beyond all fathoming. He desired to spread the Gospel message throughout the world. He vehemently yearned that, until the end of time, the preaching and catechizing of the poor and the rich, the learned and the ignorant, priests and laity, would continue everywhere. He ardently desired that all should be saved, because all are in the image of God and cost the price of Christ's Blood. These burning desires were always about his heart and formed the object of his fervent prayers to the Most High, and since they were of God, they were heard.
>
> That Lord whose eyes are fixed on the just and whose ears are

attentive to their prayers, deigned to favor his servant, inspiring him to found a Congregation of men who, since they were endowed with the same apostolic spirit as his own, would have the same aims that he himself desired and prayed for. He revealed to him that this Congregation would spread throughout the world and would last until the end of time.[42]

As anyone can see, Fr. Xifré's testimony as to the object of the Congregation is unequivocally clear. The Congregation is the result of the overwhelming apostolic zeal of the Saint, a zeal which he wished to extend to the whole world and prolong for all time. To fulfill this end, God inspired in him the idea of founding a Congregation, one whose spirit would be as intensely apostolic as his own. The idea which moved the great missionary was, above all, the salvation of souls.

Fr. James Clotet, cofounder and subdirector general of the Congregation until 1888, offers the same testimony. In his chronicle of the founding, he tells us that before the event, Claret proposed

> ... to each one separately, the plan he had of forming a Congregation of priests who would be exclusively dedicated to preaching missions and giving retreats, to the extent that the circumstances of the times would allow.[43]

In the *Life of the Servant of God*, Clotet confirms this: "He [Claret] had felt moved for a long time to form a Congregation of priests who would be dedicated to the holy missions."[44] To these testimonies from within the Congregation, we may add another from a priest who had been a close friend of the Saint since his youth, although he never joined the institute. Fr. Luis Sauquer stated that as early as 1839 the Saint had discussed with him the opportuneness of founding a missionary preaching center in Catalonia.[45]

All of these testimonies of the cofounders lead us to the same conclusion: the immediate end that really impelled St. Anthony Claret to found the Congregation was his desire to save souls, mainly through the missionary preaching of the Word of God. In contrast, he was not decisively motivated by a desire to provide the first Claretian fathers and brothers with a particularly effective means for attaining personal perfection. Not a single one of the texts in which he describes his concrete goals alludes to this secondary aim. He knew, of course, that the practice of a missionary vocation constituted a sure and effective means of attaining Christian perfection. He himself had been sanctified in it, and he realized that in inviting others to consecrate themselves to missionary ministry, he was offering them a sure road to their own sanctification. But this secondary intention was not the real motive force that drove him; rather, it was the need of souls, it was people's hunger and thirst for the Word of God. For Claret, the pursuit and realization of this end entailed the achievement of the other two ends: the sanctification of the members of the Congregation and, ultimately, the glory of God.

The Meaning of the Second Article of the Constitutions

To grasp the proper meaning of the second article of the *Constitutions,* we must bear in mind certain fluctuations in Claret's vocabulary. By the *object* of an institute, he means two distinct things. In the *historical* sense, he means the motive that, in fact, led him to found his institute, a motive that coincides with the principal occupation of the members of the institute. In this sense, missionary preaching is the object of the Congregation, as the Saint himself stated,[46] and the cofounders repeated after him. In the *theological* sense, the object of an institute includes the diverse supernatural ends toward which the missionaries should tend in achieving their concrete and immediate end. In this sense, the object of the Congregation is the glory of God, the sanctification of its members, and the salvation of their neighbors. The manner in which these three aims are incarnated in the concrete and immediate end (apostolate) helps us see how they are interrelated. All of the apostolates and apostolic life of the Congregation are immediately directed toward the salvation of the neighbor and, by means of consecration to this ministry, toward the sanctification of the missionaries, while the glory of God is incarnated in both.

This is tantamount to saying that the second article of the *Constitutions,* on the threefold end of the Congregation, cannot rightly be understood without reference to Article 63 of the second part, which deals with the means of the apostolate. The founder himself followed this procedure in explaining the object of his institute to the papal nuncio, where he fused both of these articles together: "The object of the aforesaid missionaries consists in giving mission (II, 63) throughout the world (I, 2) and preaching retreats to all classes of persons (II, 63), especially priests, students and nuns."[47] We find a confirmation of this in Claret's *Autobiography* where, in describing the motives that led him to embark on his own preaching career, he mentions the same threefold end that he later assigned to his Congregation in the second article of the *Constitutions*: "Whenever I went to a town . . . my only aim was to glorify God and save souls."[48] The Saint then goes on to give the basic outline of a typical mission sermon in which he spells out his motives for a group attending a mission.[49] He devoted himself intensely to the ministry of the Word (concrete and immediate object) for the glory of God and the salvation of souls (parts one and three of the threefold end). Since Claret was speaking to others in this section of the *Autobiography,* he made no mention of his own sanctification (part two of the threefold end), but one needs only to read the ascetic section of the *Autobiography* to form an idea of the degree to which his apostolic life sanctified him.

It might not be out of place to note here that Claret may well have derived some of his ideas from a pastoral letter by Bishop Philip Bertrán of Salamanca. The Saint had read the letter carefully, as his many underlinings and marginal notations show. Bishop Bertrán contends that there can be no other end for preaching the Gospel than the glory of God and the salvation of our neighbor. But he goes on to insist that without great personal holiness on the part of the preacher, his preaching would bear no fruit. It is quite possible that Claret had this letter before him as he wrote the chapter on his motives for preaching in his *Autobiography.* At any rate, it concurs remarkably with his own point of view and helps us understand why he should have assigned this threefold end to an institute dedicated to preaching.[50]

As we stated earlier, a strictly literal reading of Article 2 of the *Constitutions* might not provide an exact definition of the mission of the Claretians in the church (since the interrelation of the three ends of the Congregation and, above all, the manner in which they should be concretely embodied may be understood in various ways); nevertheless, a careful study of Claret's vocabulary should show us clearly that even in a literal reading, this article expresses what the founder had repeatedly and un-equivocally stated concerning the missionary character of his Congregation. In the 1865 edition of the *Constitutions* he states:

> Its object will be to seek in all things the glory of God, the sanctification of its members and the salvation of souls throughout the world.[51]

The primitive text of 1849-1857 had similarly stated that:

> Its object will be to strive in all things for the glory of God, their own sanctification and the salvation of all the inhabitants of the world.[52]

It is a pity that by failing to make a comparative study of this text with other texts of Claret's, various commentators have frequently missed its exact meaning. Thus, it has repeatedly been regarded as simply an expression of the catholicity of the Congregation; in virtue of this text, in which Claret expressed the breadth of his zeal, the Congregation is called to spread throughout the world. This is, doubtless, a legitimate conclusion, but it is not the only or even the main thing the Saint was driving at. What he expressly meant to affirm here is the missionary character of his Congregation. In fact, the trait which in the Saint's eyes distinguishes a missionary from other priests and from laity dedicated to parish ministry, is that the missionary has received as his field of work not this or that particular place or this or that particular flock but, rather, the whole world and its inhabitants.

The earliest text in which Claret expresses this conviction is his "Explanation of the Gospel Parable of the Talents," which appears as an appendix to the edition of *Advice to a Priest* published by Pla in 1846. The date is significant, since it seems that the Saint had begun that year to make up his mind concerning the organization of a group of missionaries who would act as his helpers. The Saint's words are revealing.

> The first servant signifies an Apostolic Missionary, to whom the Lord has entrusted, besides the talent of the priestly dignity, another four, which are the four corners of the earth. This He did, when He said: "Going into whole world, preach the Gospel to every creature."
>
> The second servant signifies a Pastor, to whom the Lord has entrusted, besides the talent of the priestly dignity, the further talent of a parish.
>
> The third servant is any priest to whom the Lord has entrusted the single talent of the priestly dignity.[53]

Note that this corresponds closely with what Claret wrote in 1864 in the foreword to his *Rules for Clerics Living in Community*. Again, the date is significant, since it was precisely in that year when the founder set about rewriting the Claretian *Constitutions*. In this text he tells us that what distinguishes the members of his Congregation from other priests living in community is that the former

> ...have fixed abodes in which to live and reside, but they remain there only so long as their superior disposes, or until he sends them to another town, another diocese or another country, if that should be required for the greater glory of God or the good of souls. Hence its members do not possess benefices, dignities or anything else....
>
> The latter, on the contrary, are fixed in a diocese and possess offices, benefices, curacies, canonries, dignities, professorships, etc.[54]

This amounts to saying, in the Gospel phraseology of his 1846 "Explanation," that the former have received the talents of the four corners of the earth from the Lord, whereas the latter have received the single talent of the care of souls.

Following this same line of logic, we would also have to include the Saint's refusal of the archbishopric of Cuba, which was offered him in 1849. He writes the nuncio that in so doing, "I would be tying myself down to a single archdiocese, while my spirit goes out to the whole world."[55]

If we are going to grasp the genuine meaning of Article 2 of the *Constitutions*, it must be in the light of these and still other texts that might be adduced.[56] These texts make it clear that describing the object of the Congregation as "the salvation of souls throughout the world" is equivalent to saying that it is a Congregation of Missionaries. It implies a call to realize, in all its fullness, the Gospel command: "Going into the whole world, preach the Gospel to every creature." All the members of the Congregation receive from the Lord, through the hierarchy of the church, the mission to evangelize the whole world. This is their special field of work. This is also the source of that "instability" that, as the foreword to the *Rules for Clerics* points out, distinguishes them from those who have the care of souls in a fixed place. It is likewise the reason why catholicity is an essential trait of the institute to which they belong.

IV

The Ministry of the Word

The close relationship that Claret established between Article 2 of the first part of the *Constitutions* (dealing with the ends of the Claretian Congregation) and Article 63 of the second part (dealing with the means to be employed in its apostolate) impels us to examine the latter carefully to arrive at a more specific notion of the nature of the Congregation. Indeed, we would be impelled to do so even if the founder had not established this relationship, since it is obvious that the characteristics of a missionary congregation are shaped not only by its apostolic ends but also by the type of ministry to which it is dedicated. There is a great difference, for example, between an institute exclusively dedicated to teaching and a missionary congregation founded for the evangelization of non-Christians. The formation, lifestyle, and even spirituality of both groups would differ considerably.

In fact, the researcher can easily verify this matter, since the texts in which St. Anthony Mary Claret and his first collaborators set forth the ends of the Congregation do so expressly in terms of the means they employ in the apostolate. For this reason we turn, now, to a consideration of these texts.

Earliest Claretian Ministries

The earliest witness to the Saint's intentions regarding the apostolic traits of his Congregation is a conversation he held ten years prior to its founding. At the Process for Claret's Beatification, Fr. Luis Sauquer, a friend and classmate of Claret's seminary days, testified that the Servant of God "wanted to consult his spiritual director, Fr. Peter Bach, concerning the founding of a center for missions in this country."[1]

What we have here is obviously the first seed of the future Congregation, although limited at that time to a simple mission center in Catalonia. Later, a few days before the founding, Claret explained to the cofounders his "plan to form a Congregation of priests who would be exclusively dedicated to the preaching of missions and retreats, insofar as the circumstances of the times might allow."[2]

According to Fr. Xifré, the end of the newly founded Congregation was "evangelical preaching."[3] The scope had broadened from that of a single house to that of an institute, but the aim of the institute remained the same: missionary preaching embodied in the classic forms of the day, missions and retreats.

The documents written by the Saint in the period between the above-mentioned dates concur with what his companions state.

> The principal object and occupation of the Brothers of Jesus and Mary, is to go out on missions and to give retreats at home.[4]

Earlier, in 1843, the priests of the Brotherhood of St. Mary of the Rosary were likewise dedicated to mission preaching.[5] The *Rules To Be Followed by One Who Would Become a Perfect Missionary* insist equally on dedication to missionary preaching, forbidding the missionary even to hear confessions outside missions, so as not to be tied down to just a few penitents.[6] In effect, after the founding of the Congregation the Saint wrote the papal nuncio, Brunelli, that he had been moved to found it "in view of the great lack of evangelical and apostolic preachers in our Spanish territory, the great desires of the people to hear the word of God and the many instances coming from all parts of

Spain to have him to go to their cities and towns to preach the Gospel."[7]

The 1849 *Constitutions,* published with some additions in 1857, present the same notion of the Congregation. In Chapter 10, on "the means the missionaries must employ for the salvation of souls," we are told that they must "principally" use catechism, preaching, missions and retreats, and the promotion of associations and propaganda during the missions.[8] Missions are mentioned among those matters that should command the particular attention of the director general.[9] There is a special set of regulations for the time of missions.[10] The demands of missionary life, in the strict sense of preaching in towns and villages, serve as a point of departure for the norms of asceticism.[11] The primitive *Constitutions* presuppose, then, that the habitual occupation of Claretian communities will be with preaching missions and giving retreats. And indeed this was the case: entering the Congregation and preaching missions amounted to one and the same thing. Fr. Xifré's *Instrucción importantísima,* which was revised by Claret in a number of places, was left intact in that its single stress is on the good results of preaching missions.[12] But Fr. Xifré expressly states as much in the cover letter for the *Instrucción.*

> Longstanding experience has shown that missions, supported by the authorities, are the only barrier that can successfully oppose moral degradation. This Congregation which Archbishop Claret founded has this [missions] as its object, and since its inception in 1849, has fulfilled this object, in accord with the number of its members, in different dioceses.[13]

The founder himself, in a letter inviting Fr. Domingo Ramonet to enter the Congregation, simply tells the latter to give himself over to the preaching of missions and retreats.

> It is the will of God and of the Blessed Virgin Mary that you enter the Congregation and dedicate yourself to missions and spiritual exercises.[14]

The foregoing is in perfect accord with the documents of the Holy See relating to the approval of the Claretian Congregation and its *Constitutions.* At the audience in which Pius IX granted the Decree of Praise and the approval of the Congregation, the pope was told that its aim was "the salvation of souls by means of the holy missions."[15]

One doubt arises as we read these various testimonies. Fr. Clotet's account of the foundation tells us that Claret invited the cofounders to join a congregation of priests *exclusively* dedicated to missions and retreats.[16] Was he relating the exact words of the founder or, rather, were his words influenced by the situation of the early Congregation, which was *de facto* exclusively dedicated to missionary preaching? This is a hard question to answer, although the care with which Fr. Clotet always weighed his words would lead us instinctively to give full credence to whatever he said. We have seen how the *Rules To Be Followed by One Who Would Become a Perfect Missionary,* written a few months before the founding, forbade engaging in other ministries, such as hearing confessions.[17] In fact, Claret himself refused to take charge of the church of La Merced, next door to the Claretian motherhouse but, rather, entrusted it to the care of a priest who was not a member of the Congregation. We have likewise seen that the primitive *Constitutions* describe an institute fully dedicated to missions and retreats. However, the sketch of a plan for the Brothers of Jesus and Mary, which antedates the texts we have just mentioned, states that missions and retreats should be their *principal* object and occupation.[18] Moreover, the *Constitutions* themselves, published in 1857, state that missions and retreats should be the ministries to which the members of the institute must be *principally* dedicated.[19] If it were not for the fact that we find the adjective "principal" in the earlier text for the Brothers of Jesus and Mary, we might easily suppose that it was a correction added to the primitive text in 1857. In any case, one thing remains clear: the primitive Congregation was *de facto* exclusively dedicated to the preaching of missions and retreats.

An Apostolic Profile of the Founder in 1849

When he founded his Congregation on July 16, 1849, St. Anthony Mary Claret was really doing little more than projecting on it his own conception of the apostolate as it had been developing in his mind since his seminary days. The account he has left us in his *Autobiography,* concerning the birth and development of his vocation, clearly shows that he felt a call not just to the apostolate in general but, more concretely, to missionary preaching. The beginnings of industrialization in Catalonia, the emigration of young rural workers to the cities, the strained relations between the church and the new liberal governments, as well as the aftermath and portents of civil war, were beginning to produce an acute process of dechristianization among the Catalan people. St. Anthony Claret felt called to counteract this crisis by means of his missionary campaigns. We have already noted that in a letter petitioning Pope Gregory XVI for the title of Apostolic Missionary for some of his companions, Claret states that he is so doing in consideration of "the damages suffered by the Catholic religion in Spain," damages which he has "resolved to oppose efficaciously."[20]

Claret set about his task by repeating the activities and methods employed by his predecessors, the great missionaries of the 17th and 18th centuries. Early in his Catalonian ministry, grasping the pulse of his own times, he introduced one very fruitful innovation: the apostolate of the modern press. Toward the end of this period he took another great step forward, when he came to realize the powerful role that the laity would soon be called to play in the church. This was the time (1847) when he began to sketch plans for his first apostolic associations for the laity, associations which sharply differed from the traditional lay "confraternities."

The Claretian Congregation, as described in its first *Constitutions,* mainly inherited from its founder those attitudes that he, in turn, had inherited from tradition; it was an institute dedicated, in fact, to preaching missions and retreats. Associations entered into the picture only to the extent that they had for St. Alphonsus Liguori: during missions an effort should be made to bolster the life of confraternities, so as to intensify the Christian life of the parish. The missionaries were encouraged to distribute holy cards and pamphlets but not to foster the apostolate of the press in the fully modern sense as their founder had done before them. This is the impression we gather from the *Constitutions,* but the reality was, in fact, somewhat more complex. We have already seen that Canon Caixal, who was in charge of the Religious Library, was considered by Claret as a "brother," that is to say, as a member of the newborn institute, on a par with those who were dedicated to preaching missions.[21] We also noted that when the Saint assigned patrons to the missionaries, Caixal was given St. Paul as his patron.[22] We might add that Claret also invited Caixal to celebrate the anniversary of the founding of the Congregation with the other missionaries.[23] If we see this, as it seems we must, as bolstering the strictly missionary character of the Congregation, inasmuch as Claret considered the press to be a privileged instrument for evangelization, then we are obliged to correct somewhat the rather traditionalistic impression that the *Constitutions* convey with regard to ministries. Besides missions, retreats, and the support of local confraternities, we would have to add the apostolate of the press in the modern sense in which the founder understood it. It is quite understandable that given Claret's long absence in Cuba and Caixal's drifting away from the Congregation, the institute should have hewn to the apostolic models and methods of the past, neglecting the newer apostolates of the press and lay associations. We might legitimately assume that a man of Claret's undeniable acumen and vision, if he had remained with his missionaries in Spain, would have changed things considerably.

Evolution of the Congregation from 1858 to 1870

From 1850 to 1858, the Congregation remained almost in a state of hibernation. The absence of its founder, who was named archbishop of Cuba, dealt it a hard blow. His return to Spain in May 1857, together with the election of a new general, Fr. Joseph Xifré, seemed to awaken it to new life. But it was from 1861 on that the Saint began systematically to broaden the apostolic horizons of his Congregation. In 1861, as he was engaged in writing his *Autobiography*—deliberately aimed at the instruction and formation of his missionaries—he stressed not only his itinerant ministry but also his activities as a writer and propagandist, his social works, etc. From that time on, any Claretians who felt driven to open up new paths in the service of the church could find in the pages of their founder's *Autobiography* a fertile source of inspiration: the apostolates of preaching, of the press, of promoting the lay apostolate, of social or charitable works, of teaching, of associations for priests, etc.[24] The

Saint began to introduce one direct adaptation into the Congregation in 1863, when he strongly urged his missionaries to make full use of the apostolate of the press.[25] On May 1, 1863, he asked them to take charge of the church next door to the motherhouse, which had been entrusted to the care of an elderly priest who did not belong to the Congregation.[26] At the General Chapter of 1864, he added the direction of seminaries to the list of ministries for the Congregation.

> It is most suitable to the spirit of the Congregation, that its Missionaries be dedicated to the spiritual direction of young men living in seminaries, and even to hold teaching positions there, especially in sacred rubrics, sacred eloquence and plainchant.[27]

This addition was fraught with particular importance, since the chapter, at the bidding of the founder, was discussing the criteria to be followed in drafting the new *Constitutions*. What it really amounted to was the inclusion of the ministry of seminary direction and teaching in the article on the means of the apostolate. In effect, while Claret was drafting the second *Constitutions* a few months later, he added among the Congregation's ministries that of formation of the clergy.

Indeed, the new text on the means of the apostolate considerably broadened the field of the Congregation's ministries, not only in that it added seminary formation and hearing confessions to the established ministries of catechesis and missionary preaching but also in the very words employed in the text, which reflected a change of basic outlook. The primitive *Constitutions* prescribed that the missionaries *principally* occupy themselves in the ministry of missionary preaching.[28] Now, it is clear that the word "principally" was interpreted as meaning that missionary preaching was to be a habitual occupation of Claretian houses and that ministries related to missionary preaching were the only really proper ones for the Congregation. Now the drafting of the text changed.

> In striving for the salvation of souls, let them use all means possible, especially the following: first, catechizing children, the poor and the uneducated, according to their needs; second, preaching the word of God, and giving missions and retreats to every class of people, but especially to priests, seminarians and nuns, and hearing the confessions

of all the faithful; third, directing seminaries and fostering oratory, moral theology and liturgy in them.[29]

By positively prescribing the use of all means possible, although indicating that some were preferred, the second *Constitutions* stressed the universality of means. Moreover, among the means listed as preferred, some were included that are not strictly "missionary," such as directing seminaries and hearing confessions and giving spiritual direction in their own churches.

Five years later, on July 16, 1869, Claret confirmed this broadening trend by asking Fr. Xifré to open schools, interpreting the "first, catechizing children" passage in Article 63 as follows:

> You should take a look at n. 63 in ch. 16 of the *Constitutions* and reflect on the words "catechizing children, the poor and the uneducated...." You, as Superior General, when circumstances allow and you deem it opportune, can name one or two of the better educated members to have a school for boys, so as to follow the practice of the Brothers of the Christian Schools, who have so many in France, Italy, etc., and who do so much good. I believe that at the present time they are the ones who are doing the most good for the Church and are also the ones from whom we have the most to hope for. God and the Blessed Virgin have reserved this special mission in Spain for the Congregation.... I do not mean to imply that everyone should be occupied in such schools. I only mean that a few, a very few, should. See to it that you appoint them according to their zeal or willingness.[30]

The Saint expressed the same idea in some handwritten notes that date from 1869 or 1870. After stating that he would like his missionaries, as they made their rounds through various parishes, to interest young men in the study of Latin, rubrics, and plainchant, he goes on to remark that it would be desirable "that in every mission house there be a Missionary dedicated to teach these matters, even mainly, should he feel the inclination."[31] In each house, then, there should be a priest in charge of a sort of preseminary, in order to promote vocations to the priesthood. Moreover, this priest would not have to be engaged in missionary preaching.

It is obvious that between 1861 and 1869, St. Anthony Mary

Claret had considerably broadened the field of apostolic activities to which his Congregation was dedicated. In effect, it ceased to be limited to those ministerial activities to which missionary congregations were traditionally devoted in the 18th and 19th centuries. In those times, missionary congregations were, almost by definition, clerical institutes dedicated to preaching parish missions and giving retreats. It was a phenomenon typical of this period in the history of the religious life. Following the model established in 1617 by the Congregation of the Mission (the Vincentians), a whole series of new institutes appeared: the Passionists (1720), the Redemptorists (1732), the Society of the Precious Blood (1815), and the Oblates of Mary Immaculate (1816). This is the sort of institute Saint Anthony Claret obviously had in mind when he wrote, at the beginning of the primitive *Constitutions*: "The Congregation of Missionaries, founded . . . in Vich [*sic*], shall have as its title the Congregation of the Sons of the Immaculate Heart of Mary." It is also the background to be borne in mind whenever the text of the *Constitutions* refers to the members of the Congregation as "the Missionaries."

The mere fact that the founder, in 1864, included the formation of seminarians among the ministries to which his missionaries should principally (*praesertim*) be dedicated would not, of itself, entitle us to speak of an important change, since it is well known that this is a preferred ministry for the Vincentians. Neither, perhaps, would the inclusion of the ministry of hearing confessions and giving spiritual direction in their own churches, since all of the missionary congregations, as soon as they were placed in charge of their own churches or chapels, began doing so. However, if we compare the express exclusion of this ministry in 1849 with its express inclusion in 1863, we might legitimately infer that there had been a passage from a rigidly missionary conception to a more flexible model. But the inclusion of the ministry of Christian education, as well as the fact that in 1869 the founder should have proposed as models not only the Society of the Precious Blood and the Passionists,[32] but also the Brothers of the Christian Schools,[33] indicates that the Congregation, although the *Constitutions* of 1870 would still classify it as a "Congregation of Missionaries," had already surpassed the bounds of those ministries considered proper of such institutes and had gone on to embrace others. We should note, too, that according to the founder, God had set aside the ministry of Christian education in Spain especially for his missionaries. This implied that they should devote themselves to this ministry with great intensity.

The Founder's Own Development

To grasp the fuller implications of this transformation, we must bear in mind the founder's own development during the years when he was physically separated from his institute.

His pastoral obligations as head of a vast Cuban archdiocese had forced him to confront a large number of grave pastoral problems. This led him to realize that it was not enough to send out missionary teams periodically to evangelize isolated parishes, as he had been doing. It was necessary to attack deep-rooted problems, such as the laxity of the clergy, a nominally functioning seminary, ignorance, common-law marriages, and the misery of poor farm laborers—in short, the many problems of a Christian culture in an advanced state of decay, where certain fundamental structures had to be restored. It was not a question now of saving single souls as he had tried to do in Catalonia, but of promoting the life of a whole church. From a concern for the individual soul, the Saint was moving on to a concern for the Mystical Body of Christ. At the end of this period, we find Claret writing his *Notes of a Plan to Preserve the Beauty of the Church,* a work that displays a keen ecclesial awareness. His Cuban experience had been an enriching one for him.

When he was recalled to Madrid, he busied himself with assisting the nuncio in the nomination of bishops; he created the seminary and secondary school at the Escorial; he founded the Academy of St. Michael for the intelligentsia; he promoted lending libraries for all classes; he wrote several books for the formation of priests. He personally preached and gave retreats whenever he could and envied others who were free to devote themselves full time to these ministries.[34] He received a supernatural understanding of his need to devote himself to spiritual direction.[35] Even before he had received this understanding, he would sit in the confessional from early morning until ten.[36] In 1860 he decided to remain there another hour, until eleven.[37] These were the years when he was spiritual director of St. Micaela of the Blessed Sacrament, of the queen, and of numerous priests and laity at court. He was at last allowed to experience the fruits of a priestly ministry that his vocation as an itinerant missionary in Catalonia and the Canary Islands and his episcopal duties in Cuba had prevented him from practicing habitually until that time.

In this simple description of the development that Claret underwent, we can see—anticipated by but a few years—the same path he was to point out for his Congregation. Seminary direction and teaching was in keeping with the special attention the Saint had always shown priests during his missionary campaigns in Catalonia and the Canary Islands. But in these places, given the high spiritual caliber of their seminaries, he had only to preach occasional retreats to rekindle their fervor, whereas in Cuba he had felt to the depths a need for solid priestly formation. Thus, on his return to Spain, he dedicated himself with great effort to the seminary at the Escorial. This thoroughly convinced him of the excellent service that his Congregation could render the church if, in addition to preaching, it would actively undertake the formation of the clergy. This was the real source of the addition to Article 63 of the second part of the *Constitutions.* We have already mentioned that in this he was following the precedent of St. Vincent de Paul, who had joined missionary preaching and care for clergy and seminarians in his own congregation.

The Ministry of the Claretians

We have seen how St. Anthony Claret considerably broadened the field of apostolic activities and means that his Congregation was called to cultivate in the church. In doing so, he had projected in his missionaries the experiences that had enriched his spirit during his stay in Cuba and that continued to do so during his residence in Madrid. By calling them to assume teaching activities, he was obliging his Congregation to cross over the precise confines within which the missionary congregations of the 18th and 19th centuries had traditionally fulfilled their ministries.

Does this mean that the Congregation was on the road to

becoming simply a generically apostolic institute? Or, on the contrary, without wishing to place any a priori labels on the matter, is it possible to find some connecting thread running between the personal development of the founder and the notion he had formed of his institute? We believe that such a developmental axis really did exist. The founder himself shows us this by the significant addition he made to the second article of the *Constitutions* in the 1864 edition. In this addition, the founder deduces, from the threefold end of the Congregation, a commitment of reverence, love, and obedience to the pope and the Holy See, and of steadfast collaboration with bishops in the ministry of the Word. The final form of the redaction of Article 2 reads as follows:

> Its object will be to seek in all things the glory of God, the sanctification of its members and the salvation of souls throughout the world. Hence, they shall manifest great reverence, love and obedience toward the Supreme Pontiff and the Holy Apostolic See, and shall be the steadfast helpers of the Prelates of the Church in the ministry of the Word.[38]

This mention of obedience to the pope and the Roman Curia seems to have been provoked by a particular incident. A momentary reaction of one of his collaborators against the suggestions sent by the Congregation of Bishops and Regulars for the revision of the *Constitutions* led Claret to address some strong words (*efficacem sermonem,* as the *Acta* put it) to the members of the 1864 General Chapter, concerning the duty of submission to the Holy See. The chapter, acting on this admonition, asked Claret himself to undertake the revision of the *Constitutions* in accord with the directives from Rome. During the following months, Archbishop Claret included this article in the *Constitutions.* Nevertheless, it is clear that this brief episode was simply the occasion, and that the Saint's real intention went beyond it, to include the relation of the Congregation with the hierarchy in general. Collaboration is indicated in connection with the ministry of the Word, which, as the Council of Trent taught and Claret never tired of repeating, is the principal mission of bishops. This is also the specific mission of the Claretian Congregation in the church. The Saint himself constantly held that his institute had come into being to provide the church with a group of evangelical and apostolic preachers. And, although we are anticipating matters that we will touch on later, we should recall that the first Claretian houses were diocesan centers of evangelization and that in his 1865 essay, *Notes of a Plan,* the founder offered the services of his Congregation to the bishops precisely for this end.[39] In the chapter of the *Constitutions* dealing with the students, the goal he proposes for their overall formation is that they become fit ministers of the Word of God.[40] The chapter on the novices stresses the same goal, since its point of departure in establishing ascetic norms for the novices is the mission of the preacher.[41] We should add, however, that the latter chapter seems to have been written by Fr. Xifré.[42]

Later Developments

We can already see that this balanced mentality of the founder, so profoundly missionary and at the same time so open to concrete situations, would be difficult to maintain. The institute was in danger of falling into either of two extremes: on the one hand, hewing rigidly to traditional missionary activities; on the other, losing its unified sense of mission and becoming a sort of do-all institution.

Initially, the conservative trend of sticking to the traditional means of apostolate had the upper hand. Until 1880, the missionaries were exclusively dedicated to preaching missions and retreats. A certain number of them, following the example of their founder, were also devoted to writing. But it would be no exaggeration to say that Claret's recommendations in favor of seminaries, Christian education, and the apostolate of the press had remained a dead letter up to this time. In 1883 the first foreign missions were accepted in Fernando Poo, Africa, thus emphasizing to a greater degree the missionary spirit of the institute. That same year the Claretians began working with seminarians, first in Tarragona and later in Rome. In the following year the first school was opened in Toluca, Mexico, to be followed by two more in Spain. More schools and colleges were opened in the succeeding years. Fr. James Clotet, cofounder and subdirector general of the Congregation, favored this ministry out of fidelity to the mind of the founder. Fr. Xifré, on the contrary, seems to have allowed it against his own opinion and, in fact, during the General Chapters of 1888 and 1895 strove unsuccessfully to have it suppressed.

Fr. Xifré's death in 1899 marked the beginning of a period of slow transition. In 1909 another foreign mission was accepted in Chocó, Colombia. The greatest innovation of this period was establishment of Claretian parishes. Fr. Xifré himself, shortly before his death, had accepted the first in Andacollo, Chile. He had done so despite his opinion that such ministries were contrary to the mission of the Claretians. His reason for accepting was that Andacollo was a Marian shrine in what was tantamount to a mission territory. In fact, all of the earliest parishes were accepted because they were missionary in character, such as San Antonio (1902) and San Marcos (1905), both in Texas. But by the time of the death of Fr. Martin Alsina, then Claretian superior general (1922), 50 of the 170 Claretian houses were parishes. This multiplication of parish ministries continued, according to the needs of the church, in places such as America, where there was a scarcity of clergy. Fr. Antonio Naval, a general consultor, adverted to this situation when he cast his vote in favor of accepting a parish in Peru: "We have allowed the acceptance of parishes in the United States, because it is the only means of evangelization in that country."[43]

Another ministry that underwent a strong development at this time was that of the press. The year 1906 marked the founding of the review for clergy, *Ilustración del Clero,* and the *Iris de Paz,* founded under a different name in 1889, became a weekly. One Claretian, Fr. Dueso, launched out in this apostolate through his efforts to create a Catholic daily newspaper in Spain and through his support for the Catholic news agency, *Prensa Asociada.* In 1912 the Claretian publishing house, *Editorial Corazón de María,* was established in Madrid.

The General Chapter of 1922, by the criteria it established and by its election of Fr. Nicolas García as superior general, was to have an important effect on the Claretian apostolate. Fr. García systematically pushed the Congregation toward universality in the means of its apostolate. When he left office in 1949, there were 127 parishes out of a total of 241 houses; if we exclude those houses dedicated exclusively to formation, the proportion rises considerably. Students in Claretian schools numbered 6,803 in 1935, but that number had risen to 13,594 by 1949 and, since very few of the teachers were brothers, most of those in this ministry were priests. The apostolate of the press was intensified during this period with the foundation of a few publishing houses in Latin America and of several reviews. Some new missions were also accepted: Darién, Panama (1926); São Tomé, then under Portuguese rule (1927); Tunki, China (1933).

This notable broadening of the apostolic activities of Claretians was due to the coincidence of a number of factors. The increase in parishes corresponded to the needs of the church in America. The increase, in Spain, of *colegios* (boarding schools where the children of the middle and upper classes receive their entire preuniversity education) was prompted, doubtless, by an apostolic intention, namely, the winning back of the leading classes after the Republic, but it was also dictated by the economic needs of the Congregation, which had been weakened in Spain by persecution and the civil war. However, the main factor in this changing panorama was of a doctrinal nature. Fr. García used to refer constantly to the genius of the founder's apostolic intuitions and his faculty for invention. Thus, in his *Circular Letters,* although he would periodically cite the missionary spirit of the institute, his preferences clearly leaned toward stressing the universality of apostolic means. It might be recalled that this was the period during which Claret's canonization process was drawing to a close (he was beatified in 1934 and canonized in 1950), and studies on his life and works were being intensified.

The election of Fr. García meant a victory of one model of the mission of the Claretians in the church—a radically apostolic model, but one less tied to certain ministries. Thus, while all previous General Chapters had repeatedly stressed that parish missions are the primary and principal activity of the institute,[44] the 1922 chapter, which elected Fr. García, was the first to stress the universality of ministries. The *Codex Iuris Addititii,* which came out of this chapter, gives this new formulation of the institute's attitude toward various apostolates.

> Although the Congregation accepts all means possible for the salvation of souls, among those means it has a general preference for those

which concern it most closely, that is to say, priestly and apostolic ministries.[45]

Besides being new, the formulation is, at first glance, strange. While preserving the structure of the formulation in the *Constitutions* and the traditional universality of ministries, it adds an orientation of preference for some means. But while, up to this time, it had been the custom to repeat the *Constitutions'* enumeration of the preferred means, or to speak of missionary preaching as the primary ministry, we now find included in this category all priestly and apostolic ministries, so that the emerging picture is one of a generically apostolic institute. With this, the criteria that guided the apostolic work of Claretians remained fixed until the end of the generalate of Fr. Peter Schweiger, in 1967. At that time there was a growing reaction, especially in Spain and Latin America, against what was viewed as a progressive departure from the missionary ideals of the institute.

One of the main objects of the Extraordinary General Chapter of 1967 was an examination of the original inspiration of the founder, with a view to the renewal and adaptation of the Congregation. This led to a confrontation between two opposed points of view. One, followed by the new generation, reaffirmed the missionary character of the Congregation and called for a change of direction; the other stressed the universality of means. The decrees of the chapter understandably reflect a compromise. They affirm that the institute was founded for the ministry of the Word (evangelization) and hence insist on its missionary character. This eventually led to an addition to Article 2 of the *Constitutions* as revised in the chapter of 1973.

> The aim of our Congregation is to seek in everything the glory of God, our own sanctification, and the salvation of people throughout the world, according to our distinctive missionary gift in the Church.

On the other hand, the Decree on the Apostolate of the 1967 chapter included an enumeration of all the activities to which the Claretians were *de facto* dedicated, although it also established a number of criteria for the choice of ministries. And in fact, dating from this special chapter, there began a movement of renewal in the apostolate of the Congregation, marked by an increase in new missions (São Félix [Brazil] and Humahuaca

[Argentina], in 1968; Pilcaniyeu [Argentina] and Angola in 1969; Juanjí [Perú], Cameroon, and India, in 1970; Nigeria in 1971) and by the foundation of new parishes in unchurched, dechristianized, and abandoned areas.

Claretian Ministry and Its Historic Forms

Reflecting on the data that have surfaced in our search through the texts of the founder and cofounders, we are compelled to address two different questions: first, the relationship between the proper ministry of the Congregation—the ministry of the Word—and the historic forms that it assumed in the activity of St. Anthony Mary Claret and his first spiritual sons; second, the relation between the ministry of the Word and the various apostolates to which the Claretians have been or still are dedicated.

Historically, the first form that the Claretian ministry of the Word took was the preaching of parish missions and retreats. On more than one occasion, the founder affirmed that his institute was founded to give missions and retreats, thus alluding to the models of evangelization that had been followed in Europe for two centuries. They were apostolates for the renewal of Christian life, by means of the preaching of the Gospel. It is well known that parish missions, at least according to the methods and style in which they were practiced in the agrarian society of the 18th and 19th centuries, have now ceased to exist. Does this mean that the Congregation was founded for a ministry that has died out? No. Because, as we have seen in another, more fundamental text of the founder, the Congregation was founded for the ministry of the Word or, if you will, for the proclamation of the Gospel. Preaching missions was simply the historical form that this ministry took in the 19th century.

The very same thing has happened to other institutes. It cannot rightly be said that a Congregation was founded to create schools or erect hospitals. Schools and hospitals are simply the historical forms assumed in a particular society by Christian education or the care of the sick. It is quite possible that, in some other particular society, a hospital would not incarnate, in the same manner, the type of ministry for which the institute was founded, or that it would be the only or best means of fulfilling it. And a school is by no means the only vehicle for Christian education. Apostolic institutes are obliged to evaluate periodically the effectiveness and even the meaning of their apostolic works, in the light of their respective charisms in the church.

On this point the Claretians are agreed, beyond a doubt. The Congregation, which was founded for evangelization, must periodically review its means, modes, and methods of evangelization.

Ministry and Apostolates

A more complicated question concerns the relations that exist between the ministry of the Word, for which the Congregation was founded, and the concrete apostolic activities that the Congregation initiates and maintains. It is not a question of the variety of successive forms that ministry might take but, rather, it is a question of how many apostolates the Congregation can undertake and maintain during one and the same historical period.

We have seen how the founder in the most fundamental text of the 1865 *Constitutions* (the last he wrote), calls his missionaries to be effective collaborators with the pope and bishops in the ministry of the Word. But during this very period and in succeeding years, St. Anthony Claret himself was asking his missionaries to dedicate themselves to "catechizing children, the poor and the uneducated, according to their needs; preaching the word of God; giving missions and retreats to every class of people, but especially to priests, seminarians and nuns; hearing the confessions of all the faithful; directing seminaries and fostering oratory, moral theology and liturgy in them."[46] He asked them, moreover, to devote themselves to the apostolate of the press[47] and, finally, to Christian education. Later, we have seen the Claretians founding foreign missions and accepting parishes. Either with or without parishes, we must add associations of every sort, educational, devotional, and apostolic.

Does it make any sense to speak of the ministry of the Word as the ministry for which an institute is formed, when that institute is dedicated to such broadly varied forms of apostolate? Wouldn't this be a mere word-game without any meaningful content?

No. The statement makes sense. In the mind of the founder, the choice of concrete activities is subject, first of all, to one permanent and objective criterion: the more or less close relationship of these activities with the ministry of the Word. Hence, as late as 1869, in recommending that Claretians undertake educational works, the Saint does so commenting on that article of the *Constitutions* that cites the catechizing of children and the uneducated in first place among the apostolic activities of the institute, while it cites in second place missions and retreats, which Claret calls, in this precise setting, the "primary object" of the Congregation.[48] This clearly shows that in the mind of St. Anthony Claret, the undertaking of determined apostolic activities depends, above all, on whether they are or are not vehicles for evangelization, and that there is an objective ordering of the institute toward those activities in which the proclamation of the Gospel (its "primary object") is best incarnated. We may say that all the activities undertaken by St. Anthony Claret or recommended by him to his missionaries are forms of evangelization (missionary preaching, catechesis, the press), or works that provide a privileged milieu for evangelization (Christian education), or works that complement evangelization (fostering lay movements or movements for the formation of preachers; seminary formation).

In the Service of the Word

Having made this point, which is one of fundamental importance for understanding the mission of the Claretians in the church, we can clearly see the substantial identity that exists between the mission of the institute and the personal vocation of its founder. The fact should come as no surprise, since it is well known that the characteristic gift of a religious institute in the church is nothing more than the vocation of its founder, extended in space and time. This leads us to state here some of the fundamental traits of the Saint's vocation, which we studied at some length in our first chapter. First of all, there is that living totally for the service of God, in the biblical sense of the expression, a service that takes flesh in the salvation of our neighbor by means of the proclamation of the Gospel. The Claretian is called to live exclusively for the proclamation of the Gospel. This is what characterizes him as a missionary. In effect, the Claretian Congregation is not a generically apostolic institute, but a specifically missionary institute. That is to say, it is an institute without boundaries, an institute called to be an instrument of Christ in the implanting of His church, a guerrilla movement called to intervene wherever the need is most urgent. This gives a clearly Pauline aspect to its vocation: the service of the churches by means of the proclamation (kerygma) of the Gospel. At the same time, it gives it a markedly prophetic thrust. Like an Old or New Testament prophet, the Claretian is called to a twofold fidelity: fidelity to the Word of God, which he must proclaim without flinching, and fidelity to the history in which real people live. He must preach the Gospel here and now to collaborate with Christ in the redemption of his brothers and sisters; not as the propagandist of a philosophy (still less, of an ideology!), not as the minister of an institution in search of its own power, but as a servant of God, that is to say, as a man who lives and dies for the redemption of his brothers and sisters.

V

Apostolic Life

$\mathbf{B}$y examining the testimony of the founder himself and the first Claretians, we have determined the object St. Anthony Claret had in mind when he founded his Congregation. It now remains for us to see the extent to which this object did or did not influence the idea that Claret and his earliest followers formed of the institute, as well as the structure that they, in fact, gave it.

Paging through the first *Constitutions,* we find that members of the institute are consistently and exclusively referred to as "the Missionaries."[1] The principal duties assigned to the superior general include not only the care, maintenance, and growth of the Congregation and its members but also responsibility for its mission. It is he who must "send on missions and other ministries proper of the Congregation, those members whom he in conscience believes to be best suited for them, in keeping with circumstances."[2] The Saint himself set only one criterion for admission or expulsion, namely, whether a candidate did or did not possess those "qualities indispensable for being a good missionary, capable of fulfilling the ministries of his state."[3] Postulants are asked to be ready to accept whatever place and ministry they might be sent to.[4]

The second *Constitutions* affirms these positions with greater emphasis. The founder sets only one spiritual condition for those seeking admission: they must have "an apostolic spirit."[5] Besides being industrious, discreet, and intelligent, candidates for the Brotherhood must be "lovers of the Congregation and zealous for the salvation of souls."[6] These particular recommendations are especially valuable for two reasons: first, because of the single trait required of all who are to be admitted—the apostolic spirit; second, because they are additions made expressly by the founder. This chapter, "On Those To Be Admitted," was taken from a document by Fr. Xifré, who based it on the Ignatian Examen for applicants to the Society of Jesus. In Xifré's document, there is no mention of the requirement of an apostolic spirit; therefore, on the three occasions where it is mentioned in the *Constitutions,* we are dealing with express additions by the founder.[7] This omission was obviously an oversight, since Fr. Xifré was as firmly convinced as anyone of the essentially apostolic nature of the institute. But it is significant that the founder caught the omission and rectified it.

Now, the fact that the founder, in the *Constitutions* (presupposing the postulant's will to be exclusively committed to God's service), should have set only one requisite for admission, the apostolic spirit (or, as the primitive rule puts it, the qualities indispensable for being a good missionary), is a matter of incalculable help to us in defining the character and spirit proper of the Claretian Congregation. To enter it, a candidate must have not only a general desire to consecrate himself to the service of God; he must also be animated by a lively apostolic spirit and possess those qualities necessary for being a good missionary. Since each religious institution must exercise extreme care in screening and selecting candidates in keeping with its own distinctive spirit and aims, this requirement tells us a great deal about what kind of institute the Claretian Congregation is.

Another very helpful key in determining the character of an institute is the way in which it conceives the aims of its novitiate and seminary formation programs. The primitive *Constitutions* require that during the candidate's first year in the Congregation, one of the older and more exemplary priests be assigned to instruct him in the practices to be observed both at home and in the ministry.[8] This directive is really a rough draft of what would eventually become the year of novitiate.

The 1865 *Constitutions* are, naturally, more explicit. They explain the need for a novicemaster as follows:

> It is altogether necessary that anyone who is called by God to a ministry so exalted and of such great consequence as that of the apostolate, should be adorned with virtues befitting its fulfillment. But since the effective attainment of these virtues requires a teacher and moderator, the Provincial Superior and his Consultors should choose for this outstanding office a member of the Congregation who has the requisite maturity, kindliness, discretion and knowledge....[9]

We would like to point out one of the presuppositions of this passage; namely, that the apostolic ministry demands considerable spiritual maturity and the possession of certain virtues. This is why a specially qualified priest is assigned to guide the novices in the attainment of these virtues. In the chapter on the novices, the need for these virtues is clearly spelled out.

> Nothing is so important for the Missionaries, nothing so befits them, as the adornment of all the virtues. Without them, their talent will be useless, their preaching fruitless and all their labor vain.... Since this year of probation has been established in order that the foundation of these virtues may be laid....[10]

The very purpose for the novitiate program, then, is to lay the foundation of the virtues needed by a missionary. The commentary on each of these virtues follows the same missionary perspective.

> Above all they should strive to acquire a lively faith...that faith which inflamed the prophets, strengthened the apostles, tempered the torments of the martyrs and led so many preachers to embrace poverty, abnegation and sacrifice in order to spread the kingdom of Christ....[11]
> The third virtue the young missionaries should greatly strive for is humility..., for a proud preacher is a thief and robber of God's glory.[12]

In describing the office of the prefect of scholastics, the Saint alleges only one reason for its importance. It is because his mission is "the formation of fitting ministers who, in their own time, will be instruments in the salvation of many people.[13]

A reading of these texts leads to one well-founded conclusion: the Congregation is first and foremost an apostolic institute. This is what the founder had in mind, in asking that the postulant have the qualities necessary for missionary work and, above all, a truly apostolic spirit, and in establishing as the main goal of novitiate and seminary training the formation of worthy missionaries.

Apostolic Influences on Claretian Spirituality

The short treatise on the virtues, in Chapter IX of the primitive *Constitutions,* begins as follows:

> All must be thoroughly persuaded that, to attain the conversion of sinners and the advancement of souls, solid virtues will be more helpful than learning or natural gifts. Hence they should all strive, with the help of the Lord and with full determination and effort, to attain them.[14]

The virtues recommended in the ensuing paragraphs are those that best befit missionaries.[15] This is also why the value of the virtues for edification and example is stressed.[16] We have already seen how the ideal of apostolic spirituality permeates those passages of the definitive *Constitutions* dealing with the virtues required of the novices. If the central influence of the apostolic spirit is less evident in the general ascetic section, this is doubtless due to the lesser originality of these chapters. Still, there are several indications that, even here, the Saint is fully aware of recommending these virtues with the needs of missionaries specifically in mind. In a general way this is implicit in the very nature of the virtues he has chosen. Modesty is necessary for the edification of others.[17] The ideal of poverty proposed is typically apostolic.[18] The third degree of humility is taken almost literally from a passage in which Pére Petitdidier states that this degree is proper of apostles.[19] Finally, the injunction to rejoice amid evils employs Paul's own vocabulary in describing his apostolic labors.[20]

In his second talk for the founding retreat, after a general introduction, Claret speaks of vocation and mission, taking Galatians 1:15-16 as his starting point.

> But when he who had set me apart before I was born, and had called me through his grace, was pleased to reveal his Son to me, in order that I might preach him among the Gentiles, I did not confer with flesh and blood.[21]

He then goes on to affirm the preacher's need for various virtues, and explains the foundations for a theology of mission. The third talk deals with the life-witness of the missionary, beginning with the text of I Corinthians 4:16: "Be imitators of me, as I am of Christ." The remaining talks deal with the virtues needed by a preacher: humility, meekness, chastity, mortification, zeal, and prayer.[22]

In the talks for the retreat he preached to his Congregation in 1865, Claret likewise began with the theme of mission.

> The Apostles, too, after their retreat [at Pentecost], began to speak, filled with the Holy Spirit: fire, charity, love.... You are missionaries. You must be sent, impelled. You must say, *Charitas Christi urget nos.* Fire: like a bullet, like a great wind, like the power of the sea. The Holy Spirit came as a powerful wind and fire.[23]

The second talk is entitled "The Grace of a Missionary Vocation."[24] The remaining talks deal severally with humility, meekness, chastity, mortification, poverty, obedience, and zeal.[25] All of these are seen in the perspective of a missionary vocation. Humility counteracts all the dangers of the ministry.[26] Meekness is most helpful, for, as the Saint says:

> The Missionary is commonly of a bilious temperament, easily irritated. And he has reasons enough to irritate him: journeys, cold and heat, wind and rain, as well as all sorts of people, humors, rudeness and ignorance to cope with....[27]

No doubt about it; the texts clearly and abundantly show that for St. Anthony Mary Claret, the missionary vocation is the principle and foundation for the spirituality of his religious family. This vocation is what demands such a high level of perfection in its members, dictates preferences in formation, commends the practice of certain virtues in keeping with the mission of the institute in the church, and orients these virtues by setting a strictly missionary construction on them.

In all of this, St. Anthony Claret was really doing little more than projecting his own spirit on his favorite work, giving it the hierarchy of values of his own inner world, where the call to evangelize was the center of gravity. For he, too, had put himself totally in the hands of God, asking Him to sanctify him, so that he would have the strength to meet the demands of his calling to the apostolic ministry. In the second part of his *Autobiography*, he dwells at length on this theme, in the ascetical chapters which bear the general heading of "Virtues I consider essential for an effective ministry."[28] In the introductory paragraph he states:

> ...the apostolic missionary should be a model of all the virtues; he should, in fact, be virtue personified. Following Christ's example, he should first practice, then preach.

We are well aware of how deeply the apostolic calling conditioned his spiritual life, leading him not only to prefer certain virtues, but also to opt for certain forms of prayer. It made him transform his apostolic activities into a form of unrelenting asceticism and led him to discover a special type of recollection in the midst of a multitude of persons and tasks, thus preparing him to be a great contemplative in action. It compelled him, finally, to find in his activities the occasion and object of many mystical graces and gave his supernatural experiences a decidedly apostolic orientation.[29]

Descriptions of the Institute

All of what we have said above is condensed in the various sketches in which the founder describes his Congregation, its life and spirit. In his *Autobiography*, the only traits he notes as typifying the institute in its first years are its common life and apostolic activities.[30] In the foreword to *Rules for Clerics Living in Community*, he depicts the members of his Congregation, together with the secular clerics living in community and the lay members of the archconfraternity, as forming a single army that the Blessed Virgin uses in battling Satan and extending the reign of Christ: "In the first order (of this army), there are those who form the Congregation called the Sons of the Immaculate Heart of Mary. These are priests and brothers entirely consecrated to God and the Blessed Virgin Mary, and are continually engaged in giving missions and retreats to clergy, nuns, etc., according to their rules."[31] In *Notes of a Plan*, he recommends that bishops make use of the Congregation.[32] The context is revealing: Claret is speaking of the duties of bishops, just after referring to the seminary as an ideal diocesan center for missionary preaching and retreats.[33] Finally, Claret's letters to the earliest members of the Congregation deal almost exclusively either with the spread of the institute[34] or with means of the apostolate which the Congregation should undertake.[35]

The Cofounders

The first disciples of St. Anthony Claret reflect the same convictions in their writings. Fr. Clotet's talks for the retreats of October 1861 and December 1863[36] have as their focal point the missionary vocation and its demands. Soon after this, however, Fr. Clotet began to focus on a new set of demands: those of the religious life. Fr. Xifré must have drafted his *Very Important Instruction for Aspirants* during the first half of 1862. At any rate, it first appeared in the June 10, 1862, issue of *Revista Católica* and then, after it had been retouched and enriched by the founder himself, in the issue of August 10, 1862.[37] Finally, it was edited by the founder in his short work, *An Interesting Miscellany,* in 1865.[38] Alluding to the aim of the Congregation, Fr. Xifré says that "God has chosen this Congregation so that, through preaching—accompanied by fervor, abnegation and detachment—it might serve as a guide to the blind and a way to the lost."[39] This entire *Instruction* is an invitation to embrace the apostolic ministry, which is defined, in an addition made by the founder, as "the state in which one leaves all to follow Jesus Christ, to extend His reign, and to save sinners. This is the greatest charity and this is the office of a perfect missionary."[40] The members of the Congregation are described as "ministers of the Gospel," and all who have received "the gift of preaching" are invited to join them.[41] A somewhat later document, Fr. Xifré's *Spirit of the Congregation,* in its original 1867 edition, is simply a manual for missionaries. "This book has been written," says its author, "so that you might be Missionaries worthy of your honorable title and fitting ministers of the divine Word."[42] After a brief historical introduction, the book treats of vocation, explains the usefulness of missions and retreats, and then goes on to deal with "the means whereby we may hope for good results from missions and retreats," with a stress on the virtues and ascetical means for such results.[43] All of this clearly coincides with the founder's point of view.

After this search for the meaning of the Congregation as conceived by its founder and transmitted to his earliest followers, the reader will have drawn the rather obvious conclusion. But we prefer to let the founder's authoritative voice express it, in his celebrated pen-portrait of the Claretian.

> A Son of the Immaculate Heart of Mary is a man on fire with love, who spreads its flames wherever he goes. He desires mightily and strives by all means possible to set the whole world on fire with God's love. Nothing daunts him; he delights in privations, welcomes work, embraces sacrifices, smiles at slander, and rejoices in suffering. His only concern is how he can best follow Jesus Christ and imitate Him in working, suffering, and striving constantly and single-mindedly for the greater glory of God and the salvation of souls.[44]

Above all, then, the Claretian is a man totally committed to proclaiming the Gospel. His love, as the founder stated in his 1865 retreat, is the same as that of Pentecost: a powerful and overwhelming flame that sets fire to everything in its path. The pains and sufferings which the Saint includes in his pen-portrait of the Claretian are the very ones he attributes to apostles and prophets elsewhere in his *Autobiography*.[45] The Claretian works and suffers with Christ; all that he does is aimed at fulfilling the ideal proposed in Article 2 of the *Constitutions*: "the greater glory of God and the salvation of souls." This essentially apostolic character of the Claretian in the pen-portrait stands out in still bolder relief, if we compare it with another pen-portrait— that of St. Paul—drawn by Claret in his *Autobiography*.[46] Like Paul, the Claretian is driven by zeal from place to place. As Paul "preached, wrote and taught in synagogues, prisons—everywhere," so the Claretian makes use "of all means possible." Like Paul, the Claretian "works and suffers" every sort of pain. As Paul "was never daunted," but "rejoiced in tribulations," so "nothing daunts" the Claretian, since he "delights in privations, smiles at slander, and rejoices in suffering." There can be no doubt about it: with this, we have come to the true picture of the ideal Claretian.

Apostolic Life

The lifestyle of the newborn Congregation was deeply conditioned by its essentially apostolic character. "In this college we are living a truly poor and apostolic life," writes Claret to his friend Caixal, describing the Congregation during its first few weeks of existence.[47] Fr. Xifré tells us that during the founding retreat, "they spoke and made proposals concerning the apostolic lifestyle the Missionaries should observe in private and in public."[48]

Naturally, this apostolic character radically affected the spirituality of the institute. In the letter just cited, the founder links poverty with the apostolic life. In the *Autobiography*, he mentions common life and ministry as two of its typical elements.[49] To these we may add obedience to mission[50] and the rule of always going two by two and on foot.[51] We will treat of these matters in dealing with the apostolic rule of the Congregation. One very important trait of the early Congregation is the fact that for the first Claretians the year was divided into two distinct parts: the first and longer part was dedicated to apostolic mission campaigns; the second, shorter part was dedicated to rest and to spiritual and pastoral preparation. Each of these parts of the year had its own special regulations, dealt with in separate chapters of the *Constitutions.*[52]

The frantic pace of the founder's own life, during his ministry in Catalonia and the Canary Islands (let alone the heroism of his years in Cuba), could hardly be surpassed. His carefully planned and methodical campaigns always began toward the end of September, in autumn, and continued uninterruptedly through Lent and Easter. But then, a fortnight later, he would begin his "Month of May" preaching. During the summer, he conducted a series of retreats for priests and sisters, as well as a series of clergy conferences; however, work must have been even more demanding at that time since the Saint has left us fewer data concerning it. The campaign in the Canary Islands lasted uninterruptedly from March 1848 until May 1849.

Claret's missionaries, however, adopted a somewhat more moderate rhythm of life: the preaching phase always began at the end of summer and ordinarily ended at Easter. This practice is already recognized in the primitive *Constitutions,* which prescribe a retreat "at the end of summer, before beginning the missions," and another, upon returning, at an unspecified date.[53] This was, in fact, the rhythm of life followed by the first Claretian communities. Toward the end of September, most of the priests dispersed to begin their apostolic campaigns.[54] They would ordinarily begin returning around mid-April, although they would sometimes prolong their campaign into May, after making a retreat in Passion Week or Holy Week.[55] This pattern of life was initiated in the very year of the foundation. On September 1, 1849, the Saint wrote his friend Caixal that he was making a three-day retreat with six members who were leaving on mission the following week. Some had remained home to conduct retreats for various communities and clergy groups, but they would all have to be on the road by the Feast of All Saints.[56]

For this period of missionary campaigns, the Saint wrote a special set of regulations in the *Constitutions*. These regulations set the working timetable in such a way that the missionaries might have an indispensable amount of time for personal prayer and devotions, but the latter were reduced to recitation of the breviary, a half hour of morning meditation, and two examens of conscience. During meals, if they were alone, they should read a chapter from the Bible and another from the *Imitation of Christ*.[57] On the other hand, in view of the absorbing occupations of these days, these regulations were rather flexible. Meditation was positively limited to a half hour, after which the missionaries were to take turns saying mass for the people, while those who were not so occupied would hear confessions.[58] Reading at meals could be omitted if they were eating with others.[59] The General Chapter of 1862 had determined that on retreat days there should be three more meditations and a talk.[60] In 1864, when the founder inserted this prescription of the General Chapter in the *Constitutions*, he qualified it by adding that during the time of missions, it should be observed if possible.[61]

During the remaining months, from April or May until the end of September, they spent their time resting or making pastoral preparations. The priests followed an intensive round of conferences: an hour of moral theology in the morning, an hour's class on preaching in the afternoon, and a half hour of mystical and ascetic theology at night, according to the directives in the primitive *Constitutions*.[62] In 1864, studies in Sacred Scripture, casuistry, and liturgy were added.[63] This does not mean, however, that they totally abstained from apostolic activities—at least one priest had to preach the "Month of May" services and, in keeping with the wish of the founder, this was the proper time for giving retreats.[64] The register of the mother-house at Vic shows that there were always two sets of retreats, one for clergy, the other for laity, during these months at home.

As anyone can see, the lifestyle of the first Claretian communities could not have been in better keeping with the missionary character of the institute. Everything was centered on the ministry. We know of no other institute in which the continual dedication to prayer, missionary activities, and pastoral preparation for the ministry was so all-absorbing. Shortly after the foundation, Claret joyfully writes:

> We can go no faster than we're going. We are extremely busy from four in the morning until ten at night. We are so busy, in fact, that—like an endless chain—one occupation interlinks with the next.[65]

The Claretian House

One consequence of St. Anthony Claret's essentially missionary concept of his Congregation may be seen in the way he conceived the nature and mission of its houses. During the very first year of the institute's existence, the Saint was already considering three other foundations.[66] Almost immediately upon his return from Cuba to Madrid, he began to send a steady flow of requests to the two Claretian major superiors, Frs. Xifré and Clotet, urging them to expand the Congregation. He invited them to found a house in Oviedo;[67] he offered them a section of the Escorial;[68] he approved a foundation in Barcelona;[69] he himself took the initiative in founding the house in Segovia;[70] he requested a foundation in Oran[71] and one in Algiers;[72] he approved the foundation in La Selva.[73] He made the first suggestions for foundations in America and sent the first petitions for foundations in the New World to Fr. Xifré.[74] On the other hand, although he was pleased to see his missionaries established in France, he remained faithful to his decision not to ask the rulers there for anything, especially since he did not wish to recommend his missionaries to the protection of the Empress Eugénie de Montijo de Gusmán, a native of Granada.[75]

On all of these occasions, the Saint has a consistent view concerning the motives that should govern the expansion of the

Congregation. These foundations are needed because of the great good that preaching will bring to the dioceses in question. The foundation in Oviedo should take place immediately, so that the priests (accompanied by a brother) can begin to spread out, two by two, to preach throughout the diocese.[76] The house at the Escorial would be most useful since, being situated in the center of Spain, missionaries could be sent from it in all directions.[77] On July 1, 1861, he asks them to become established in the center of Spain, since the need is great everywhere in the country.[78] Likewise, it is because of the incalculable good that their preaching will do that he asks them to found a house in Oran.[79] Clearly, according to the mind of the founder, these houses should be established for the purpose of fulfilling the urgent needs of the church in various regions.

For this same reason, the Saint does not want to have more than one house in each diocese: "I must tell you that as long as there is a single house in each province or diocese, it will be enough, because with our scant numbers we have to do a great deal."[80] Moreover, at a time when there was such a shortage of evangelical workers, the Saint requests that no houses be founded in cities where the Jesuits are already established: "In places where the Jesuits have been unable to work . . . , we should enter, as it were, under the wings of the bishops."[81] Nevertheless, he does feel that each diocese should have a Claretian house.[82] For this reason, the Saint asks that each community should have no more than twelve priests, counting both the old and the young, and that when they go beyond this number, they should form a new offshoot.[83]

This shows us St. Anthony Claret's thinking on his communities, on their mission in a diocese, and on the relationships that should bind them with the bishops and secular clergy. The Claretian community is made up of a small but very active group of missionaries, "because with our scant numbers we have to do a great deal."[84] Since their aim is to collaborate with the bishops in the ministry of preaching,[85] these communities must maintain close relationships with the hierarchy. The bishop of Barcelona, in asking the Spanish government for its approval of the Claretian house at Gracia, described it as "an auxiliary of the seminary, for the preparation of candidates for Ordination."[86] This was not merely some sort of legal subterfuge; it was the plain fact of the matter. The first Claretian houses had a twofold aim. In the first place, they were the missionary centers of the diocese, under the bishop's orders, since they could not preach missions without the license of the bishop. In the second place, during the time when the missionaries were resting from their mission campaigns, priests, candidates for Orders, and the laity made retreats in these centers. Thus we can understand why Claret, in his *Notes of a Plan*, suggested that bishops allow the foundation of Claretian houses as diocesan centers for evangelization.[87] This tended to create fraternal and cooperative relationships between the first Claretians and the local clergy.[88] It was also one of the reasons why the Saint thought it most useful to have the Claretian scholastics live together with students at the diocesan seminary. This common life would tend to establish friendly ties with future pastors.[89]

From this same point of view, an interesting and significant sidelight is thrown on a characteristic early Claretian structure: the quasi-residence. This was a small community established only for a determined time in a particular place, to serve as a center for the evangelization of a given area. Ever since they were included in the primitive *Constitutions,* quasi-residences were not well understood by the Roman censors. One of them, Fr. Augustin Theiner, an Oratorian, wrote: "It seems fitting that they do away with this specious and airy entity called a quasi-residence."[90] Fortunately, this suggestion was not followed, and the structure was maintained in the second *Constitutions.*[91] The quasi-residence was an essentially apostolic institution. Living far away from the house that was their domicile, the missionaries could set up a mission center dependent on the domicile, while they were working in the territory of the quasi-residence. They did not need canonical permission in this case, since it did not involve a foundation, properly so-called; all that was needed was a mission to evangelize, given by the bishop. As if this were not enough, the founder himself, in effect, created "flying communities," whose members were sent out in groups, thus forming small, itinerant communities.[92] The Saint wanted at least some of these groups to assist in the evangelization of the diocese of Oviedo. During the summer months instead of returning to the motherhouse in Vic, they would remain in the diocesan seminary, giving retreats.[93]

No doubt about it: in the mind of the founder, there was nothing conventional about Claretian houses. They were centers of evangelizing activity, in response to the needs of the church. What counted in them was not the stability essential for the monastic life but, rather, the mobility demanded by the apostolic life. In the foreword to his *Rules for Clerics Living in Community,* Claret also insists on the lack of stability for members of the Congregation, as opposed to the stability of secular clergy assigned to parishes.

> They are different, in that those of the first order [the Congregation] have fixed houses in which they reside, but they [the Missionaries] remain there only during the period set by their superior, or until he sends them to another town, diocese or country, as required by the greater glory of God and the good of souls.[94]

This is why, contrary to the prevailing custom of other institutes, the Saint asks that his communities should not have a great many members. The lifestyle he has chosen for them demands that they spend more than half of the year outside the house, and he recommends that they establish quasi-residences, where their ministry will keep them far from their house of origin. To forestall some of the difficulties that this might involve, he orders them to make a retreat before and after their apostolic campaign. He also requires that they should not go off alone but, rather, that they should form small "flying communities," in which they must follow a rather full working schedule, although always allowing sufficient time for the practice of the fundamental acts of personal piety.

Naturally, to the extent that the apostolic horizons of the Congregation broadened under the impulse of the founder, some of these characteristics had to be moderated. Thus it is obvious that the priests dedicated to education or seminary formation had to adopt a certain kind of stability of life, by the very nature of their ministry. But one characteristic could never disappear: the *apostolic* aim of all houses belonging to the institute.

Priests, Deacons, and Brothers

The conclusions we have been drawing on the basis of numerous texts and events concerning the apostolic and, more specifically, the missionary nature of the Claretian Congregation, now oblige us to broach the question as to whether it is or is not a clerical institute.

The very first Claretians were all priests who left their parishes to commit themselves to the ministries of itinerant evangelization. Very soon after this, the first brothers entered, to be followed some years later by scholastics. At present, dating from the Special Chapter of 1967, the institute accepts the permanent diaconate as a possible Claretian vocation. The inclusion of students among the membership of the Congregation need not detain us here, since this is not a permanent vocation but merely a preparatory phase for life and ministry in the institute as a priest, deacon, or brother. In contrast, the presence of lay members dedicated to the service of God and collaborating with the other members in the mission of the institute does raise some questions on their own role and their relationship with the priests and deacons in the institute. Before we formulate these questions more exactly and attempt to give them a satisfactory response, we would do well to recall some historical data.

The question of the date of admission of the first brother, Miguel Puig, has not yet been unequivocally settled. Fr. Mariano Aguilar, in his *History,* had written that the first brother was admitted in 1857.[95] In the passage cited, Aguilar speaks of Bro. Juan Jorda i Verdaguer; but in two later books, Aguilar states that the first brother entered in September 1849 and the second, Bro. José Pla, in 1852.[96] In his more recent *History of the Congregation,* Fr. Cristóbal Fernández corrects the statements in Aguilar's first book, while he seems not to know of the others. Fernández states that the brothers must have entered during the first days of the institute;[97] but certain other expressions he uses seem to imply that this should be understood somewhat broadly, since the first person who really did those tasks that would later be considered distinctive of Claretian coadjutors was a layman, Miguel Iter, who was temporarily associated with the Claretians before his ordination to the priesthood outside the Congregation.[98] The data that we have access to lead us to suppose that Bro. Miguel Puig entered rather early, probably in 1850, although Fr. Clotet tells us that during the illness of Fr. Fábregas, which, in its gravest phase, lasted a month and took place precisely during September, the sick man had to be attended to by the first priests, since there were no brothers. Thus we are forced to exclude the earliest date suggested by Fr. Aguilar.[99] In fact, toward the end of April 1850 the institute numbered twelve members, all of them priests.[100]

We have tried to pin down the date of entry of the first Claretian brother because we would like to know whether or not, when the founder left his sons to take up his post in Cuba, he left behind him merely a group of priests or an institute already composed of priests and brothers. There is no point in seeking to clarify the matter from the primitive *Constitutions*, since we only have access to the 1857 edition, "*newly* augmented." And among the additions made at that time, we must reckon the two chapters on the brothers.

Judging by one of Fr. Clotet's remarks, it would seem that the founder himself had already received the first *Ajudant* (adjutant or helper), the prototype of the future coadjutor brothers.[101] His reception, nevertheless, since it was an isolated case, did not lead the Saint at that time to expressly formulate the role that the brothers were to play in the life and ministries of the institute. That this role and its formulation underwent a process of evolution should come as no surprise; this was the case in other fundamental aspects of Claretian life. The first missionary and sacerdotal seed of the institute, as it developed, brought with it the unfolding of new possibilities, which had been, at first, merely latent. Among these possibilities was the incorporation of lay members into the apostolic action of the Congregation.

In 1857 at the signing of the acceptance of the augmented *Constitutions*, we find among the signatures, as members of the Congregation on a par with the priests, the names of three brothers: Miguel Puig, José Pla, and Rafael Viñolas.[102] We should note that Article 5 of these *Constitutions*, which was probably augmented at this time, expressly states: "And it shall, moreover, consist of missionary priests and adjutant brothers." Furthermore, that same year (1857) two chapters on the brothers had been added to the end of the 1849 text.[103] The 1862 General Chapter introduced a significant correction into Article 5. Wishing to insert a mention of the students and, at the same time, to reaffirm the missionary character of all members of the institute, the chapter decided to revise the text as follows: "And it shall, moreover, consist of priests, students and adjutant brothers."[104] In practice, the first consecrations and taking of private vows were made by both priests and brothers but not by students.[105] In 1864 Saint Anthony Claret described his institute as being composed of priests and brothers in these significant words in the foreword to his *Rules for Clerics*.

> In the first order are those who form the Congregation called the
> Sons of the Immaculate Heart of Mary. These are priests and brothers
> entirely consecrated to God and the Blessed Virgin Mary, and are
> continually engaged in giving missions and retreats to clergy, nuns, etc.,
> according to their rules.[106]

These words of the Saint are doubly significant. Not only do they affirm the equality of the total consecration of priests and brothers; they also assign both groups to missionary ministry. We must now try to clarify how this assignment is to be understood.

It is well known that the relation between priests and brothers differs considerably, according to the type of religious life and institute involved. In the monastic life, which is characterized by a type of life and not by any specific ministry, ordination does not (theoretically) add any difference. In antiquity, the greater part of the monks were laymen and the abbot was not necessarily a cleric. The same situation recurs in the Rule of St. Francis, which likewise stresses a type of existence, rather than a ministry. The situation of brothers among canons regular was somewhat diverse, since it involved a movement whose starting point had been priesthood and the care of souls, and which had moved toward a form of religious life into which laymen were incorporated in a marginal and complementary manner with respect to a fundamental aim of this type of religious life, namely, ministry. This phenomenon is even heightened in institutes of clerks regular, or clerics living in community, which appeared in the church around the time of the Council of Trent. Some of these institutes state that they were founded for the "sacred ministry," namely, for activities proper of ordained ministers: preaching and the administration of the sacraments (mainly in churches belonging to the institute), priestly leadership of associations, etc. In this context, lay members came to be incorporated as "coadjutors" of the priests. Thus it happened that the missionary Congregations that appeared later reproduced this same type of "Coadjutor Brother." To arrive at a better understanding of this phenomenon, we should bear in mind the sharp distinction—both in theology and ecclesiastical practice—which was drawn, from Trent to the 19th century, between functions proper of the priesthood and those proper of the laity.

This automatically suggests the question: What is the role of the brother in the Claretian Congregation? Is it a case of a layperson helping a priest in the fulfillment of the (priestly) mission of the institute or, on the contrary, one of a layperson who is consecrated to the service of God to develop, in his own (lay) fashion, their common mission? The answer to these questions depends on how we answer another: Is the Claretian Congregation a priestly or clerical institute or is it a missionary institute in which priests, deacons, and laypersons develop their own proper ministries in collaboration with each other?

Historically, the answer might seem obvious. The 1857 *Constitutions* speak of "Adjutant Brothers" in the article on the members of the Congregation,[107] while they refer to them as "Coadjutor Brothers" in the last two chapters,[108] although they call them "adjutants" in Article 152.[109] The second *Constitutions* refers to the brothers as "coadjutores."[110] This was obviously the name that was applied to them in the Congregation, a custom reflected in the texts that Fr. Clotet had been writing for them, and it was from these texts that the nomenclature passed into the *Constitutions.*

The structure of the *Constitutions* reflects a change of mentality. The first *Constitutions,* written for the original, exclusively priestly, group, contains no chapter on the brothers, since all rules were addressed to priests. Hence, when it was decided to publish them nine years later in 1857, two chapters of particular norms for the brothers were added, by way of an appendix. In contrast, in the second *Constitutions,* the chapter on the students and another for priests were added, so that the spiritual and disciplinary rule became a common text for all.

Nevertheless, there are other data that reveal another direction. In the founder's description of his Congregation, in the foreword to *Rules for Clerics Living in Community,* he speaks of "priests and brothers entirely consecrated to God and the

Blessed Virgin Mary and continually engaged in giving missions and retreats.[111] Note carefully that the founder does not refer to the brothers as "coadjutors," and that he equally represents priests and brothers as engaged in missionary ministry.

The history of the ministries entrusted to Claretian brothers likewise points in various directions. On the one hand, they were given domestic chores. On the other hand, in the motherhouse at Vic, both a priest and a brother were in charge of organizing the series of retreats given there.[112] Later, Fr. Xifré wanted the brothers to take main charge of the ministry of Christian education. And, in fact, during the first half of the 20th century, there was a generation of Claretian teaching brothers who directed the ministry of education as their proper responsibility.

The fact that the brothers gradually became "coadjutors" and that most of them became involved in domestic work can largely be explained by historical factors. In the first place, the mentality still prevalent in the 19th century left little room for ministerial activities on the part of lay religious, except for those purely lay communities of brothers and sisters dedicated to teaching or charitable works. Secondly, the social origins and lack of education of many limited them to domestic work. Hence we can see that the unfortunate custom of assigning brothers to the subsidiary position of being "auxiliaries" to priests, while it was in some sense inevitable, must nonetheless be seriously reviewed in the light of present-day ecclesiological attitudes, which have changed radically.

The whole question must be reformulated on the basis of the ministry proper of the Congregation. Is this ministry something intrinsically sacerdotal, so that a lay member can only contribute to it collaterally, as a coadjutor? Indeed, there are occasions when the founder speaks of the "sacred ministry" to which his missionaries are dedicated. He does so in his *Autobiography,* in the account of the life of the original group at the time of the foundation. This is quite understandable—up to a certain point, as we shall soon see—since it was a small group made up exclusively of priests.[113] In *Selfishness Overcome,* a short work written and published in Rome toward the end of his life, the Saint classifies his Congregation among a group made up of the Jesuits and "the many Congregations of Clerks Regular," such as the

Oratorians, Vincentians, Redemptorists, and Passionists, "consecrated to giving missions and retreats to all social classes, catechizing, hearing confessions: in a word, to the sacred ministry."[114]

But while it is certain that Claret, in seeking a group in which to classify his Congregation, ranked it among the "Clerks Regular ... consecrated to ... the sacred ministry" of giving missions and retreats, catechizing, and hearing confessions, we should bear in mind that this was the most recent group in the church in which he could include them. Two other factors entered into the classification of the Congregation.

1. The radical element in the origin and life of his institute is, as he states in the *Constitutions,* "the ministry of the Word," and this is a mission of the whole church, which each Christian must endeavor to carry out in his own fashion. The *Constitutions* always refers to the members of the Congregation as "missionaries," and to their activities as "ministry." In this connection, it is highly significant that, whereas the first *Constitutions* describes the members of the Congregation as "missionary priests and adjutant brothers," thus suggesting a priestly image of its mission, the second *Constitutions,* in keeping with a decision of the General Chapter of 1862, deleted the adjective "missionary" before the word "priests" and simply stated that its members are "priests, students and coadjutor brothers."[115] It is evident that the chapter, presided over by the founder, wished to reaffirm by this that the term "missionary" applied equally to all members of the Congregation, whether priests or not. In doing so, they broadened the notion both of mission and ministry in the Congregation.

2. We should note that the concrete ministerial tasks that the founder was recommending to his missionaries as particular forms of the "ministry of the Word" were not exclusively sacerdotal. In the first place, he recommends catechesis,[116] and catechesis, even at that time, was not something restricted to priests, since he himself recommended it to laypersons of both sexes.[117] Nor could we call Christian education an exclusively priestly ministry. Yet in 1869 Claret recommended that his missionaries undertake it, precisely as an application of the ministry of catechesis, and drawing his inspiration from the example of the Brothers of the Christian Schools.[118] The same is true of the

Catholic press, which he also forcefully promoted.[119] In those days, missions and retreats were certainly priestly ministries, and this goes a long way toward explaining the clerical tinge that the institute assumed. But at present we know that they are not, since there are many nonpriestly and even lay institutions dedicated to evangelization campaigns and retreats.

The conclusion is obvious: the Claretian Congregation is not a priestly or clerical institute, founded for ministries proper of the priesthood ("sacred ministry"); rather, it was founded for evangelization in all its forms. Its members—priests, deacons, or laypersons—collaborate in a common mission, each of them according to his proper gift. In it there are no coadjutors as a separate class, since they are all one another's helpers. It is a generically missionary institute. The clerical or priestly tinge it once had was something that came to it from the outside, from the ecclesial context in which it developed.

VI

From Mission to Religious Life

From the very moment in which he discovered his vocation, St. Anthony Claret understood his life in terms of total dedication to the preaching of the Gospel. He attached the same meaning to the form of life he proposed to his confreres, both during the retreat he preached to them at the founding of the Congregation and in the earliest *Constitutions* he drafted for them. The missionary's life must be totally consecrated to evangelization. It must be a life fully committed to God in following Christ, the Prophet of the Father. In somewhat differing form, this was simply one more embodiment of the ideal of total dedication of one's existence to the service of God that has characterized the religious life since the dawn of monasticism. The difference in this case, as in that of St. Dominic, St. Ignatius, and so many others, was that the "service of God" was centered on the ministry of the Word.

But there was more to it than this. Both the founder and his earliest companions, from the outset of their life in common, felt called to a life of evangelical perfection. Above and beyond the universal call to holiness, they had an added awareness that the preaching of the Gospel must be grounded on a previous personal experience. Preaching, in other words, should mean bearing witness. St. Anthony Mary Claret repeatedly states that, in a missionary, the Christian life should shine forth in a pronounced manner. "The apostolic missionary should be a model of all the virtues."[1] He should above all be a man of charity: "The virtue an apostolic missionary needs most of all is love."[2] The reason for this, according to the Saint, is that the pentecostal explosion of zeal must issue from a great love for God and neighbor. This ministry, of its very nature, presupposes great generosity of spirit, since it implies a readiness to renounce everything for the sake of the Gospel.[3]

Finally, the way of life espoused by the Saint and his first followers was characterized by the practice of the so-called evangelical counsels, namely, those vocational charisms which have *de facto* accompanied the various forms of life dedicated to the service of God and which have, since the 12th century, been considered the distinguishing mark of every religious community. St. Anthony Mary Claret was firmly convinced that celibacy, poverty, and obedience were necessary for a life completely dedicated to the preaching of the Gospel. In his own life, these traits derived from his personal mission. He did not look upon celibacy as a special problem. The reason for this was not merely the fact that celibacy was already entailed in the priestly rule of life he had undertaken when he applied for admission to the subdiaconate; rather, it was because his markedly Pauline notion of a vocation to preach the Gospel—involving a constant readiness to be uprooted and on the move—was incompatible with the ordinary demands of married life. It is likewise clear that today's Claretian does not commit himself to a celibate life simply because it is a matter of church law. (There are, after all, lay Claretians not bound by that law.) But neither does a Claretian undertake celibacy simply because a canonical form of the religious life requires a vow of chastity; rather, it is because he regards celibacy as a "built-in" consequence of his being called, like Paul, to the instability and mobility of an all-absorbing missionary vocation.

But if we can say that Claret, so to speak, took celibacy for granted, the reasons for his insistence on *poverty* might not

seem so clear. In fact, we may look upon poverty as a touch-
stone that makes the connection between mission and evangelical life stand out in boldest relief. For the Saint, poverty was an
essential part of the apostolic life, something based on the very
meaning of mission. He treats of this at great length in his *Autobiography*: to be a missionary, one must be really poor.[4] The
biblical texts which had awakened his vocation referred not only
to preaching the Gospel, but to poverty.[5] To his way of thinking, this implied that poverty was a typical element of the missionary vocation. In the economic system of the church of his
day, a secular priest might legitimately enjoy the income of a
benefice, curacy, or chaplaincy. In contrast, a missionary, even
if he were a priest, must forego all this. Moreover, as Claret saw
things, the missionary, like St. Paul, should even refuse to be
supported by the labors of his own ministry. This was one of
the distinctive traits of the form of apostolic life he proposed
to his first followers. A short time after the founding he joyfully
wrote his friend, Canon Caixal: "We are leading a truly poor and
apostolic life in common."[6]

From the very outset of the Congregation, then, celibacy and
poverty were two of the fundamental traits of Claretian life, just
as they have been of every form of life publicly consecrated to
the service of God in the church. The reason is, of course, that
celibacy and poverty are the two fundamental means whereby
the Christian breaks through the conditioning factors of secular
life, to create a liberated form of existence exclusively oriented
toward God. Obedience, on the other hand, does not seem to
have formed a part of Anthony Claret's personal experience, except in his working in close communion with the hierarchy.
Nevertheless, from the very foundation of the institute, obedience was stressed in all its breadth, including its ascetical and
disciplinary aspects. Seen in this perspective, there is a close connection between obedience and community life. Something similar happened in the formation of the Society of Jesus. Ignatius
and his companions first professed only poverty and celibacy as
the essential traits of their apostolic life; but when they decided
to found an institute, they added the vow of obedience.

In the first *Constitutions*, drafted in 1849-50—the Claretians'
first year of existence—we can see that they were already prac-

ticing what are commonly called the three "evangelical counsels." Thus, from its inception, the Congregation was not only an institute of evangelical life but expressly adopted those three life-traits which, ever since the 12th century, have characterized the profession of the religious life. The fact is, then, that the Congregation, from a theological and existential point of view, was in practice a religious institute, although canonically it was simply an apostolic society of common life. Bearing this in mind, we may honestly say that both the apostolic mission and the evangelical life of the Congregation were born at one and the same time, on the day of its foundation.

From its very outset, then, the Congregation was doing in practice what religious, properly so-called, were doing: living in celibacy, poverty, and obedience. There was nothing particularly odd about this. In the church, celibacy has arisen mainly as an exigency of total consecration to the ministry (St. Paul), while obedience and poverty have formed the two fundamental chapters in any rule of apostolic life. But over and above this, there was a deliberate attempt in the nascent Congregation to copy certain organizational and spiritual features of existing religious institutes. Already in its first *Constitutions* we can see that the ascetic rules it prescribes are at least partially inspired by those of the Society of Jesus. In the second *Constitutions* nearly every paragraph in the ascetic section shows some contact with Jesuit authors or spirituality. In the section on government, a number of rules are derived from either the Jesuit or Redemptorist *Constitutions.*[7] Occasionally, too, the founder would propose that his missionaries adopt this or that practice from the Vincentians[8] or, later, from Congregation of the Precious Blood.[9] In *Selfishness Overcome,* Claret refers to his own Congregation, along with the Oratorians, Piarists, Vincentians, Redemptorists, and Passionists.[10]

This indiscriminate lumping together of religious orders, congregations of simple vows, and societies of common life shows clearly that in the mind of St. Anthony Mary Claret, his own Congregation resembled these institutes in two respects: (1) in that it was an institute approved by the Holy See and destined for a worldwide mission; (2) in that it was an apostolic institute, in which the life of evangelical perfection must be oriented to

serve the exercise of an apostolic vocation. Note that the brief
history of the religious life that the Saint outlines in this book
represents all of these different institutes only because they
were founded to remedy the current ills of the church. He glar-
ingly omits any mention of monastic orders, whether eremitic
or communal. After an allusion to St. Augustine, he leaps ahead
to the mendicant orders (Dominicans, Franciscans, Mercedarians, and Trinitarians), continues with the Jesuits, and ends by
speaking of the various later congregations.[11] All of these later
groups, he writes, "practice the mixed form of life; all are dedicated to missions, retreats, catechesis and the confessional, i.e.,
to the sacred ministry."[12]

How the Vows Were Understood
in the Primitive Congregation

Certain more or less late assertions by Frs. Xifré and Clotet
attribute the lack of vows or any other form of commitment
in the beginnings of the Congregation to a fear of the complica-
tions that this might provoke with the civil government. Fr. Cristóbal Fernández has alluded to these assertions in his history of
the early days of the Congregation, where he explains its juridical situation up to the year 1870.[13] Neither Xifré nor Clotet
ever expressly states that St. Anthony Mary Claret had begun
by envisioning the founding of a religious congregation, properly so-called, with mandatory vows. In fact, they even seem to
imply the contrary at times. In any case, since they limit themselves to citing this single external cause, they might well give
the impression that the juridical situation of the early institute
depended solely on this external cause. Since this is a matter of
some importance from a historical point of view, we believe that
it is necessary for us to sort out the facts with great care.

There is no doubt that the times were unfavorable to religious
institutes; the troublesome laws enacted in 1835 had proscribed
them throughout the kingdom of Spain. As late as 1851 the new
Concordat had expressly recognized only the Vincentians and
Oratorians (institutes without public vows), as well as a third,
unspecified group, approved by the Holy See, in order to collaborate with the hierarchy in the ministry of preaching.[14] (As Pius
IX showed in his allocution of September 5, 1851, his intention

was to reestablish in Spain the religious institutes that had been disestablished in 1835.) Under these circumstances, even though the political climate had changed considerably by 1848, a Congregation that seemed to be just a simple association of priests would have the best chances for survival. This motive must have been in the back of the founder's mind in 1849, when he declined to impose any official bond on the members of his institute. The drafting of Article 44 of the first *Constitutions* was a response to this situation, as Fr. Xifré has clearly pointed out.

But when we reformulate the question to ask not just the motive for not having any public commitment in the primitive institute but, more concretely, for not having any religious vows, public or private, we believe that the alleged reason of the opposition of the civil authorities does not explain everything. The point is that Claretian events and documents seem unanimously to suggest a deeper reason, namely, that the taking of public or private vows had no part in the idea of the institute as St. Anthony Claret *originally* conceived it. It would arrive at that stage later, by a natural process of evolution.

In his *Autobiography,* St. Anthony Claret tells us that his aim in 1849 was to found a "congregation of priests" dedicated to preaching missions.[15] On two occasions, Fr. Clotet repeats these very words in describing the Saint's original proposal to the cofounders.[16] This is a fact that deserves consideration, given the customary care with which Clotet weighs his words. The outlines of the talks for the founding retreat are significantly titled, "Exercises for the Clergy."[17] All Claretian documents relating to the Congregation describe it unanimously as an institute dedicated to missionary preaching. For example, the dilemma posed by the Saint to Fr. Ramonet, when he invited the latter to join the Congregation, was the same one he had posed to the cofounders: namely, *not* the dilemma between being a diocesan priest or a religious priest but, rather, between being a parish priest or a missionary priest.[18] This alone, then, the missionary vocation, distinguishes a Claretian priest from any other in those documents where the Saint establishes any such comparison.[19] In as late a text as the 1865 *Constitutions* he still speaks of the "apostolic spirit" as a condition for entering the Congregation, making no express mention of the religious spirit.[20] In *Notes of a*

Plan he refers to the Congregation in the section dealing with diocesan institutions.[21] In contrast, there is not a single text before 1862 in which the Saint alludes to the possible taking of vows, even privately. But the clearest proof of the fact is that as late as 1862, Claret expressly states in the formula for vows that "one is free to take them and, hence, that one could belong to the Congregation for all his life without taking them."

Obviously, if it had only been a question of fear of possible government opposition, we would be hard pressed to explain the silence about vows in internal documents addressed only to members of the Congregation. Without leaving the circle of influence of Claret himself, the Adoratrices, the Sisters of the Immaculate Conception, and the Carmelite Sisters of Charity had already come by that time to take vows, some of them from their very founding and with no knowledge of the civil government, although the founder of the Sisters of the Immaculate Conception did not include the matter of vows in their first *Constitutions.*[22] For the Claretians, on the contrary, the introduction of the vows—first private, then public—was something of a novelty. This is borne out in a letter of Fr. Currius to Fr. Sala.[23] On a number of occasions Fr. Xifré proposed the matter somewhat timidly, fearing that some would not be prepared to accept it, as indeed some did not in 1862.

Having mapped out the concrete stages in the historical evolution of these facts, we must ask ourselves what they mean. They mean, basically, that the germinal idea for the institute had not yet revealed all its potentialities, not even in the mind of the founder. St. Anthony Claret, always focusing on the missionary vocation, had been considering the founding of a mission center for Catalonia as far back as 1839. From this he had gone on, through a series of groups of collaborators, to the foundation of a Congregation of missionary priests in 1849. An integral and distinctive part of that Congregation was made up of those elements of the religious life (celibacy, poverty, obedience, and fraternal life) that are required for an apostolic vocation lived in its fullness. Hence, as we noted above, both mission and evangelical life were born at the same time in the Congregation, on the very day of its founding. This explains the particular stress in this institution on the practice of evangelical life that Claret had always recommended to priests, calling them to a special imitation of the Lord since they were so closely bound to Him in carrying out His ministry. Still, his own personal experience had not led the Saint to take even private vows; his total consecration to the Lord and the Blessed Virgin in carrying out his ministry was enough for him. Moreover, the fact that he had been forced to live apart from his spiritual sons for a very long time had prevented him from seeing the reinforcing power that the taking of public vows could add to their commitment and consecration to the apostolate. In the spirit and life of the Congregation, however, the characteristic elements of the evangelical life—the practice of celibacy, poverty, fraternal life, and obedience—were so explicit that they would eventually lead to religious profession by an internal and, so to speak, natural evolution. The same has happened in a great number of religious institutes of apostolic life: their specific apostolic aim has led them little by little to the canonical religious state.

There is nothing particularly strange about this. Quite often, in the history of the religious life, founders do not initially have a clear awareness of all of the elements—even important ones—that will eventually constitute the definitive profiles of their institutes. God continues to show them further implications little by little. In the beginning their idea is very simple: they perceive an urgent need in the church and envision an institution destined to respond to that need. In this initial idea, the spiritual element is predominant; the other elements appear gradually by derivation. St. Francis of Assisi had only one ideal—to live according to the Gospel. St. Ignatius Loyola was obsessed with a will to serve the church. Experience gradually showed Francis the need for giving a certain organization to his manner of evangelical living; while Ignatius was to spend years of prayer and reflection on the best manner in which to regulate some important aspects of the life of the Company of Jesus. St. Anthony Mary Claret saw the need for founding an institution dedicated to missionary preaching and he also saw, from the first moment, that if his missionaries were going to carry out that task, they would have to follow a rule of celibacy, poverty, and obedience. Whether they would need to take public vows to reinforce that evangelical life in the service of the apostolate was a problem that he does not seem to have explicitly considered at the time. It was an issue that would surface gradually, with the passage of time.

First Wishes for Religious Vows

The idea of transforming the primitive apostolic society into a religious Congregation, properly so-called, began to appear spontaneously in the writings of the first members. The oldest document of this sort is the formula of private profession made by the Servant of God, Fr. James Clotet, in 1861.

> I shall make my vows to the Lord. With the help of God I promise to observe chastity, poverty and obedience in the sense in which they are expressed in the *Constitutions* of our Congregation, remaining free, however, in doubtful cases, so as to avoid anxieties and scruples. Pronounced at Gracia, before the altar of the Blessed Virgin, on Holy Thursday, the 18th day of March, in the year of the Lord 1861.[24]

We would call this the oldest document *of the institute* referring to religious profession. Years earlier, while the founder was in Cuba, his secretary, Paladio Curríus, had written on his own initiative to Fr. Sala, proposing the idea that the missionaries should consecrate themselves to God by public vows. Currius' words show, however, that he is aware of proposing something novel. We believe that Currius acted under the influence of M. Antonia París, the foundress of the Claretian Sisters, who at that time was under Currius' spiritual direction. M. Antonia had perceived prophetically that Claret would found two apostolic communities, of women and of men. She interpreted this in the sense of an order with two branches, the only kind of religious life she knew at that moment, and in fact started her community as a cloister of nuns with solemn vows. Obviously, for the men's branch Currius imagined that the Congregation already founded by the Saint at Vic could develop into a religious order with vows.[25]

Fr. Mariano Aguilar informs us that ten days later, on March 28, 1861, Fr. Xifré spoke to the bishop of Vic on the convenience of having all members of the Congregation take perpetual vows, subject to the will of their superior, upon finishing their year of probation.[26] Evidently, Frs. Xifré and Clotet had reached a previous accord on the matter, otherwise we would be at pains to explain this coincidence. We cannot substantiate which of the two had the original idea concerning the vows.

The bishop, as one might have expected, did not deem it opportune that he alone should decide in a matter of such importance and recommended that Fr. Xifré should consult with the founder first. We do not know why Fr. Xifré did not follow through immediately on the bishop's suggestion, despite the fact that he wrote the Saint three times during these days, once on March 25, three days before speaking with the bishop, and again on April 8 and 14. St. Anthony Claret answered all three letters in his own letter of April 20, without any mention of vows, a clear proof that nothing had been said to him about them.[27]

This did not stop a growing trend among the missionaries in favor of the idea of taking private vows. In a letter from Segovia on April 29, 1862, Fr. Donato Berenguer asks Fr. Xifré's permission to take a vow of poverty—a sure indication that he had already taken vows of obedience and chastity.[28] Like Fr. Berenguer, others must have been taking vows during the period between March 1861 and July 1862, although we cannot say how many did so, since we totally lack documents of the matter. (We say that we lack documents on the progressive taking of vows between these dates, because the list of members published by Fr. Fernández in his history of the Congregation,[29] p. 481 f., cannot refer to these months. Fr. Fernández notes that the words *Con Vs*—"with vows"—were added to the names of some missionaries *later,* by Fr. Clotet. We may add, with greater precision, that we know these words were a later addition, since they appear in connection with Fr. Maciá, who had not made a private profession as late as March 1863, as we read on p. 490 of the same work by Fernández. The mention of vows in the list of members is, hence, later than the latter date.) The founder must have gradually become aware of all this, since he had frequent dealings with the community in Segovia. Nevertheless, there is no mention of this fact in the correspondence between the Saint and Fr. Xifré.

Clearly, then, the idea of taking vows spread from the motherhouse in Vic, and its able propagandist and probable father was none other than Fr. Joseph Xifré. What motives lay behind this development? Two, above all. First, during the first decade of the Congregation it had become clear that something was needed to reinforce the commitment that bound the missionaries to the institute. The freedom they always had to leave it if they so chose and the virtual impossibility of the superiors being able to expel those they thought to be unworthy had given rise to some serious mishaps. Fr. Xifré, above all, felt the need to bind the members of the institute more closely to it for its own good. Second, the perfection with which obedience and poverty were already practiced in the Congregation seemed to favor taking vows to enhance and safeguard the existing practice. Both of these motives appear in the various texts that allude to this question.

On April 2, 1862, a year after his consultation with the bishop of Vic, Fr. Xifré wrote to the founder, proposing the celebration of a general chapter. On April 11, the founder answered, accepting the proposal, fixing a date, and promising his presence.[30] The chapter was held from July 7 to July 14, 1862. During it Fr. Xifré must have put forth his own proposal of making vows obligatory for all. A more moderate position— whether it was suggested or merely approved by the founder, we do not know—prevailed: No one would be obliged to take vows, but the chapter members committed themselves to promote the practice and not to elect as director or subdirector general anyone who had not taken vows. For the time being this agreement was to remain secret. The Acta of the chapter resolve:

> That there be a reserved decree, whereby all of us here present are committed to promote the taking of vows by all the Sons of the Congregation, and not to elect anyone to the office of Director or Subdirector who has not done so. And let this agreement remain under a signed, secret oath.[31]

When the Roman censors received the Acta of the chapter, they judged it inopportune that a decision of such importance for the life of the institute be kept secret.[32] What the censors failed to understand was the serious motive which had led the chapter members to keep silence on the matter, namely, the fact that some of the missionaries were not ready to accept the idea of vows, as their indecision during the following months would show. We believe that this internal problem was what moved the founder at this time to counsel Fr. Xifré that: "As regards vows, you should proceed with great circumspection, as I see you are already doing."[33] At the same time, the chapter had decided that the year of probation should begin and end "with some ceremony" (unspecified), to officially mark the candidates' entry into the Congregation.

After returning to Madrid and then following the royal retinue to La Granja, Claret drafted an "Act of Consecration to God, to Jesus Christ, and to the Blessed Virgin Mary," for the ceremony marking the end of the year of probation. In it, the candidate committed himself to keep, "with all possible care," the commandments, the evangelical counsels, and the *Constitutions*. The original text by Claret states this and nothing more.[34] As one can see, the actual practice of the evangelical life, which had been an essential element of the apostolic spirituality of the institute since its first days, was hereby solemnly affirmed in this official commitment, although it was not made the object of a vow. At the same time, the Saint drafted a "Formula of Vows Counseled for the Members of the Congregation," which began with the following explanatory note:

> These vows are free, so that no one in the Congregation is obliged to make them. Thus, one might very well be a member for his whole life without being bound by vows. But experience has shown that members who have not bound themselves by vows, when they have some temptation against their vocation, give in to it and leave.... Moreover, it has been observed that those who have bound themselves by vows remain quite content, without ever having a temptation against their vocation.[35]

A second explanatory note made it clear that the vows in question were perpetual but that the superior general could dispense from them and that they were to be taken with that proviso. They were to be taken after a second period of probation for those who had already made the Act of Consecration.[36] As this text clearly shows, the vows had only an ascetic and personal character, but they added a greater firmness to the public act of consecration. For the time being, the Saint did not think that they should be obligatory for all: "Thus, one might very well be a member for his whole life without being bound by vows."

Fr. Xifré could not have been very happy with the solution arrived at by the chapter, since a simple consecration would not guarantee the kind of stability he believed necessary for a religious institute. Therefore, immediately after the chapter during the retreat he preached to the community at Gracia, he proposed that Frs. Reixach, Ramonet, Quintana, and Portell take an oath to remain perpetually in the Congregation.[37] It is possible that Xifré consulted with Claret on the matter, although we cannot be sure, since we do not have Xifré's letters to the Saint. We have mentioned Claret's letter of August 22, 1862, where he states: "What you say about the consecration seems quite good to me. As regards vows, you should proceed with great circumspection...." The opening words may refer to the oath of permanence. The priests in question were agreeable to Xifré's proposal. Later, when Xifré received a draft of the formulas of consecration and profession transmitted through the good offices of Fr. Serrat, the superior of the house at Segovia, he corrected the former, striking out the words "Jesus Christ" and replacing the Saint's more general "Blessed Virgin Mary" with "the Heart of Mary," while adding the twofold oath of perpetual permanence in the Congregation and refusal to accept dignitary titles. All of this is, in fact, missing in the text of Claret sent through Fr. Serrat to Fr. Xifré.[38] Upon receiving the corrected text, the founder approved it without further ado.[39]

The state of the new institute, as it now appeared after these decisions, was described in the minutes for the audience at which Pius IX definitively approved it on December 22, 1865.

Mons. Claret y Clara, Archbishop of Trajanopolis and Confessor of the Queen of Spain, has founded, in the diocese of Vic in Spain, in 1849, the Institute of the Missionaries of the Immaculate Heart of Mary, whose object is the salvation of souls by means of the holy missions. Its members are free to take simple vows, but they must make an oath of stability and of not accepting ecclesiastical dignities.[40]

The Claretian Congregation received definitive pontifical approval, then, as an apostolic society of common life.

A Religious Congregation

The final step toward transforming the institute into a religious Congregation, properly so-called, was likewise taken by

Fr. Xifré. He first discussed the matter with the subdirector, Fr. Clotet, and with the other general consultors, and then convoked an extraordinary meeting of the priests of the Congregation in Prades. The discourse which he delivered on this occasion is preserved for us in Xifré's own words in his *Chronicle of the Congregation.*

> 1. We have all embraced the apostolic life with a mind to persevere in it until death. 2. We have embraced it in order to avoid the innumerable dangers of condemnation which are to be found in any other state. 3. We have embraced it because we are convinced and can feel that God is given incomparably more glory and more souls are saved than in any other profession. 4. We have embraced it, finally, because we have felt called to it, after previous competent counsel and even, invitations.
>
> Sirs: we are in the Congregation for the aforesaid reasons, but our Congregation does not constitute a religious state, since we lack profession of the three perpetual vows and the pontifical approval of that profession and of our Constitutions. We are presently no more than a middle term.
>
> Would it not be more fitting, useful and meritorious to shape the Congregation into a true, religious state?
>
> By doing this, without undertaking any further duties, we would gain more merit, increase our personnel and spread more easily throughout the world. What do you think of this?
>
> To this, with no discordant voice, they all responded, with consoling emotion: "This is what we wish"—all of them agreeing, with those who had been somewhat hesitant raising their voices with the greatest enthusiasm. The response, consequently, was: "We shall have recourse to the Holy See."[41]

This document is highly revealing. Fr. Xifré and his consultors wished to convert the institute into a religious Congregation. Until then, says Fr. Xifré, it had only "embraced the apostolic life." This conversion was being sought for two distinct reasons: (1) because of the greater merit a religious gains in virtue of his vows and (2) because of the conviction that in this way, by reinforcing the ties that bound them together, they might spread more readily and obtain more vocations. Fr. Xifré was obviously afraid that some would not accept this step, but was pleasantly surprised to find that all accepted it wholeheartedly.

"Before anything else," Fr. Xifré continues, "our Father Founder was apprised of this." And, in fact, the petition to the

Holy See was sent to the Saint, together with a letter in which Fr. Xifré explained the matter to him. This letter is one of the few articles of correspondence from Xifré to Claret that we still possess. It is in the archives of the Congregation of Religious, among the position papers on the *Constitutions*. In it, Fr. Xifré states:

> I believe that the moment has come when the Congregation must take the final step in arriving at the perfection to which it is called, a step which, to my way of thinking, it can no longer put off. It does not seem good to me to do things half-way, or to stand still along the way. I mean to say that our Institute must be a religious order in which the highest perfection exists; but for this, neither the oath nor the optional vows will suffice. It is indispensable that they be obligatory in the act of profession. Thanks be to God, all do this before the community on the day they make their consecration with the approved oath; but this is not obligatory, and hence, we are lacking something for the desired end. What we need is for His Holiness to approve, grant and decree what we ask in the accompanying petition. We have cosigned Your Excellency's will and conformity, in the belief that this would meet with your approval.[42]

Fr. Xifré included another request for some slight changes in the *Constitutions* and begged the Saint to engage the intervention of Bishop Franchi and the Spanish bishops.

This letter was written from Prades on November 14, 1869. On December 16 of that year the founder answered, repeating what he had already stated in an earlier letter to Fr. Clotet—a letter which, unfortunately, has not come down to us. As soon as he had received Fr. Xifré's letter, the Saint had passed it and the accompanying documents on to Monsignor Franchi, an old acquaintance from the Nunciature in Madrid, then secretary of the congregation for extraordinary ecclesiastical affairs.[43]

These documents were accessioned on December 1, 1869, as the annotation on the protocol shows. On December 7, they were sent to the bishop of Vic, who was in Rome at the time, for his opinion. Perhaps on that same day or on one of his visits to the Congregation of Bishops and Regulars, the official asked the founder the nature of the vows that were to be taken, and annotated the minutes for the Holy Founder as follows:

His Excellency, the Bishop, has told me by voice that the vows would be simple, thus the Institute cannot be reckoned among the true Religious Orders.[44]

The doubt had arisen after reading Fr. Xifré's petition, which had three main points:

First, that the members of our Congregation be obliged to take three perpetual vows in the rite of profession.... 2. That the Constitutions be definitively approved and confirmed.... 3. That the Congregation be ranked among the Orders of Regulars and that its members be esteemed and held as true religious.[45]

Fr. Xifré's petition that the Congregation be numbered among regular orders lent itself to some confusion. The common practice of those days was to lump all institutes of common life under the general heading of Religious Orders, somewhat as the man in the street does in our own times. Thus, in the *Annuario Pontificio* for 1866, under the heading of Religious Orders, we find Canons and Clerks Regular (Theatines, Barnabites, Jesuits, etc.), Religious Congregations (Passionists, Redemptorists, etc.), Ecclesiastical Congregations (Oratorians, Vincentians, Marists, etc.), Monks, and Mendicant Orders. The Claretians, although they are not mentioned in the 1866 edition, would have been classified in all likelihood among Ecclesiastical Congregations (societies of common life), and would hence have come under the general heading of Religious Orders. Among Fr. Clotet's notes there is one on the division of Religious Orders into Canons Regular, Monks, Ecclesiastical Congregations (societies without vows), Religious Congregations (with vows), and Religious (lay) Institutes.[46]

As anyone can see, the designation "Religious Orders" was applied improperly to all institutes of common life, with or without vows, in the sense that we speak of institutes nowadays. Nevertheless, the law distinguished carefully between religious, properly so-called—those with solemn vows—and improperly so-called—those with simple vows. According to Canon Law, congregations with simple vows were not properly Religious Institutes. The practice of the Sacred Congregation was somewhat fluctuating: sometimes it applied the law for Regulars to congregations, sometimes it did not.

All of this, however, does not clarify the meaning of Fr. Xifré's petition in a fully satisfactory way. In asking for two distinct things—obligatory profession and the request that members of the Congregation be considered as *"true* religious"—he seems to imply that what he wanted was a profession of solemn vows. Nevertheless, in his letter to the founder he states that to be true religious, Claretians needed obligatory profession.

> Our Institute must be a religious order in which the highest perfection exists; but for this, neither the oath nor the optional vows will suffice. It is indispensable that they [the vows] be obligatory in the act of profession.[47]

It is quite possible that at that time Fr. Xifré had not been thinking of the question of the different quality, solemn or simple, of the vows and that for him, at that time, true religious meant those with simple vows. But if this were the case, it is hard to understand why, in his petition to the pope, he asks for obligatory profession and consideration as true religious, as if he were asking for two diverse things.

The official of the Sacred Congregation of Bishops and Regulars understood him to be asking for solemn vows and hence he asked the founder, during one of the latter's visits to the Sacred Congregation, what sort of vows they were to be. The Saint responded that they were to be simple and the official drew the conclusion we related above. Pius IX, in an audience granted to the secretary of the Sacred Congregation on February 11, 1870, definitively approved the *Constitutions,* corrected them to state that obligatory profession, together with the apostolic consecration, would come at the end of the year of probation. From this moment, the institute ceased to be, in the nomenclature of the age, an Ecclesiastical Congregation, and became a Religious Congregation.

The first official profession, judging by Fr. Clotet's notes, was made on August 11, 1870, by Fathers Reixach, Soler, Llambés, Prums, Puig, and Novellas, with Brothers Pla and Villalta. Another followed on August 12, and on August 28 Fr. Xifré made his profession in the hands of Fr. Clotet, and then proceeded himself to receive the vows of all of the other members of the house at Prades.[48]

We have no document to tell us what Fr. Xifré's reaction was on receiving the decrees from Rome. If this was what he had sought, then he must have been content with them. Prompted by certain ideas and even official statements on the not properly religious character of institutes of simple vows, he would write years later, on November 26, 1890, to Fr. Batlló, the procurator general, asking him to sound out the authorities on the possibility of transforming the Congregation into an order with solemn vows. He was moved to do so in the desire that the Claretians should be religious in the full sense of the word, and that he could die in the knowledge that he had left the institute in a completed state. Xifré felt that this would obviate certain defections and erroneous notions on the part of those who thought that simple vows were not sufficiently binding.[49] His idea never came to fruition, however, doubtless because the sounding he had asked for turned out to be negative. Consequently, the Congregation remained definitively constituted as its founder had decided, as an institute of simple vows.

The Meaning of This Evolution

The history of the developmental process that led to the transformation of the apostolic society of 1849 into a canonically Religious Congregation in 1870 is of itself revealing. Nevertheless, it will not be out of place if we briefly comment on its meaning here.

Let us first make one thing clear: the process we are speaking of affected only the juridical constitution of the institute, and not directly its vocation and spirit. For since the first day of its foundation, its members were men radically and exclusively committed to God in the ministry of the Word and, as an expression of this radical and exclusive commitment, embraced celibacy, poverty, fraternal life, and obedience. All of this was an integral part of the Claretian vocation and spirit, as its founder and his first companions understood it. The chapters on chastity, poverty, and obedience already appear in the first *Constitutions,* and their observance was strictly practiced.

Where a long process did, indeed, take place was in the idea of taking religious vows, by means of which the Claretians committed themselves, in the presence of the community, to uphold those aspects of the evangelical life that they were already practicing. This idea began to surface with some vigor among the missionaries at Vic, in 1861, and it was decided that it should be recommended to all, the following year. The founder drafted the formula for the free taking of vows and thus it came to appear in the *Constitutions* of 1865. In November 1869 the members of the institute, at Fr. Xifré's proposal, unanimously accepted the idea of making profession obligatory, thus giving rise to a Religious Congregation. The founder adopted the idea, sought the aid of those bishops in whose dioceses his missionaries had houses, and personally carried out with the Holy See the steps necessary to obtain its approval. A few months later, on his deathbed, the founder himself made his profession.

Once the unanimous petition of the membership had been accepted by St. Anthony Mary Claret and the Holy See, the institute became, juridically, a Religious Congregation. With this, during the lifetime of its holy founder, and with his approval and personal intervention, the institute completed its canonical evolution.

That the missionaries themselves should have taken the initiative in this process might seem surprising, but it is understandable in view of the early history of the Congregation. Its founder, ever since 1850, had lived physically on the margin of the institute, either in Cuba or in the royal court. It was normal, then, that the superiors of the Congregation were the ones to feel the need for obligatory religious profession. St. Anthony Claret accepted the petition, prudently moderating the process by which it was carried out.

All of this, however, does not mean that the history of this evolution lacks great importance for defining the physiognomy of the institute. This history confirms once more what we already know from other sources, namely, that the very first thing about Claretians, the root of their being in the church, has been the missionary vocation. It was from this vocation that they felt moved from their first day to practice that evangelical life which would later take on the form of public profession of vows. Apostolic mission explains and specifies Claretian religious life: the Claretian Congregation is a missionary institute ordained to preach the Gospel. The common concept of religious life, identical in its essential elements in all institutes, although embodied in diverse concrete forms, is specified in the Claretians by apostolic mission, just as it is in the Jesuits and in modern missionary congregations. However, religious profession adds a special depth and particular characteristics to the missionary apostolate of the institute.

These considerations have brought us to touch upon the relationships that exist between religious life and apostolic vocation in religious institutes founded for an external ministry. This is a decisive question for an understanding of the proper identity of such institutes, yet it is one which is rather frequently ill stated. For example, it is not a rare case to see the relationship between religious life and apostolate stated as if it were an exact analogue with the relationship between prayer and ministry or, in terms that ultimately derive from Greek philosophy, between contemplation and action. In other cases, it is understood as equivalent to the question of the relationship between community commitments ("observances") and external ministry. The first of these statements reflects a "contemplative" conception of religious living; the second, a monastic or conventual one.

By religious life we understand a type of Christian existence exclusively consecrated to God, in such wise that those who are engaged in it renounce every other type of relationship on which a form of Christian existence in the world might legitimately be based. This orientation toward God (*re-ligio* in the sense meant by Lactantius and St. Augustine), constitutes the unique *raison d'etre* of this kind of Christian life. To put the matter in more specifically Christian terms, there is an attempt to live only for Christ and His concerns; that is to-say, for Christ and His church. Hence, every form of religious life entails a service to the church; it is, of its very nature, ministerial. It is radically ministerial, as a form of life in which evangelical values flower forth visibly and publicly. It is also ministerial, in most cases, by the undertaking of some specific ecclesial ministry for which the institute was founded: an intercessory ministry, among "contemplatives"; an external, apostolic, or charitable ministry, in institutes founded for these works.

From what we have just said, it can be seen how it is possible to distinguish between religious life and any sort of ministry in institutes founded for ministries. It is not the works (prayer or apostolate) that define the religious but, rather, the exclusive gift of oneself and one's life to God, so as to do what He wills of us. The effective dedication to different ministries is, nevertheless, a distinctive expression of one's self-gift to God, since it is God who calls one to these ministries (intercession or external activity) and, hence, the religious enters an institute founded for this service. Religious life and ministry are founded in the concrete, thus giving rise to determinate, specific forms of religious life. What we call "apostolic life," in the modern sense of that expression, is nothing but a specific form of religious life.

We cannot, however, even in this context, say that "religious life" and "ministry" are equivalent terms. By "religious life," we mean a type of Christian existence; by "ministry," we mean a type of activity. One is a religious, according to the type of life one leads. Hence, we cannot say that an intense dedication to some activity (prayer or external ministry) suffices, of itself, to make one a religious. There are plenty of lay Christians intensely dedicated to prayer and apostolic activity, who neither are nor pretend to be "religious." But, on the other hand, the religious life, in institutes specifically determined by a ministry, is a life oriented toward that ecclesial ministry. One is celibate and lives in common to be able to dedicate oneself more freely to that ministry. Thus there is a mutual interaction between religious life and ministerial activity. The religious life demands that celibacy, the profession of Christian poverty, and fraternal life be visibly manifested in the ministry. The ministry demands an orientation of personal and group life toward that ministry.

When we speak of the religious life as a type of Christian existence, we refer to an objective reality, which arises from the orientation of that type of life toward certain values. This is what really constitutes religious life as a specifically differentiated form of Christian life. Just as what constitutes marriage as a state of life is an objective and public relationship between a man and a woman, rather than the quality or intensity of their feelings for one another, so also what constitutes one a religious is the accepting of celibacy for the sake of the Kingdom as a way of life, whether in anchoretic solitude or in community and not, properly speaking, the quality or intensity of one's own subjective relationship with God. Subjective communion with God does not itself create the religious state of life. With faith, hope, love, the life of prayer, and so forth, we are on the plane of the Christian life in general, a life that may be subjectively more intense in secular Christians than in religious. But it is likewise certain that the concrete form of religious life is in the service of the Christian life, so that without the latter, the former loses its meaning and value.

Christian communion with God is effected in charity, with that twofold dimension that is explicit in the two commandments of love. Charity—the love of God and of the neighbor in God—is the soul of all Christian life. Love is, then, the soul of all apostolic life. Love has two dimensions: prayer and service. But there is one, *exceptional* form of Christian life, in which service is fused with prayer. That is to say that, to aid the church interiorly, through a ministry of intercession, certain Christians are called by God to renounce all exterior activity. Think of how much the community of believers has been enriched by such persons as Anthony the Hermit, Teresa of Avila, and Thomas Merton. What Christianity cannot legitimately do is to suppress all orientation toward the neighbor (toward the church), under pretext of giving oneself totally to God or working only for one's own salvation. A type of religious life oriented exclusively toward prayer is a form of religious life in the service of the church and humanity by means of the ministry of intercession.

We have said that this type of religious life—dedicated exclusively to prayer—is exceptional, because the Pilgrim Church is at once a community of worship and a community of mission, and in this type of religious life, only the first dimension is made visible. In the other, specifically determined type of religious life, of institutes consecrated to apostolic and charitable activities, both poles of charity (God and the neighbor in God) and both dimensions of the church (worship and mission) are made visible. As an expression of Christian life, the apostolic life is more complete. On the other hand, we simply cannot have a type of religious, or even generally Christian, life without prayer, because prayer is the unsuppressible expression of the theological virtues of faith, hope, and charity. What happens in the apostolic life is that prayer is determined by a total orientation of life to an external ministry; hence, on the level of both the community and the individual, prayer assumes those forms and times that are proper to an apostolic spirituality.

This is the general theological context in which the Claretian tradition, vocation, and spirit are set. Called by God to evangelization, the Claretian embraces celibacy, poverty, fraternal communion, and, among the aspects of this communion, obedience, so that he may give himself more freely to the service of the Word. For the Claretian, the "religious" means a radicalization of the "missionary."

Having arrived at this point, it is fitting that we examine the texts of the internal tradition of the institute, starting with those of the founder, to see how this question has been understood throughout the historical development of the Congregation.

In the mind of the founder, the question seems to have been resolved with a simplicity and a decisiveness that are truly instructive. For him the entire life of the institute is ordained to the apostolic vocation, and it is precisely this orientation that creates among the Claretians the exigencies of the religious life. We saw this at sufficient length when we studied the way in which the Saint organized his Congregation, giving it structures proper of an apostolic institute. Let us merely recall that both of the *Constitutions* he drafted take a missionary aim as their point of departure, and from that point of departure they regulate the entire personal and community life of the missionaries. The system of life in and outside the house, the forms of prayer, the type of government, and the formation of students, are all proper of an essentially apostolic institute. However, the other side of the coin is that the manner of carrying out the apostolate must be animated by the spirit of evangelical perfection, which the Saint considers to be essential to the apostolic ministry. Recall his strong statements in the *Autobiography* and the *Constitutions* on obedience,[50] on the demands of apostolic poverty,[51] and on detachment from the world, which he inculcates with such insistence in the chapter on impediments to the sacred ministry.[52]

The same idea is reflected in the *Spirit of the Congregation,* by Fr. Joseph Xifré. This whole work is based on the conviction that mission is the central element in Claretian spirituality. Its entire ascetic teaching is inspired by the exigencies of the apostolic vocation. The sanctity it postulates for the Claretian is that of the missionary, and it sees even the evangelical counsels within this perspective.[53] But here, too, the obligation to practice evangelical perfection, a life of prayer and detachment, are unequivocally expressed.

The rules traced out by the succeeding superiors general of the Claretians have followed this same direction. Frs. García, Maroto, and Schweiger insist that the religious life of the Claretian is centered in apostolic mission. Fr. García dedicated a circular letter to show how the apostolate is the primary trait of the Claretian spirit,[54] and he had previously taught that the goal of the apostolate is the fundamental precept of Claretian life.[55] His entire ascetic teaching takes this statement as its starting point.[56] He once stated that "our contemplation is directed to the apostolate."[57] Fr. Maroto speaks of the "essentially missionary character" of the institute.[58] Fr. Schweiger, too, has dealt with the apostolic end of the Claretians as the goal of their life. He tells us that the Claretians' life of union with God is indispensable for the attainment of the specific end of the Congregation, which is the apostolate.[59]

Hence, the religious life of the Claretian cannot be rightly understood unless it is seen as springing from and ordained to apostolic mission and, consequently, inasmuch as it entails as its typical expression, the ministry. Fr. Alsina had said as much, and Frs. García and Schweiger repeat it: a Claretian is not a good religious unless he is animated by the apostolic spirit and strives constantly to ready himself for ministerial work.[60] The same fathers general constantly recall the spirit and manner in which this apostolate—the fundamental law of Claretian living—should be developed, so as to be considered an integral part of the religious life, deriving from that life its fullness and efficacy: the practice of the evangelical counsels, especially obedience; self-denial; the spirit of union with God and frequent converse with Him; detachment from the world. The texts are so many and so precisely to the point that it would be useless to cite them here.

Let us simply note how Fr. Schweiger, in one of his last circular letters, dealt with the question of the identity that should exist between the religious consecration and the apostolic mission of the Claretian:

> The renewal of the religious life and the updating of the apostolic ministry, since both of them are united by nature and by history, are not two parallel things that must be treated independently, for the one supposes the other. In our case, as in that of a number of other Institutes of apostolic life, our specific apostolic end leads us to the generic end of the religious life. Founded for the ministry of the Word, we have embraced the evangelical counsels since the beginning of the Congregation, and only gradually during the course of its first twenty years of life, has our Institute evolved to become a religious Congregation properly so-called and juridically complete. Whence it may be deduced that, in our Congregation, the apostolic ministry is intimately united with the religious life, in such a way that, in renewing the former, we must always bear the latter in mind, and vice versa.[61]

After this brief but instructive excursus through the texts of the Claretian tradition, it is hoped that the reader will feel that our conclusions have been fully justified. The teachings of Vatican II on the relations between religious life and apostolic mission in institutes such as the Claretians were already familiar to the Claretians, thanks to the teachings of their holy founder, teachings that were repeated and developed by his successors in the highest level of government of the Congregation that he founded.

VII

The Claretian Community in the Church

One of the richest and most revealing veins in the thought of St. Anthony Mary Claret is made up of his ideas on the nature of the church. In sharp contrast with social and juridical models that dominated the ecclesiology of his day, Claret insistently dwells on the most inward aspects of the mystery of the church.

Strongly imbued with the teaching of Paul, he sees the church, above all, as the prolongation of Christ: not simply as the historical continuation of the earthly Christ but as the presence on earth of the risen Lord. In his *Notes of a Plan,* he writes, echoing certain notions he derived from Bossuet: "The Church of Jesus Christ, extended and communicated, is Jesus Christ in his fullness."[1]

This conception of the nature of the church was fully in accord with the Saint's preferred method of presenting the reality of Christian existence, as a communion of life with the Incarnate Word.

But if the image of the Mystical Body, so familiar to Saint Anthony Claret, defined the church as a living communion with the risen Lord, another image, equally dear to him—that of the Spouse—brought him face to face with his Lord. In effect, the

133

Church-Spouse is the alter ego of Christ, his helpmate and complement, but from a diverse point of view: that of the redeemed creature. The Saint stresses that the church, like a new Eve, has been born of the rib of the new Adam, Christ crucified. So deeply related are these two events, the mystery of the Death of Christ and the birth of His Spouse, that throughout his work, *The Clock of the Passion,* based on a similar work by St. Alphonsus, Claret cannot refrain from thinking of the church.[2] He likewise spoke of this in *Notes of a Plan* and in *The Two Standards.* It is precisely because she is born of Christ and because she is His Spouse that the church deserves our love, veneration, and filial obedience.[3]

If we were asked to indicate the motives that led St. Anthony Claret to delve so deeply into the doctrine on the church that he struck its richest and most solid veins, in clear contrast with the tendencies in his milieu, we would have to list three. First, there was the Saint's instinctive preference for the spiritually most fruitful concepts in theology. He seems to have been gifted with a sure instinct that led him to find the most beautiful and fruitful theological ideas. Second, we must bear in mind the force of his mystical experience, which frequently focused on the Eucharist, the center of the sacramental life of the church, precisely at that juncture where the church is eminently realized as sacrament and as living communion with the risen Lord. Finally, we must mention his very long and rich pastoral experience. His apostolic vocation had sensitized him to the needs of the people of God. This was always his principal preoccupation. In Catalonia and the Canary Islands, he had oriented his ministry to confirming and strengthening the life of local churches. In his Cuban mission, the pope had placed him over a vast diocese beset with equally vast and pressing problems. Up to that time he had been mainly concerned for the salvation of individual persons; now, he began to be concerned for the general good of the people of God. It was no longer sufficient for him to move from parish to parish, preaching; he had to organize the life of the local church, reform the clergy, create religious communities, establish educational centers and social concerns groups. Later in Madrid, as counselor of the queen and steadfast collaborator with the nuncio, he felt called in some way to help the whole Spanish church.

(In this connection, consider his significant reaction to the eucharistic grace: "I must pray and confront all the evils of Spain, as the Lord has told me."[4] The next day, the Lord told him just what evils were, indeed, going to trouble the Spanish church.[5]) The First Vatican Council would bring him to a concern for the renewal of the whole Church of God.[6] It may be seen, then, that his experience of the church had gone on developing in concentric circles, ever widening until they reached ecumenical dimensions. In the center of all this development as its source was his experience of union with Christ through the Eucharist.

We have chosen to list these indisputable facts from the spiritual life of St. Anthony Mary Claret because we believe that they will help us understand the idea the founder had concerning the ecclesial mission of his institute.

An Institute for the Church

With these preliminaries, we can better understand the living sense of church that motivated the founding of the Claretian Congregation. This sense shines through visibly in the expressions the founder used in his many letters to the Holy See and the nuncio in Madrid explaining the origins of his work. As early as 1845 he had begun recruiting missionaries and associating them with him in his work of evangelization, moved, as he wrote, "by the damages that the Catholic Religion was suffering."[7] In 1849, shortly after founding his Congregation, he explained to the papal nuncio that he had done so:

> In view of the great lack of evangelical and apostolic preachers in our Spanish territories and the great desire on the part of the people to hear the word of God.[8]

In the 19th century the church in what had traditionally been considered the bastions of Old World Catholicism found itself beset by grave problems. On the ideological level liberal laicism was tending to corrode men's consciences and irreligion was growing and becoming evident on all sides. The apostasy of the bourgeoisie, which came with Encyclopedism and the French Revolution, was soon followed, from 1848 on, by the apostasy of the working masses, who had been forced to live in conditions close to slavery. Significantly, it was in 1848 that Marx and

Engels issued *The Communist Manifesto*. Liberal governments harassed the church with a number of penalizing laws, not only despoiling it of its goods but, much more gravely, suppressing its religious orders. In Spain the laws of 1835 had deprived the dioceses of the evangelization centers that had been built up during the previous century. This was followed by the exile of several bishops and the virtual orphaning of most dioceses, owing to the government's deliberate policy of not promoting successor bishops when sees fell vacant.

In Europe, 1848 also witnessed a swing back to religion on the part of the conservatives, who feared the consequences of the various labor movements. The greater part of the bourgeoisie began to become conservative, and once more latched onto the church as a force for moderation, one that could be most useful in keeping the masses calm. Rulers and bishops both began exalting the peacemaking and counterrevolutionary function of preaching and Catholic education. In Spain the government in the hands of the moderates began to permit the founding of a number of apostolic, educational, and charitable congregations. The vitality of the church, held back until this time, now began to manifest itself once more in a great variety of initiatives.

Anthony Claret founded his institute of missionaries to reanimate the people of God, who had been scattered and leaderless for some time. He wanted his group to be closely associated with the chief shepherds of the church. There was a historical motive at work here, one that has not yet been put in full relief. With regard to the pope, there was a growing movement in the Catholic Church that advocated a return to greater adherence to the See of Peter. In the 18th and early 19th centuries, a good number of French, Austrian, and Spanish bishops had favored regalism, a movement that, under the pretext of assuring the privileges of the crown, tended to nationalize the church in their countries. Felix Torres Amat, nominated bishop of Astorgas in 1843 by the Spanish government, was well known for his anti-Roman ideas.[9] Clashes with the liberal revolution, as well as the dismantling of ecclesiastical structures by civil governments, caused not a few Catholics to turn their hopes toward Rome. Spanish seminarians, especially in the northeast of Spain, crossed the border and headed for Rome, since Spanish law forbade their ordination in Spain. The establishment of the Italian republic in Rome and Pius IX's flight to Gaeta aroused the emotions of Catholics and strengthened their adherence to the See of Peter. Thus there developed an internationalist and Roman wave of feeling in the.European church, one which Rome reacted to through the intelligent and ceaseless efforts of Pius IX in favor of total centralization. One of Claret's friends, Antonio Palau, constantly defended the interests of the church and especially those of the Holy See through his *Revista Católica,* published in Barcelona after the 1840s, and accustomed Spanish Catholics in numerous articles and commentaries to broaden their ecclesiastical views to include a worldwide appreciation of the church. In France the ultramontane (Roman) movement waxed strong, while on the liturgical front, the monks of Solesmes waged their campaign to impose the Roman Liturgy over the Gallican Rites. Catholicism came to be a synonym for theological, ritual, and disciplinary uniformity. Years later in Madrid, St. Anthony Claret, then confessor to Queen Isabel II, would repeatedly complain of regalist tendencies among the civil authorities. His complaints reflected not only his deep adherence to the pope but also his desires for a church free from state controls.

A similar process took place among the Spanish bishops. As we have seen, a number of them were either exiled, on leave, or confined to locations far from their dioceses. In 1841, of the seventy-four Spanish dioceses, only ten had bishops.[10] (For this very reason, St. Anthony Claret, in his *Autobiography,* refers to his relations with his "prelate," rather than with his bishop. Prelate could refer to a priest with an honorary or jurisdictional title, such as Vicar Capitular, Ecclesiastical Governor, etc.) The civil government had tried to impose its own nominees as bishops without counting on Rome. This led to a reaction among Catholics to regroup and consolidate around the legitimate bishop as successor to the Apostles.

It is within this historical and ecclesiological context that we must place both Claret's strict personal and ministerial dependency on his prelate, as well as the addition he introduced into Article 2 of the 1865 *Constitutions* stating that his institute should profess reverence, love, and obedience toward the pope and the Holy See, and should be the steadfast helpers of the prelates of the church in the ministry of the Word. We speak of the historical context here not to discredit but, rather, to understand more fully the reasons that shaped this attitude, for the reasons that motivated the Saint in this matter were of a theological and generic order. Anthony Claret had a strong Catholic sense of the Petrine ministry in the church and of the apostolic succession of bishops. If the church was for him a mystery, and certainly much more than a visible and hierarchical society, it is equally sure that he regarded the ministry of the episcopate and Petrine primacy as the axis around which, by the will of God, ecclesiastical communion is to be expressed. During the sessions of Vatican I a few months before his death, Claret declared that he was ready to shed his blood not only in defense of the primacy of the See of Rome but also in defense of the personal infallibility of the pope, whenever the latter should propose a doctrine as contained in revelation. This brings us face to face with an important datum in the ecclesiastical tradition of the East and the West: the bishop incarnates the unity of the local church. In Catholic tradition, the bishop of Rome is called to be the visible sign of all ecclesial communion, the point of encounter and dialogue, an active factor for unity.

Collaborators with the Bishops

In making his Congregation strictly dependent on the See of Peter and in defining its mission as one of collaboration with bishops in the ministry of the Word, the Saint was guided, moreover, by a doctrinal position of a more concrete nature: the relationship between the ministry of the Word and the office of bishop. Anthony Claret insistently repeated that the preaching of the Gospel is the most important aspect of a bishop's ministry. In *Notes of a Plan,* for example, he wrote to his brothers in the episcopate:

> Preaching has always been considered as the principal obligation of bishops, in accord with the Council of Trent [ses. 5, c. 2 *de ref.*]. And Jesus Christ, who is our model, left us an example when he said, "I must announce the Good News of the Reign of God" [Luke 4:43]. This is confirmed by the Apostle Paul, when he assures us, saying, "For Christ did not send me to baptize, but to preach the Gospel."[11]

In his *Autobiography* Claret describes how, during his ministry as archbishop of the Cuban church, he gave particular importance to the preaching of the Word of God.[12] Evangelization took up far more of his time and energies than administration did. In the excerpts from the life of Archbishop Pedro de Castro, which he included in *Notes of a Plan*—and hence, recommended to bishops—he noted how catechesis, missionary preaching, and clergy conferences were the principal means used by de Castro in his reform of the archdiocese of Seville.[13]

The ministry of the Word is hence the bishop's gravest obligation. Moreover, the pope, for the entire communion of the church, and the bishop, for his own church, have an official preaching mission that entails a responsibility for the public proclamation of the Gospel. It is from this that the Saint derives the notion of mission that he so energetically proposes. This does not mean, however, that the Saint had a markedly "clerical" conception of the apostolate. Since 1847 Claret had been fighting for and organizing the apostolate of the laity, and in his earlier series of booklets addressed to various family members, he had stressed the importance of catechesis by both the father and mother. Claret never thought that the layperson acted in the name of or with the delegation of the priest or bishop. But a vocation to proclaim the Gospel by word and life witness is one thing, and it belongs to every Christian; it is quite another to be a preacher or evangelizer through a special calling in the church. The latter supposes a public ministry that must be publicly recognized by the ecclesial community through the bishop and must necessarily involve collaboration with the bishop's ministry. This is clearly the motive that led Claret to place his Congregation of Missionaries in close dependence on the See of Peter and in collaboration with the chief shepherds of the church.

It is important for us to underscore this fact. Not once did the founder of the Claretians ever state that the relationship between his Congregation and the bishops was a consequence of its priestly character. Certainly, the priests and deacons of the institute have through ordination a further cause for collaboration with the bishops. But the Claretian Congregation is not bound to the episcopate simply because it is a clerical institute dedicated to "sacred ministries" (and its founder never said so) but, rather, because it is a public institution consecrated to evangelization. Some of these forms of evangelization are priestly, but others (catechesis, education, the press) are not. In our own times, the very preaching of missions and giving retreats, which in Claret's day were exclusively sacerdotal ministries, are now being carried out by laypersons.

Traditional theology, with varying nuances and emphases, has always distinguished three aspects in the ministry of bishops: teaching, sanctifying, and governing. This doctrine, already sanctioned by the Council of Trent, received further confirmation in the teachings of Vatican II. The bishop teaches in the name of Christ; that is to say, the proclamation of the Gospel becomes magisterium through the exercise of the bishop's office. But at the same time Christ, through the bishop, continues to sanctify His church by means of the administration of the sacraments and, through the bishop's government, leads the people of God toward their heavenly home. Since the Claretian Congregation has the ministry of the Word as its special ministry, it is evident that its collaboration with bishops is directly engrafted into the prophetic function of the episcopate, namely, the proclamation of the Gospel.

For the Church Universal

Founded to serve the church in the ministry of the Word, the Claretian Congregation has felt called from its very first day to spread throughout the world, establishing itself wherever the needs of the people of God might call it. Geographic universality is one of the characteristic traits built into the profile of his institute by the founder himself. The original *Constitutions* insists on this in its definition of the end of the Congregation:

> Their object will be to seek in all things the glory of God, their own sanctification and the salvation of all the inhabitants of the world.[14]

This expression was to pass almost literally into the text of the definitive *Constitutions*: "to seek the salvation of souls throughout the world."[15] These words struck the Roman censors as somewhat odd, doubtless because they had not grasped their exact meaning.[16] The text did not mean to imply that the missionaries must dedicate themselves, in fact, to work for the salvation of each and every human being on earth but, rather, that their zeal must be universal in scope, like the charity of which zeal is but the other side of the coin, and hence that they must be ready to work for the salvation of their neighbor in any part of the world, regardless of nationality, culture, or class. That Anthony Claret regarded universality as a distinctive trait of his Congregation can be seen from his description of the end he had in mind when he founded it.

> The object of the aforesaid missionaries consists in giving missions and retreats to all classes of persons, especially priests, seminarians and nuns.[17]

This universalist and profoundly catholic spirit of the institute is no more than a reflection of the catholicity of spirit of the Saint who brought it into being. In 1839, when he could not preach in Catalonia because of the political revolutions going on there, Anthony Claret went to Rome to put himself at the disposal of the *Propaganda Fide,* resolved that he be sent wherever the church might need him. Toward the end of 1869, urging Fr. Xifré to send missionaries to America, the young and promising vineyard, he expressed a desire to go there himself to work for the church, despite the fact that his age and the illnesses he was then suffering from seemed to stand in his way.[18] When he was nominated archbishop of Cuba in 1849, he had offered to go there with a group of his companions to work for the evangelization of the island, but he had demurred from accepting a dignity that would tie him down to a particular place.

> This would mean tying myself down and confining myself to a single archdiocese, while my spirit goes out to all the world. But, even in this tiny dot on the map, I would not be able to preach as much as I would like to, for I have seen with my own eyes the many affairs which an archbishop must attend to.[19]

This universality of the Claretian spirit is of Pauline parentage: to serve the church wherever one is needed, with no fixed abode. A natural consequence of this generous openness of Claretian zeal to all the needs of the church is the readiness the missionaries must always have to move from one place to another. The Saint has dealt with this in the foreword to his *Rules for*

Clergy Living in Community. After indicating the points on which missionaries coincide with this other branch of secular priests entrusted with the care of souls, he goes on to write:

> They differ, in that the former [missionaries] have houses in which they live and reside, but only remain there for the time that their superior tells them to, or until he sends them to another town, diocese or nation, as may be required by the greater glory of God and the good of souls. Hence the members do not have benefices, dignities or anything else of that sort, so that they are entirely in the hands of Divine Providence, as were the holy Apostles.[20]

Guided by this higher principle of the good of souls, the Saint throughout his lifetime was continually asking Fr. Xifré to found houses wherever the need of the church was most urgent: in various provinces of Spain, in Oran, in Algiers, in America, etc.

In effect, however, the catholicity of the Claretian Congregation is not limited to demanding that its members be disposed to serve the church in every part of the world; it also involves them in an openness to contemporary spiritual currents and movements throughout the church. In this respect their founder has left them an outstanding example. He—genuine Christian that he was—not only nourished himself at the purest source of Christian spirituality, the Sacred Scriptures, but also kept in continual contact with the most important schools of spirituality in the church. Spanish, Italian, French, Portuguese, English, and German books formed part of his ascetic library. He attentively read Jesuit, Franciscan, Carmelite, Augustinian, Dominican authors—and many more. The Saint always remained sensitive to the varied riches that the Holy Spirit had lavished on the most diverse national and religious milieux. Fr. Peter Schweiger pointed this up in one of his most closely written circular letters:

> In the natural order, one must admire in the Saint the great harmony of mind which disposed him to such a truly universal and catholic breadth of spirit, in virtue of which he was open to the whole Church, in his doctrine, as well as in his life and apostolate. In his spiritual teaching we find elements of the most diverse schools of spirituality, mainly those of St. Teresa of Jesus, the Jesuit ascetical writers, St. Alphonsus Liguori, the French school, the Portuguese spiritual writers and those of other nations, such as William Faber, Bartholomew Holzhauser and others.[21]

In the Local Church

Total availability to serve the church wherever the need is most urgent does not mean living merely peripherally as regards local churches. On the contrary, it means being fully involved in the diocese or city to which the will of the Lord should send one. For the service of the universal church is ordinarily accomplished by means of service to local churches.

Relationship with the local church is another typical trait of the Claretian. Obviously, this is a trait of every apostolic institute, since all of them are called to work in various dioceses; but in the Claretians it is a particularly notable trait, by will of their founder.

The Claretian motherhouse at Vic was founded as a diocesan institution. The bishop of Vic could describe it as such to his diocese in a circular letter written in 1850. The same was true of all the earliest houses. All without exception, whether in Spain, Algiers, or Chile, were diocesan centers for missionary preaching and retreat houses for clergy and laity. For this reason the Saint recommended that there be no more than one in each diocese and that they should be undertaken "under the bishops' wings."[22] This recommendation was particularly meaningful with regard to foundations in Spain since, according to the terms of the Concordat of 1851, the civil government allowed the foundation of only a single house to assist the bishop in preaching and the bishop had to assume responsibility for that house. It responded, moreover, to the Saint's notion of the mission of a missionary community in a diocese. In the second edition of *Notes of a Plan to Preserve the Beauty of the Church,* he had recommended that bishops strive to establish a missionary house in their dioceses, with the twofold end of preaching missions to the people and giving retreats to the clergy and laity. In a footnote he remarks:

> The Missionaries called "Sons of the Immaculate Heart of Mary" are dedicated to these holy, apostolic tasks, and thus each bishop should strive to acquire one of their houses for his diocese. These Missionaries have their main house in Vic, Catalonia. This is the residence of their Superior General, to whom one may apply for a foundation.[23]

In following this procedure, the earliest communities were

fulfilling the aim expressed in their *Constitutions* of being "stal-
wart helpers of the bishops in the ministry of the Word."[24] The
Claretian house became a center for apostolic outreach and
priestly spirituality, thus making a priceless contribution to the
vitality of the diocesan church.

Fitting a Claretian community into the life of a diocese demanded not only collaboration with the bishop but also living
fraternally with the priests of the diocese. Claretians lived with
diocesan priests both when the latter made retreats at their
house and when Claretians came to give missions in various parishes during mission campaigns. This presupposed that members have and can develop a lively sense of fraternity. To foster
friendship with diocesan priests, the founder recommended on
one occasion that Fr. Xifré consider sending some of his scholastics to take their studies in the diocesan seminary.[25]

Community-Church

The relationship between the Claretian Congregation and the
church is not limited to the ministry, although that is the prime
reason for the Congregation's being in the people of God. The
Congregation, founded to serve the church, belongs to the
church as one of its institutions dedicated to implanting and
renewing the church through the ministry of the Word—a ministry it carries out on the general, provincial, and local levels.
But we may go even further and say that the Congregation of
Missionaries founded by Anthony Claret is, in itself, Christ's
church: above all, because it was born of listening to the Word
that calls to the following of Christ and to the proclamation of
His Gospel; or, to speak in more "pneumatic" terms, because it
is born of a charism granted by the Holy Spirit for the good of
the whole church. On the general and provincial levels, its members are united ecclesially by this communion in vocation and
spirit.

In the local community there is something more. For a Christian community of any sort consists in bringing the business of
"being church" to the level where Christians whose lives and
persons are oriented by the charism of celibacy actually live together in a group. The local Claretian community arises from
and is ordained to ministry; hence, relationship to ministry is

the basic criterion for its foundation, for the type of community it is, and for the relationships and norms that characterize it. The Claretian community is radically a group of missionary companions, as is the case with the Jesuits, as well. Nevertheless, it would be wrong to conclude that the Claretian community is something merely functional. For it is nothing more than the concrete mode in which a group of men who feel united by the same missionary charism realize and embody the common Christian vocation to communion. And communion cannot be reduced to the merely functional; it is essential and central to Christianity.

Gathered together in a local group because of their common vocation and spirit, the Claretian house is a group of disciples of Christ, who, in communion, listen to the Word of the Gospel; seek the saving will of God here and now; pray (although the time allotted to community prayer is limited because of the group's apostolic character); strive to establish fraternal, mutual relationships; and cooperate in the ministry. All of this amounts to saying that the Claretian house is church, for the church exists wherever the Word is proclaimed and heard in faith, wherever a group of disciples is united in a search for God's will, wherever two or three are gathered in the name of Jesus. It is church, moreover, by its essential orientation toward the rest of the church, by its Pauline preoccupation for all churches and by its communion with the bishops of the church.

What we have been saying is the fruit of a theological reflection based on the concrete data that characterize the Claretian community. It is certainly not something that the founder explicitly formulated. Indeed, it would be strange if he, living in the mid-19th century, should have arrived at any adequate expression of the theology and spirituality of living in communion. The Catholics (and among them the founders) of that time had managed to formulate a somewhat narrow disciplinary concept of community, probably as an initial reaction against the individualism that had exploded in the French Revolution. Nevertheless, when we read what the Saint wrote in the chapter on fraternal charity in the *Constitutions* (the only properly original chapter of the spiritual Rule), we notice how the norms stated in it faithfully echo those of St. Paul and are inspired by Paul's theology of the local community as the Body of Christ. The chapter, in fact, begins with the biblical motifs of "image" and "body": "As images of God and members of one and the same body, let them love one another."[26] One might ask whether "body" as used here has an ecclesial or merely sociologic meaning. Did the author expressly wish to echo Paul on the Body of Christ, or was he simply speaking of a group or an institution? Clearly, he was referring to the Body of Christ. His own words confirm this. First, the metaphor of the body is preceded by that of "image," which is clearly biblical. Second, from the fact of belonging to just any social body, one cannot deduce, as the Saint does, that its members must love one another as Christ loved us. Third, Claret goes on to cite Romans 12:10-11, 1 Corinthians 12:25, 12:12-23,[27] as well as a few other texts of St. Paul. We are thus fully in the context of Paul's doctrine of the local church as the Body of Christ.

Historical Perspective

The church, which not only apostolic institutes but all institutions of religious life are meant to serve, is the real, living church, the church that moves in history. Not only each individual institute but, more generally, the very forms of religious life arise as a response to the needs of the people of God in various times and places. Concrete data that affect a local church or a whole period of history cause a founder or foundress to become aware of a permanent or long-lasting need in the community of the faithful.

St. Anthony M. Claret had a vivid awareness of the way in which his Congregation fitted into the historic flow of the church. He showed this in one of his last short works, *Selfishness Overcome,* published in Italian by the Saint during his last stay in Rome, where he was attending the First Vatican Council. In the seventh chapter of this short but revealing work, he says:

> Through the special care and providence which God our Lord shows toward the Church militant, in all times He has sent and still sends men according to his own heart, full of grace and teaching, to confront the errors which the evil one has invented and suggested to his impious followers.... I shall cite but a few of them here.... At the same time that Pelagius was born, so was Augustine, the great Doctor of the

Church.... At the beginning of the 13th century, the Church found herself beset by three most grave illnesses, but the Lord sent three sound and timely doctors to cure her, three most valiant captains to wage war on the enemies of Jesus, Mary and mankind. These three heavenly emissaries were St. Dominic, St. Francis of Assisi and St. Peter Nolasco, each of whom founded a religious Order or family.... Sometime later, the proud and restless Satan once again reared his head, using Luther, Calvin and their followers to disturb the peace of the Church, and immediately the merciful God awakened and called St. Ignatius Loyola and the Company of Jesus, who claimed the fullest of victories. Notwithstanding the triumphs of the Company of Jesus over demons and wicked men, it has been necessary, in order to stem the tide of impiety, for God to send others. This He has done through the many Congregations of Clerks Regular which have since been founded: the Oratory of St. Philip Neri, the Piarists of St. Joseph of Calasanz, the Priests of the Mission of St. Vincent de Paul, the Redemptorists of St. Alphonsus Liguori, the Passionists of St. Paul of the Cross and finally, the Congregation of the Sons of the Immaculate Heart of Mary, founded on July 16, 1849 and approved on December 22, 1865.[28]

Apart from its 19th-century apologetic clichés (the tide of impiety and the triumphs of Catholicism), this paragraph is notable for the sweeping vision in which it has the religious institutes take their place in the history of the church. It provides us with a confirmation of the founder's conviction that his favorite work was fundamentally oriented toward the service of the church. His Congregation, of its very nature, tends toward the good of the people of God as its reason for being. Throughout the course of history, the Claretians must strive to discern the concrete means by which they may best serve the church in its most urgent needs and in the diverse social contexts in which these needs arise. Since religious institutes are born out of contact with a human spiritual need and, frequently, in opposition to some particular evil afflicting Christianity, they cannot remain in the church as monuments to past victories; rather, they must prove their continual adaptability to commence new battles. This seems to be the basic meaning of the passage just cited.

It would not be out of place, however, to ask just which concrete needs the Congregation aimed to remedy. The situation that called the Congregation into existence was the lack of evangelical and apostolic preachers, a lack that was common to the

whole church in the 19th century but most acutely felt in the
Spanish church because of the suppression of the older religious
orders, which had been the traditional promoters of centers for
evangelization.[29] This was the immediate occasion, discerned by
Anthony Claret during his seminary studies and his missionary
ministry in Catalonia and the Canary Islands. Later, while reflecting on the rise of various religious institutes, the Saint discerned some deeper and more general roots of need. Often, he
discovered, the foundation of an institute came not only as an
answer to supply some lack of Christianization but as a positive
attack on grave evils that were troubling the people of God.
Looking about him, the Saint wished to discover the deepest
reasons Providence could have had in suggesting to him the creating of his own missionary institute. It is interesting to note
that, instead of dwelling on such episodic phenomena as the lack
of missionaries or the serious difficulties that the church was en-
countering in most European states, he rather sought out the
roots of the problem in a cultural phenomenon of the western
world that was to exercise a prolonged and incisive influence on
Christianity: the rise of new directions in philosophy and historical studies on Christianity. We can see this clearly in the résumé
of a talk he delivered to his missionaries in 1865.

> In all times God has had a special care for his Church, but more
> singularly in some than in others. When Pelagius was born in Britain,
> St. Augustine was born in Tagaste. When the Albigensians came to the
> fore, God sent St. Dominic and St. Francis with the rosary. When
> Luther began to divulge his errors in the year 1521, that was the year
> in which St. Ignatius was wounded in Pamplona.
>
>   In the mid-19th century, when Strauss, Hegel and Schelling have
> published their Pantheism in Germany, and M. Renan has written
> against the Divinity of Jesus Christ in France, the Blessed Virgin has
> founded her Congregation in Spain.[30]

There can be no doubt about it: Claret had hit upon the core
of the problems that were affecting the proclamation of the
Gospel and the life of the church. Hegel's monistic idealism was
the radical denial of the Christian faith. If heretofore the Encyclopedist Enlightenment had aimed at denying this or that specifically Christian doctrine, what was now being proposed was
the annihilation of the very distinction between God and crea-

tures. All was reduced to a single reality, of which concrete beings were the successive moments, the totality of which, in becoming, was God. Religion was swallowed up in philosophy. This evolutionary criterion was to become the determining factor in the exegesis of the New Testament under the influence of the theory of Hegel. It is perhaps for this reason that the Saint mentions David Strauss, the author of the celebrated *Life of Jesus* (1835-1836) and the first to incorporate into the exegesis of the Gospels the mythologizing activity of human groups, side by side with Hegel. Positivism, too, was leading men of culture not only to deny one or another miraculous incident but also to deny the very center of Christianity: faith in the Incarnation. The thesis of Renan, to which the Saint refers next in this passage, was an instructive example.

In all of this, the thing that mainly preoccupied Claret was the threat it posed to the faith of the people. In two of the mystical experiences he had around this time, he saw Protestant propaganda as one of the particular threats to Spanish Christianity. In describing the second of these experiences he added the significant words, "Protestantism, *or rather,* decatholicization."[31] The fact was that repeated experience since his years in Cuba had taught him that Protestant propaganda, which was knowingly accepted by the liberal elite, did not end with the evangelization of that part of the people who were the most lukewarm in their faith but, rather, simply with their decatholicization. The propaganda tracts of those days were frequently blatant, anticlerical attacks, aimed at defaming persons and institutions. In the popular forum, where the same persons and institutions formed the already overworked targets of liberal and socialist propaganda, the dissemination of these tracts only added fuel to the fire. The people were in danger of losing their Catholic faith without replacing it by accepting the teachings of Protestantism.

In fact, Hegelian monism and the works of Strauss and Renan were by no means the only phenomena that concerned the Saint or related to the founding of his institute. In the mid-19th century, in reaction to Hegel's idealism, another movement of even greater consequence arose: socialism. A year before the founding of his Congregation, while Claret was totally engaged in evangelizing the Canary Islands, another pair of German intellectuals, Karl Marx and Friedrich Engels, had unleashed *The Communist Manifesto* on the world. This coincidence escaped the notice of the Saint, otherwise he would surely have mentioned it in the talk we referred to above. The only revolutionary rumbles he felt were the new hopes being awakened in the masses. He was amply acquainted with the plight of the working classes, since he himself had been a worker in one of Barcelona's great textile factories during sufficiently troubled times. Like many other young men of his time, he had left his home town, where work followed the rhythm of a family shop, for the excitement of the big city, teeming with factories and workers.[31] This is not to say that Anthony Claret had any firsthand experience of the direst sufferings of the working class of his day, since his status as a student at the Lonja and his position in the factory put him in a privileged group. But around him he could see how his companions were losing the quiet faith of their fathers as they were caught up in the hubbub of their new surroundings.[32] Within himself, his continual preoccupation with mechanical work brought on a dryness of spirit and a vocational crisis of which he has left us a personal record.[33] In the colonialist, agrarian society of Cuba, he had met a very different set of work problems, and had managed to remedy them adequately.[34] But it was in Madrid that the Saint began to detect in the Spanish people some of the unmistakable signs of what was soon to happen. The Andalusian countryside was just beginning to awaken from its lethargy, with cries more disturbing than its marvelous *cante flamenco*. Perez del Olmo, a blacksmith from Loja (Granada), had begun to preach social liberation, and those same liberals who had shown themselves such loyal sons of the French Revolution in despoiling the church of her goods now saw their own interests threatened, and they reacted with ruthless repression.[35] This episode, painful as it was, was no more than an initial warning signal of a more general condition that was affecting the entire Iberian peninsula: the *Manifesto* of Marx and Engels had crossed the Pyrenees.

St. Anthony Claret, recently arrived at the court of Madrid, soon discerned that this popular revolution was going to confront the Christian conscience with far more pressing problems than those occasioned by the earlier, liberal revolution or the impoverishment of the church through the disenfranchisement of its holdings.[36] One of the best informed historians of the Spanish Church in the 19th century has called attention to the fact that Archbishop Claret was the only Spanish bishop who realized the gravity of the uprising at Loja, an event "which should have left its mark in blood and fire on the later pastoral activity of the episcopate."[37] Claret was not so much concerned for the losses of the past or for the persecutions that might follow as he was for the phenomenon of the dechristianization of the masses that would accompany the awakening of the workers' consciousness. That this conviction was not simply the fruit of his penetrating intuition but that of the prophetic lights he had received in prayer we know from his own spiritual notes.

On September 23, 1859, while he was reading from the Book of Revelation, the Lord told him of the evils that were about to befall mankind.

(1) Protestantism, communism....
(2) The four archdemons that will make fearful inroads: the love of pleasure, the love of money, independence of the reason, independence of the will.
(3) The great wars and their consequences.[38]

Two years later, on the day after he had become aware of his great Eucharistic privilege, the Lord revealed to him the ills that would beset the Spanish people in particular.

On August 27, 1861, in the same Church, during Benediction of the Blessed Sacrament that I was conducting after Mass, the Lord let me know the three great evils that were menacing Spain: (1) Protestantism, or rather, the loss of the Catholic spirit; (2) the Republic; (3) communism.[39]

That same day he communicated this message to the superior general of his missionaries and to the foundress of the Claretian Sisters. He wrote the former as follows:

I tell you that three calamities are threatening Spain: Communism, the Republic and Protestantism.[40]

This is not the place to present a complete analysis of Claret's position vis-à-vis the incipient redress of social wrongs. We know that while he was in Cuba he was painfully aware of the misery and ignorance of the farmworkers and did as much as he could to remedy their needs. He wrote two books on this theme, preparing himself by painstaking research in an area in which he was really a novice. To this same end, he founded a model ranch and trade school, called the House of Charity, at Puerto Principe, and established licensed credit unions for the poor of his archdiocese.[41] He realized that the Christian faith was being attacked in Cuba through the miserable conditions in which the farmworkers lived. In Madrid, however, the social propaganda that reached him was openly revolutionary in character, and took the form of a direct attack on the church and its teaching. Antireligious propaganda, defamation of the clergy, and the denial of the Christian faith were fundamental themes in contemporary Spanish socialism. The passages excerpted by the Saint from the various tracts that he cites in his *Autobiography* leave little doubt as to the virulence of anti-Catholic propaganda.[42] His reaction was foreseeable. Leaving to one side the social problematics—which, in their new dimensions, the holy archbishop was not prepared to understand—he focused his attention on the religious questions involved. Claret could not at that time have foreseen the many evolutionary changes the concept of society would undergo up to our time, especially those aspects of a new kind of society that was as yet only in embryo. Nevertheless, it is interesting to note how the Saint had gone to the heart of the matter in singling out, among the greatest evils which were going to beset humanity, the love of riches, selfish pleasure, and the rebellion of reason and the will. This was a general set of phenomena that the Saint had noticed since the first years of his Catalonian ministry.[43] It was a temptation that would appeal to all alike, whether rich or poor, industrialists or simple workers. Furthermore, the phenomenon had begun to manifest itself with capitalism among the leading classes who, in turn, provided the motive for the reaction of the proletariat. Later, Popes Leo XIII, Pius XI, and John XXIII in their various social encyclicals, as well as Pope Paul VI in *Populorum Progressio,* identified capitalist selfishness, proceeding from a materialist conception of life, as the root of some of the gravest evils of our times.

Claretians: a Congregation or a Movement?

What we have said thus far does not cover the entire matter. We might go further and say that in considering the relationship of the Claretians to the church, we have passed over certain fundamental data without which the image of "the Claretian" in the church would remain greatly impoverished and even mutilated. If the Claretian institution (by which we mean the Congregation of Missionaries) is seen exclusively or primarily as a canonically well-defined Congregation, namely, as a self-sufficient entity, then something essential to "the Claretian" has been left out of its proper image. We say this because although it is true that, canonically speaking, the outlines of the *institution* are well enough defined (a male Congregation of simple vows, dedicated to evangelization), the distinctive *charism* of the founder tends to overflow these limits handily. In what sense? In the sense that the personal vocation as well as the spiritual and apostolic vitality of Claret far exceed the limits of that special work of his which was gradually transformed into the Claretian Congregation.

During his lifetime, Anthony Claret was continually instituting or proposing the creation of numerous works dedicated to the apostolate: the Apostolic Society of the Heart of Mary (lay apostolate: 1847), the Religious Library (publishing apostolate: 1848), the Congregation of Missionaries (1849), the secular institute of Cordimarian Filiation (1850), licensed credit unions in Cuba (1852), the Claretian Missionary Sisters of Mary Immaculate (1855), the Academy of St. Michael for intellectuals and artists (1859), Parish Lending Libraries (1869)—the list could go on.

The Saint was not only working tirelessly in his own ministry but awakening and fostering the apostolic work of many others, priests, sisters, and laypersons. This is a distinctive trait of his spirit. We may conclude from this that his sons and daughters in the church are called to imitate his example in this, by making an individual effort to stir up in others an awareness of the Christian vocation to evangelize. But even this, good as it might be, would not be enough, because Claret wanted to form a full association in the apostolate for the service of the church, surpassing the barriers that would distinguish within it the various sorts of vocations involved: priestly-lay, secular-religious.

Here we touch upon one of the most genial and masterful insights of St. Anthony Mary Claret with regard to the mission of his institute in the church. Precisely because he had founded his

Congregation to serve the Spouse of Christ effectively as an association of priests and brothers consecrated to the ministry of the Word, he soon realized that the activity of his missionaries (above all, in the area of service) would be vigorously reinforced if the Congregation were encompassed by a larger apostolic movement.

This idea begins to emerge in the Apostolic Society of the Most Holy and Immaculate Heart of Mary in 1847. It is, then, something very deeply rooted in the Saint's being. At that time he saw it as an apostolic association in which groups of priests and laypersons, men and women, would work together.[44] Doubtless, we cannot identify this priestly nucleus with his future Congregation, since he was then separately organizing teams of missionaries consecrated more directly to evangelization, and it is these latter groups that formed his first essays in that direction. St. Anthony Claret does not precisely define the status of the priests in the 1847 society, although we can form some notion of it from the broad range of their ministries, which are not limited to those of a group of missionaries but extend to priests involved in the care of souls and in other possible activities. It is likely, however, that if Archbishop Echanove's narrowmindedness had not aborted this marvelous project, some of the priests involved in it would have gone on to form part of Claret's Congregation of Missionaries. Even if this did not happen, it is clear that the missionaries would have maintained close fraternal ties with the apostolic society. It is noteworthy that when he drafted the *Constitutions* for his missionaries in 1849, St. Anthony Claret followed the general lines and carried over many of the particular elements of the statutes he had written for the ill-fated society.

Something similar occurred in connection with the birth of the Congregation in 1849. The Saint had always planned on organizing its work in a harmonious fashion, arranging side by side one group dedicated to itinerant preaching, another group running retreat houses, and yet another group organizing the apostolate of the press—each of these groups serving the others. The apostolate of the press was entrusted to the direction of a "brother," Canon Caixal, whom the Saint considered as a member of his institute on a par with the others, although Caixal was not regularly involved in missionary preaching. But Claret had also begun to organize the life of the community at Vic, establishing two sets of "conferences," one of them internal for the members of the Congregation, the other external for clergy who did not belong to the Congregation.[45] This, too, would probably have led to the establishment of a collateral organization, although the Saint did not expressly allude to it at the time. It is clear, nevertheless, that the ideas that he had cherished earlier regarding the creation of a broader apostolic association were still at work in the depths of his being, waiting for better days. The founder's separation, when his institute was barely fourteen months old, limited his work to the central nucleus of his missionaries. Caixal went his own way, concentrating independently on the Religious Library, and relationships with clergy and lay associates dwindled in the absence of Claret, around whom they would have gathered cohesively.

The idea would again emerge, although the time was still not ripe, in 1864, when the Saint was drafting the second *Constitutions,* which were to give his institute its definitive shape. He expounded his plans, not in the *Constitutions,* which were due for immediate submission to the Holy See for approval, but in the foreword to his *Rules for Clergy Living in Community,* which were published that same year. According to the ideas expressed in the foreword, the Congregation of Missionaries, now solidly structured as something autonomous with its own life, was to be but the central nucleus or axis of a broader apostolic organization. In this organization, three different branches were to coexist: the missionaries, fully consecrated to God and the Blessed Virgin Mary; a second branch of priests dedicated to the care of souls or other fixed ministries, living in community; and finally, a much more numerous group of laypersons, this time incorporated into the Archconfraternity of the Immaculate Heart of Mary. As we can see, what this amounted to was a restatement under new forms of the basic notion of the society of 1847. But let us consider the Saint's own words on the subject:

> Mary is, to the enemies of our souls, like a terrible army, well ordered
> and set in battle array. The armies of earthly kings are composed only
> of soldiers, but the army of Mary, queen of heaven and earth, is
> composed of angels and of those who devoutly honor her Immaculate

Heart and have enlisted in her archconfraternity. In an army there are soldiers who belong to different corps. . . . In the archconfraternity there are three distinct orders, and each one has its special set of regulations which it fulfills exactly, and together in the Immaculate Heart of Mary, they form an admirable ensemble and a perfect and formidable whole against the enemies, the world, the flesh and the devil. . . . We have said that in the Archconfraternity there are three orders. In the *first* there are those who form the Congregation called the Sons of the Immaculate Heart of Mary. They are priests and brothers entirely consecrated to God and the Blessed Virgin Mary, and continually engaged in giving missions and retreats to clergy, nuns, etc., according to their rules. In the *second* order there are those who form the Institute of secular priests living in community, according to their own special regulations. In the *third* order are all the other faithful devoted to Mary who have enlisted in her Archconfraternity, having as their principal rule the Holy Law of God, which they strive to keep with the greatest exactitude, making a great effort, moreover, to faithfully fulfill the duties of their state and to recite those devotions prescribed by the Archconfraternity and daily recite one part of the rosary out of devotion to the Blessed Virgin Mary.[46]

Let us, for the moment, pass over the fundamental relationship of this great apostolic organization to Mary under her title of the Immaculate Heart, as well as certain expressions the Saint uses in describing the role which the laity was to play in it. Desiring to enlarge the bounds of this organization considerably by including in it the great number of the faithful who already belonged to the archconfraternity (a well-established, highly popular movement), Saint Anthony Claret assigned to them as their distinctive traits those already required of them for entry into the archconfraternity. But it is clear that among this mass of people consecrated to the Heart of Mary in such a broad-based organization, he would distinguish an elite core group, who had a more decidedly apostolic vocation that offered greater possibilities for service. We must not forget that at this time Archbishop Claret was deeply involved with the Academy of St. Michael and that in 1864 he had founded the first Popular Lending Libraries, which he had entrusted to the care of laypersons. As regards the secular clergy living in community, we should bear in mind that in those days this was the only possible method to organize them and put them more decidedly on the road to evangelical perfection. Since those days, the evolution of the religious life has brought secular institutes and similar groups into existence, thus opening up new possibilities for the realization of Claret's original idea. The Saint himself had been one of the precursors of this evolution in his plans for the institution of the Daughters of the Most Holy and Immaculate Heart of Mary.

But for all the twists and turns of history, the essentials of this bright and fruitful intuition remain quite viable: in the mind of the Saint, the Congregation of Missionaries is only the axis of a much broader apostolic organization. Without prejudice to the theological and canonical constitution proper of the Congregation of Missionaries, "the Claretian" stands for more than a Congregation: it was meant to be *a movement.*

VIII

Spirituality

When we speak of spirituality in the present context, we do not mean a school of spirituality in the strict sense; there are few—very few—of these in the church. Rather, we mean the ensemble of traits that characterize the way a Christian actually lives his life in the Spirit or, in the case of a group united by a common calling, the overall way in which its members tend to express their Christian experience, precisely as a result of their common calling in the church. Thus we speak of priestly, lay, or married spirituality, or the spirituality of a religious order. In this last case, the main factors that unify its spirituality are: the group's mission in the church, first discovered by its founder or foundress as a personal vocation; then the further spiritual experience of the founder or foundress; and finally, the development that these have undergone in later tradition (Saints and theologians).

The Experience of Pentecost

Anyone who intends to embark on a study of Claretian spirituality must begin with Pentecost, that great experience of the Spirit sent by the risen Lord, which drove Peter to proclaim that God has "raised up ... and made both Lord and Christ, this Jesus whom you crucified" (Cf. Acts 2:1-41). But why go as far back as the origins of the church? Mainly because Pentecost is more than just an isolated incident in the past: it is a paradigmatic experience that is being constantly repeated in the church. All of the church's proclamation and service must flow from an experience of the living Christ; every particular vocation among the people of God must proceed from the charisms distributed by the Spirit of the Lord. But in studying Claretian spirituality, there is a reason much closer to us in time: the experience of the Spirit that was manifested most forcefully in Anthony Claret, the founder of the Claretians. The first of these manifestations took place during those seminary years when the Saint was discovering his call to evangelize. We have already studied this experience at some length in the first chapter of this book. We need only recall here that it consisted of a prolonged series of lights and impulses that the Saint received, especially while he was reading the Scriptures: lights and impulses that moved him to commit himself totally to Christ in the ministry of the Word. These phenomena were of a pneumatic and prophetic character.

In this case, too, the incident involved was paradigmatic: each Claretian must come to grips with it to illuminate and orient his own experience. In making this transposition, what counts is not the extraordinary elements in the event (the prophetic lights and impulses) but, rather, its fundamental meaning. It should be noted that the founder himself made just such a transposition of his personal experience into the life of his institute by describing it in his *Autobiography,* which he wrote at the insistence of the superior general of his missionaries, as a guide for their formation. In fact, during some lights he received while praying, on September 24, 1859, he was given to understand that the fundamental texts for his own vocation—Luke 4:18 and Matthew 10:20—contained a message not just for him but for his missionary companions as well.[1] On two important occasions—first, while writing on charity in his *Autobiography* and second, in the first talk for the retreat he gave his missionaries in 1865—Claret presented some general reflections on what we have called the experience of Pentecost in missionary spirituality.

It is much the same with the Word of God. If God's Word is spoken only naturally, it does very little; but if it is spoken by a priest who is filled with the fire of charity—the fire of love of God and neighbor—it will wound vices, kill sins, convert sinners, and work wonders. We can see this in the case of St. Peter, who walked out of the upper room afire with the love he had received from the Holy Spirit, with the result that through just two sermons he converted 8,000 people....

The same Holy Spirit, by appearing in the form of tongues of fire above the Apostles on Pentecost, showed us this truth quite clearly: an apostolic missionary must have both heart and tongue ablaze with charity.[2]

While Claret had chosen the paschal experience of Paul (Gal. 1:16) as his point of departure in explaining missionary spirituality to his earliest followers at the founding retreat in 1849, he focused on the community experience of Pentecost during the retreat he preached to them in 1865.

The Apostles, too, after their retreat (Pentecost), began to speak, filled with the Holy Spirit: fire, charity, love....

You are Missionaries. You must be sent, impelled. You must say, *"Charitas Christi urget nos."* Fire: like a bullet, like a great wind, like the power of the sea.

The Holy Spirit came as a mighty wind and fire.[3]

A number of concepts are implicit in this text. First of all, at the basis of the missionary vocation there is always an action of the Holy Spirit: one must be sent and impelled. Beneath the surface of the church's ministerial activity, there is a powerful, volcanic force: the Spirit of Pentecost. The Saint uses various images to suggest the power of this force: the explosion of energy that launches a bullet, the driving surge of the wind and waves. This same power that the Apostolic Church experienced continues still to stir the people of God.

Applying this to the individual, we would say that there is always some action of the Spirit at the origin of a missionary vocation, since any and every Christian vocation is the fruit of a charism granted by the Spirit for the good of the whole church. This brings us face to face with the charismatic dimension of the church. In a special sense, the proclamation of the Gospel (an integral part of any vocation) is closely related with the Spirit because—as the various accounts of the appearances of the risen

Lord show and the closing passage of Matthew sums the matter up—every proclamation of the Good News is based on an experience of the life of the risen Lord. It is a form of witness.

This is exactly what St. Anthony Claret had in mind in the two texts just cited. Missionary proclamation must proceed from an irresistible impulse, born of communion with Christ. This communion must reach such a pitch of intensity that the impulse will have the eruptive force of the grace of Pentecost. If we were to fall into the trap set by the Greek dichotomy of action/contemplation, we might be tempted to say that in this case the proclamation of the Gospel must flow from an intense interior life; but were we to do so, we would run the risk of reducing the richness of Christian experience to an all-too-intimate and individualistic level. The interior life is indeed involved, but there is much more to it than that, namely, the experience of Christ in all its fullness. And this is brought about through prayer, through the orientation given by celibacy, through poverty, through the interpersonal relationships that form the dynamics of community life, and through the ministry itself.

Claret stresses the central role that charity plays in this experience. The presence and action of the Spirit are manifested in the impulse of love that draws us out of ourselves and into communion. In the context of a missionary vocation, charity is transformed into an impulse to serve the Gospel. Claret tells us this in his ideal portrait of a missionary.

A Son of the Immaculate Heart of Mary is a man on fire with love, who spreads its flames wherever he goes.[4]

It is a matter of knowing God and making others know Him; of loving Him and making others love Him; of serving Him and making others serve Him.[5] "Loving consists in doing and suffering," as Claret frequently said and wrote. By this he meant that love is an impulse that urges us to act in proclaiming the Good News and to bear the sufferings that this entails.

Obviously, although Claret has chosen to stress the central importance of love in missionary spirituality, we must not forget that underlying this love is the other great theological dimension of Christianity: a faith that recognizes the presence of God in man's individual and collective history and in the Word He utters and the Grace He offers to human beings. Toward the beginning of his *Autobiography,* describing the powerful impression he felt at the thought of the eternal destiny of mankind, the founder of the Claretians highlights the influence of faith on his apostolic zeal: "I simply can't understand how other priests who believe the same truths that I do . . . do not preach and exhort. . . . I wonder too how the laity, men and women who have the faith, can help crying out."[6] In the 1865 *Constitutions,* Claret included a paragraph by the superior general, Fr. Joseph Xifré, on the importance of faith and hope in the formation of Claretian novices.

> Let them above all strive to cultivate a living faith, since without it, it is impossible to please God, for faith is the foundation of the Christian life. It was faith that inflamed the prophets and strengthened the apostles in persecution, torment and even death. It was faith that eased the sufferings of the martyrs and led so many preachers to embrace joyfully poverty, self-denial and sacrifice, in order to spread the reign of Christ. . . .
>
> Secondly, let them have great trust in God, hoping to obtain from Him all graces.[7]

Servants of the Lord

The Pentecost experience of Anthony Claret and his companions is closely related to another most important aspect of Claretian spirituality: the call to serve God. We have discussed how the Saint discovered his vocation above all in the Isaian oracle on the Servant of Yahweh, which Christ himself used in formulating his own vocation, and how, years later, Claret felt that this prophetic text also defined the vocation of his missionaries. The text itself speaks precisely of an anointing by the Spirit. A servant is someone who has been chosen by God and anointed by His Spirit.

Since the 4th century A.D., monks and nuns have been called "servants and handmaidens of God." From that time on, the religious life has been traditionally defined as a form of existence committed to the service of God. Setting aside the Hellenistic notion of the service of God as something done without relation to the world or history or, rather, in conflict with them, we should concentrate on the biblical notion of the service of God: we serve God when He associates us with Him in His saving work. The service of God is the salvation of human beings. Claret, like Paul and like—saving the immense distance between Him and any mere man—Jesus of Nazareth, felt chosen to proclaim the Good News of salvation to his neighbor.

We are not going to dwell on these notions. We only want to focus on the total and radical way in which Anthony Claret committed himself to God for this task. In his second talk for the founding retreat he began by citing the text in which Paul, reacting to the criticisms of Judaizers, reaffirms his vocation: "But when he who had set me apart before I was born and had called me through his grace, was pleased to reveal his Son to me, in order that I might preach him among the Gentiles, I did not confer with flesh and blood" (Gal. 1:15-16). Claret understood this passage as an affirmation of the resoluteness with which Paul committed himself to his mission. *"Mai pert de vista la sua vocació!"* he writes: "He never loses sight of his vocation!"[8] This reminds us of the portrait of St. Paul that Claret has left us in his *Autobiography*.

> But the zeal of St. Paul has always awakened my deepest enthusiasm. He went from place to place, a vessel of election, carrying the teaching of Jesus Christ. He preached, wrote, and taught in synagogues, prisons—everywhere. He worked and made others work, in season and out of season. He suffered scourgings, stonings, persecutions of all sorts, as well as the fiercest calumnies, but he was never daunted; on the contrary, he so rejoiced in tribulations that he could say that he did not wish to glory, save in the cross of Jesus Christ.[9]

Some of the concepts and above all the stirring rhythms of this description are carried over into his ideal portrait of a Claretian:

> I tell myself: A Son of the Immaculate Heart of Mary is a man on fire with love, who spreads its flames wherever he goes. He desires mightily and strives by all means possible to set the whole world on fire with God's love. Nothing daunts him; he delights in privations, welcomes work, embraces sacrifices, smiles at slander, and rejoices in suffering. His only concern is how he can best follow Jesus Christ and imitate Him in working, suffering, and striving constantly and singlemindedly for the greater glory of God and the salvation of souls.[10]

All of this sets one fact in bold relief. For the Saint, a missionary is one who, in response to a call and following an impulse of the Spirit, commits his whole person and life to God, to cooperate with Christ for the salvation of his neighbors. Claret himself lived at this more-than-exemplary, incredibly high pitch. He lived only for his mission. Anyone who has read his *Autobiography* cannot fail to come away from that experience convinced of the extraordinary intensity of his action, his heroic constancy, and his acute sensitivity to the needs of the church at every stage in his life.

Claret seems to have understood his whole life precisely in the same way that Paul understood celibacy: as an exclusive ordering of his life and person to "the things of the Lord" (1 Cor. 7:32). And celibacy, indeed, is a radical part of Claretian spirituality. This is what makes a Claretian, radically, a religious: living only for the Lord and the things of the Lord, namely, His church.

With Christ, Like Christ, In Christ

In *Mystic and Man of Action,* we have spoken at length on the strong Christocentrism that characterized Claret's spiritual experience,[11] hence we need not dwell on that theme here. But we should say something about the way in which the Saint projected this central image of Christ on the spirituality of his Congregation.

We mentioned above how in 1859, Claret came to understand in prayer that the prophetic texts in which he had discovered his own vocation—especially Luke 4:18—equally defined the vocation and spirit of his followers.[12] This obviously means that at the root of the Claretian's mission and spirit lies an association with the Lord in His saving work. The mission of Jesus, the Son-Servant-Prophet, is the very source of the mission of the church and indeed of every mission in the church.

In Claret's talks to his missionaries and in other missionary writings where he works out, in outline form, a theology of mission, his main focus is on Christ, the Envoy of the Father. "The Father sends his Son," is the central point in the second conference Claret gave during the founding retreat.[13] In his *Letter to a Missionary,* he clearly explains which mission he means.

> In no other matter has the Lord our God so manifested his love for us miserable exiles in this valley of tears, than in sending us his only

begotten Son to redeem and save us, and to become the head and model of other missionaries. "God so loved the world that he sent his only Son." Nor did the divine Majesty of Our Lord Jesus Christ ever find in this world a task more pleasing to his eternal Father, or more glorious, than that of being Savior of the world.[14]

The Son's mission, then, implies incarnation, passion, and resurrection. The whole temporal existence of Christ is, in effect, mission; not just the word He preached or the miracles He performed or even the passion He underwent, but His whole temporal existence. In Christ, mission and existence are utterly identical, because His whole life *is* Word, gift, and proclamation of grace. His whole life is the encounter of God with the Man in whom all men must encounter God. We are evidently in the presence of one of those Pauline Christologies of descent (in the mission of the Son) or, rather, of a Johannine Christology, since the earthly life of Christ is reincorporated into the theological reflections involved, as an epiphany.

Christ calls His apostles, and in them and with them, He calls us, the missionaries of His church, as Claret goes on to say:

This ministry [saving souls] —so sublime, so holy and so divine—Jesus Christ has been pleased to entrust to the Apostles and to apostolic missionaries, when he says: "As the Father has sent me, I also send you." And he has wished, as St. Jerome tells us, that we, too, should be saviors of the world. See if there is any honor like that which Jesus Christ bestows in admitting us to his apostolate and in sharing with us his title of Savior of the world.[15]

"Jesus Christ Himself was sent from God, and Jesus in turn sent His Apostles," he repeats in his *Autobiography*[16] and in his talks for the founding retreat. He is obviously not talking about a parallel mission associated with that of Christ. The Father has but one Envoy, one only Word, and there is but one saving action, unique and unrepeatable: that of Jesus Christ who died and rose once for all. By Christ's own will, apostolic mission is inserted in this, His unique mission; the apostles are the witnesses of Christ, the heralds of His message and His grace. When they are faithful to their vocation, they are collaborating with Christ in the salvation of their brothers. This is what Paul himself said, when he included preaching in the series of acts that form the divine plan of justification (Rom. 10:14-15).

Before all else, the missionary receives a call from the Lord: Follow me. Claret had this in mind when he added the following line to Fr. Xifré's Very Important Instruction: "The missionary life is one in which we leave all things in order to follow Jesus Christ, to extend His reign and to save sinners."[17] This is one of the fundamental elements of the celebrated description of a Son of the Heart of Mary written by the founder: "A Son of the Immaculate Heart of Mary is a man . . . [whose] only concern is how he can best follow Jesus Christ and imitate Him in working, suffering, and striving constantly and singlemindedly for the greater glory of God and the salvation of souls."[18] Here, again, we find the theme of the following of Christ, which is essential for an understanding of the Christian life, and a central issue in that visible and institutionalized form of discipleship that we call the religious life.

Sharing in the vocation of Christ, the Envoy of the Father, presupposes a sharing in His grace, in the same Spirit with which He was anointed in the epiphany at the Jordan. In his *Well-Instructed Seminarian,* Claret explains this in his remarks on the priestly spirit.

> The ecclesiastical spirit is nothing more than a sharing in the spirit of God, bountiful and near. . . . Jesus Christ Himself received the Holy Spirit, the priestly spirit, the spirit in whom every priest must live and work. The Holy Scriptures say: "The Spirit of the Lord is upon me" (invisibly, since the hypostatic union; visibly, since the baptism in the Jordan); "therefore, he has anointed me": anointed me as teacher, prophet, savior and lawgiver. The Saints are anointed by the grace and gifts of the Holy Spirit, but Jesus Christ was anointed by the Holy Spirit Himself, as the fount and fullness of all graces, so that from His fullness we have all received, as from an overabundant source.[19]

In another sense, Christ is not only the source but also the object of mission. The apostles and missionaries proclaim none other than Jesus Christ. St. Anthony Claret calls this to mind in the second talk for the founding retreat, where he traces out a theology of apostolic mission. The central text he uses, Galatians 1:15-16, states that Paul was predestined and called by God, who "was pleased to reveal his Son to me, in order that I might preach him among the Gentiles." Claret expands this thought in his *Letter to a Missionary,* where he alludes to the three states in which the Word is communicated: "The Word should be considered as existing in three states, incarnate, sacramental and preached."[20] It is the same Incarnate Word that is given in the sacrament of the Eucharist and in the Word of the Gospel. In this respect, we may recall an expression found in Origen and Augustine: "It is no less the Word of God than it is the Body of Christ."[21] If Christ is the Word of the Father and if, in Him, the Father has spoken His definitive Word, then all of the church's preaching must have Christ as its object. And Christ is given in the word of the church when the missionary word evokes faith in its hearer or leads a believer to conversion. In both cases, the reception of the Savior in the Word should culminate in His reception in the Eucharist.[22] This is the entire aim of missionary activity.

Given these premises, we can understand the intensely Christocentric character of an asceticism such as that which St. Anthony Mary Claret lived and taught. For him, apostolic life and the following of Christ are identical. One must leave all—boats, nets, father, the counting table—and follow Him. This not only implies joining His group; it means setting ourselves to learn in His school and allowing ourselves to be molded by His words and example.

As we read through the primitive *Constitutions,* one aspect of them strikes us: their constant reference to the conduct and teaching of Christ. Articles 54 (detachment from family), 69 (disinterestedness), 71 (poverty) and 83 (love of enemies),[23] all recall sayings of the Master. In Article 64 the Saint makes the following recommendation: "Let the Missionaries never forget that they must be true imitators of Jesus Christ in all the virtues, but especially in obedience."[24] In this same article he proposes several examples of the obedience of the Lord, especially His obedience unto death on the cross. In Articles 68 and 72 he reminds his missionaries of the real poverty of the Son of Man, exhorting them to copy it. In Article 77 he proposes the modesty of the Savior as a model.[25] Still more, in Article 54, he asks them to live only for Christ, dead to the world, and self. Article 57 invites them to love what the Incarnate Word loved, and to identify with His sentiments. In Article 82, speaking of fraternal

charity, he uses some Pauline expressions to describe the relationships that should exist between the members of the Body
of Christ.[26]

When he set about redrafting the *Constitutions* in 1864, he
was forced to be more concise, to put them in the form of a
code of law, according to the criteria established by the board
of censors in Rome. This meant that the founder had to substi-
tute short rules and brief scriptural texts for the longer ascetic
commentaries of the earlier *Constitutions.* Nevertheless, even in
this concise text we can see, although in more sober dress, the
same insistence on the fundamental rule of the imitation of
Christ. In a key text addressed to the novices, he proposes that
they adopt, as the ideal of their spiritual life, Paul's statement in
Galatians 2:20: "The young Missionaries, in leaving the world,
should also leave their own will, so that having entered the Congregation, each of them may be able to say with the Apostle, 'It
is no longer I who live, but Christ who lives in me.'"[27] The principle of imitating Christ is expressly stated in the chapter on
poverty, "in imitation of Jesus Christ, who had nowhere to lay
his head,"[28] and in the chapter on interior mortification, where
the Claretian is invited to follow Christ by carrying the cross of
self-denial.[29] As a motive for obedience, he proposes the example of the Lord Himself: "For the sake of Jesus Christ, who for
our sake became obedient unto death, even to death on a cross,
let all obey. . . ."[30] The third degree of interior mortification is
that of being crucified with Christ.[31] Finally, speaking of fraternal charity, the Saint again cites Paul's statements on the mystical Body of Christ, reinforced this time by a reference to the
Lord's commandment of love: "As images of God and members
of the same body, let them love one another, thus fulfilling the
Lord's command: 'This is my commandment, that you love one
another as I have loved you.' Let them be concerned for one
another (1 Cor. 12:25), anticipate one another in showing respect (Rom. 12:10), and support, serve and help one another."[32]
What makes this all the more important is the fact that most of
these new texts have been expressly added by the Saint to material he took in good part from other ascetic authors. Still
more, the idea of the imitation of Christ seems dominant in his
selection of ascetic rules; for example, Article 9 of the chapter

on modesty, which is taken from a meditation on the modesty of Christ. In his *Autobiography*, he offers the example of Christ as the motive for the norms for mortification of the eyes which he describes there.[33]

This constant recourse to the words and example of Christ in the norms of the *Constitutions* corresponds to a rule of behavior that Claret always followed in his writings to his missionaries. It can be seen in his talks for the founding retreat: the example of Christ is cited at the beginning of nearly every one of his talks.[34] The same is true of the retreat he preached in 1865.[35] In the *Letter to a Missionary*, which is the introduction to his *Mission Sermons*, he lays down some fundamental norms of apostolic asceticism, always keeping his sights on the Lord. The missionary is told to pray frequently, as Jesus did;[36] to continually observe and imitate the humility and meekness of Jesus;[37] to contemplate His persecutions and His patience.[38]

Claret's reading of the Bible, which he always understood within the real-life perspective of his missionary vocation, gave him an image of Christ that was predominantly prophetic. Since Claret dwells so insistently on the mission of the Son, he closely links the prophetism of Jesus with the divine Sonship. But his concern is with the Son as sent into the world, with Him who speaks in the Father's name. At the same time, his initial notion of the imitation of Christ was a copying of the concrete behavioral traits of Jesus, as revealed in the Gospels. Little by little, Claret's own mystical experience led him to interiorize the image of Jesus. His contacts with masters of spirituality, especially those of the French school, led him to manifest a preference for assimilating the spirit of Christ, for attuning his own sentiments with those of Christ.[39] Claret's mystical experience was to culminate in experiencing Christ living in himself.[40]

But if the Bible gave the Saint a prophetic image of Jesus, the Eucharist brought him face to face with the risen Christ who lives in His church. Throughout his life, Claret continued to develop a concept of the church in which its interior and mystical dimensions predominated. For him the church is primarily the Body of Christ, the communion that the Lord fills with grace.[41] This helps us understand why his keenest experience of the presence of Christ took place while he was celebrating the Eucharist and why, in turn, immediately following one of his highest mystical graces connected with the Eucharist, he was led to confront the most serious evils that beset the church in Spain.[42]

It is worth noting here that the Eucharist and the Bible were, for Anthony Claret, the two channels through which the Spirit flooded him with special graces. In both *Constitutions* he recommends that the students daily partake in the celebration of the Eucharist, and on various occasions he urges all to spend some time in prayer and meditation before the Blessed Sacrament.[43] He also asks that the students read a few chapters of the Bible every day.[44]

The Intercession of Mary

Here again we encounter another typical trait of the Claretian spirit: the patronage exercised by the Blessed Mother of the Lord over the ministry of the Claretians in the church. The founder experienced it in an exemplary, although extraordinary form, in his vision of the Blessed Virgin, who appeared to him and helped him through an excruciating temptation against chastity that came at the very moment when his missionary vocation was awakening and when the spirit of evil would have nipped it in the bud.[45] The Blessed Virgin was also involved in the birth of the Congregation of Missionaries. We know this through Fr. James Clotet, a cofounder and attentive annotator of everything that concerned the institute and its founder.

> It was through Mary's inspiration that it [the Congregation] was founded. The writer of these lines heard it from the lips of the Founder himself. Preaching to the community at Vich [*sic*; 1865] on the occasion of a retreat, he spoke to the Blessed Virgin and said: "You founded it, do you not remember, Lady? Do you not remember?" And he said this with such a tone and naturalness that it was obvious that, at that very moment, he was having a very lively recall of the precept, words and presence of the Mother of God.[46]

Perhaps it was on the basis of this experience that, years later, the Saint developed a general thesis according to which the Blessed Virgin always intervenes, alongside her Son, in the foundation of religious institutes, thus raising up valiant allies for the church. He expounded this idea in *Selfishness Overcome*, a life of St. Peter Nolasco, the founder of the Mercedarians.[47] He had already stated this orally to his missionaries toward the close of a talk he gave at the 1865 retreat, after showing how the various religious institutes were born during some crisis in the church.

> Toward the middle of the 19th century ... the Blessed Virgin founded her holy Congregation, so that her Heart might become a Noah's ark, a Tower of David, a city of refuge and a sacred propitiatory.[48]

It is quite likely that this was the talk during which Claret spoke the words we referred to above, concerning her being the Foundress of the Congregation.

Still later, on Ascension Thursday, 1870, a few months before his death, as he was praying before the altar of the Blessed Virgin, he received an illumination in which he saw his Congregation of Missionaries as the "arms of Mary," working for the salvation of their neighbor.[49] This means that toward the end of his life the Saint saw his institute as being doubly related to the Mother of the Lord: (1) it was founded through Mary's intercession in favor of the church; (2) it is called to be the instrument of the Blessed Virgin in her work for the church.

The Congregation, since its foundation, is also related to Mary, inasmuch as she is mentioned in its title and is honored as its patroness. Her patronage is mentioned expressly only in the 1865 *Constitutions.*[50] The primitive *Constitutions,* as revised and published in 1857, state:

> This Congregation of Missionaries, first founded in the mission house of Our Lady of Mercy in the city of Vich [*sic*], shall bear the title of "Congregation of the Sons of the Immaculate Heart of Mary" and shall have as its Patron St. Michael the Archangel....[51]

It is quite likely that the omission of the patronage of Mary in this text arose from the fact that her inclusion in the title implied that she was the patroness. Fr. Xifré, alluding to a note that the Saint jotted down on the same day in which God inspired him to found the Congregation, comments:

> He revealed to him that this Congregation would spread throughout the world and would last until the end of time, and that it should have as its titular and principal patroness the Heart of Mary, wherefore its members should be called Missionary Sons of the Immaculate Heart of Mary.[52]

In keeping with what we said in chapter 2, we believe that the idea for the foundation (and, according to Fr. Xifré, the title and patronage of the Blessed Virgin) came to the Saint while he was preaching in the Canary Islands in 1849. If we run through the list of the various missionary associations that Claret planned or organized before founding the Congregation, we will notice that the first of them was called the Brotherhood of the Virgin of the Rosary and the Blessed Virgin was to be its "Mother, Directress and Captainess."[53] In the series of documents addressed to various pre-Congregation groups,[54] Document VI refers only to the "Apostolic Fraternity,"[55] while Document VII, dating from 1847 or 1848, speaks of the "Brothers of Jesus and Mary."[56] These are the only documents of this period that mention the specific title of the organization in question.

Anthony Claret always included the Blessed Virgin in the title of his various organizations: the two religious institutes and the secular institute that recognize him as their founder; the Apostolic Society of the Heart of Mary (1847); the (Cuban) Association of the Name of Mary; the Association Against Blasphemy. Among the few of Claret's organizations that do not include Mary's name in their title, the Religious Library, the Academy of St. Michael, and the Popular Lending Libraries were, nonetheless, consecrated to the Blessed Virgin. One might well suppose, then, that the Congregation of Missionaries would have Mary as their titular patroness, under one or another of her titles. But why did the Saint choose the particular title of the Heart of Mary? Fr. Xifré tells us that when Claret received the inspiration to found the institute, he understood that it should be so named. Anthony Claret had already come in contact with the devotion to the Heart of Mary in 1831, when he enrolled in the Congregation of the Sacred Hearts, under the direction of the Jesuits at Manresa. Incorporated with the Pious Union of St. Eustace in Rome, one of the objects of this group was to honor Mary and implore her protection. According to the tract writers of the time, the devotion was directed toward the physical Heart of Mary as the symbol of her love. Later, the Saint joined the third order of the Servites. In the manual of traditional prayers used by the group in Vic, there was frequent reference to the compassion of the Heart of Mary. Finally, he came in closer contact with the devotion to the Sacred Hearts in the Jesuit Novitiate in Rome. But all of this seems to have had little impact on him since as late as 1847, he does not so much as use the expression, "Heart of Mary." What does surface in the early years of his ministry is a constant tendency to speak of Mary as the Mother of Fair Love, *Mater pulchrae dilectionis,* or Mother of divine love, expressions common enough in Italy and related there with the devotion to the Heart of Mary.[57]

The decisive impulse seems to have come to him from the Parisian Archconfraternity of the Most Holy and Immaculate Heart of Mary. His friend Anthony Palau, the founder of the *Revista Católica* and a future bishop, persuaded Claret, toward the beginning of 1846, to join and espouse the cause of the arch-confraternity. In 1846 and 1847 the Saint devoted his efforts to founding archconfraternities of the Heart of Mary associated with the Parisian core group. When Claret completed his evangelization of the Canary Islands, Bishop Codina deemed that the best memorial for that memorable missionary campaign would be to establish the archconfraternity in every parish in his diocese. The Saint, in turn, would later found it in every parish in his own archdiocese of Santiago, Cuba.[58] In 1846 he published a *Brief Notice on the Archconfraternity* to promote a publicity campaign. It is very instructive to note that while he had systematically called an association dedicated to the service of God in the world "The Association of Philomenas" until 1847, he suddenly begins referring to them as "Daughters of the Most Holy and Immaculate Heart of Mary." In a letter to his friend Caixal, dated January 6, 1847, he still refers to them as "the Philomenas";[59] in another letter to Caixal, on August 18 of that same year, he refers to them as the "Nuns of the Most Holy and Immaculate Heart of Mary."[60] In 1847, too, he planned the Apostolic Society of the Most Holy and Immaculate Heart of Mary.

The adjectival phrase, "Most Holy and Immaculate," is an evident proof of the influence of the Parisian archconfraternity, which always used it in reference to the Heart of Mary, in contrast to Spanish or Italian piety, which did not. Of even greater importance is the fact that the *Annals of the Archconfraternity* occasionally refers to members of the association as "Sons of the Immaculate Heart."[61] With these data before us, we begin to understand what moved Claret to give this title to his Congregation of Missionaries, to his future secular institute, and to the apostolic brotherhood he was planning in 1847. M. Duffriche-Desgenettes, the founder of the archconfraternity, spoke of the devotion to the Heart of Mary as a formidable arm of the apostolate, which sinners could not resist. This is precisely how Claret saw the matter, too: as an effective instrument in the service of evangelization.[62] It was the apostolic effectiveness of the devotion, then, that led him to choose the Heart of Mary for the title of his Congregation.

Note, however, that for Claret the Heart of Mary signified the total person of the Blessed Virgin, understood from the standpoint of her love[63] and of her work in favor of the church (Parisian archconfraternity).

These are the fundamental and permanent data defining the relationship with Mary, the Mother of the Lord, in the spirituality of the Claretian Congregation. The founder regarded the birth of the Congregation as a result of Mary's intercession in favor of the church, and hence he consecrated it to her. Mary's intercession accompanies the institute in its struggle for the Kingdom of God. Obviously, the Saint lived his devotion to the Blessed Virgin within the context of the Catholic piety of the 18th and 19th centuries, a piety that stressed the mother-son relationship between Mary and Jesus and exalted the unique privileges of the Mother of God. To this the Saint added his experience of Mary's intercession in favor of his personal missionary vocation and that of his institute. This experience, in which the Blessed Virgin of Nazareth was seen as associated in the charismatic genesis of the Congregation and as continuing alongside it in its journey through history, can easily fit into a theological vision far different from the one Anthony Claret received from the church of his day. There is no doubt that the missionary vocation is closely related to a more biblical image of Mary, as she embraces virginity as an expression of radical poverty; is left behind by her Son when He sets out to proclaim the Kingdom and create His own "family" on the basis of a communion in the will of the Father (Mark 3:31-35); and finally reenters the Gospel precisely as the prototype of the disciple who hears the Word and makes a total commitment to it (Luke 1:26-55; John

19:25-27), so that she might be present in the nascent church (Acts 1:12-14).

The Church

It is easy to see how important relationship with the church is in the spirituality of a group of disciples of Christ who are called and moved to dedicate their lives and persons to the proclamation of the Gospel. This is equivalent, after all, to saying that they orient themselves vocationally in a profound commitment to the church. In fact, when we spoke of the constituent elements of the vocation of the Claretian Congregation, we had to spend a long chapter on the theme of the church. We began that chapter with a consideration of the various images of the church that Anthony Claret continued to propound throughout his life: Church-Spouse, Church-Body of Christ. We likewise noted that in the ecclesiology of the Saint, the mystical and interior aspects of the church predominated over the sociologic and juridical aspects. Another equally significant idea in Claret's ecclesiology was his notion of the church as holy, inasmuch as it is a gift of God, but constantly in need of reform in its members. Claret worked out this notion largely through his contacts with Mother Antonia Paris who, under his aegis, became foundress of the Claretian Missionary Sisters.

Bringing this theme down to the level of actually lived experience—the real level of spirituality—the Claretian's relationship with the church seems to be characterized by two traits, both of which were visible in the founder: responsibility and communion. Before going into these in detail, let us rapidly review the common ecclesial elements with which these distinctive traits must be associated. The Claretian knows that his own baptism was not merely the beginning of a relationship, in grace, with the Triune God but an incorporation into a living church journeying through history. His relationship with God is realized not only *in* the church but also, sacramentally, *through* the church. The call to give himself utterly—his whole person and life—to the service of God (religious life) reorients him toward the church. In effect, his profession is an oblation of himself to God, the same oblation he made in his vocational decision, an oblation made through the church and the community of disciples into which he is incorporated. (I discuss this theme at length in a forthcoming book, *Discipleship: A Theology of Religious Life.*)

This is where the particular traits of the Claretian spirit, vis-à-vis the church, fit in. The Claretian vocation is a missionary calling to proclaim the Gospel. While the Christian vocation always entails a reference to mission and proclamation, the fact of "having been chosen by God in the womb" ([Gal. 1:16] cited in Claret's 1849 retreat talks), to dedicate oneself and one's life to proclaiming the Kingdom, fills one with a deep sense of responsibility. This is only reinforced by the additional fact of being incorporated into a missionary community recognized by the church. This phenomenon was particularly powerful in the life of Anthony Claret. Moved and impelled by what he himself calls his "universal charity,"[64] Claret lived in a state of constant alertness to the needs of the church.

> Seeing that the Lord, out of sheer good will and no merit on my part, was calling me to stem the torrent of corruption and cure the ills of a moribund society, I thought that I should dedicate myself to studying and gaining a thorough knowledge of the maladies of this social body.[65]
>
> As I was giving missions, I ran into all sorts of needs, and as each new need arose I wrote a booklet or pamphlet on the subject.[66]

In fact, then, the Saint always showed signs of a keen sensitivity to the different situations and needs of whatever local church he happened to be working in. This is the only way we can begin to explain not only his truly inspired intuitions in the apostolate (promotion of the lay apostolate, women's ministries, the press, the publishing house, licensed credit unions, the Academy of St. Michael) but also the great variety of his ministries in different times and places: Catalonia, Canary Islands, Cuba, Madrid. Even in his intimate dealings with God in prayer, the needs of the church came very forcefully to the fore. His decisions to found the Society of the Blessed Virgin Against Blasphemy in 1845 and the Congregation of Missionaries in 1849 both came to him in prayer, as a response to the lights he received at that time. If we read the notes he made on the lights and graces he received in prayer, we will note that a good many of them refer to his ministries.[67]

A second aspect of Claretian spirituality vis-à-vis its relationship with the church is the sense of communion with the people of God, a sense that was very strong and lively in the founder.

This is manifest in his awareness of the historic movement of the church, which we just spoke of. We refer not only to his attention to various needs of the church but also to the movements that were then arising in the church. This is what led him to adopt means for the apostolate being promoted by others in Italy, France, or Spain; e.g., he derived the idea for the Pious Union of Prayers from Vincent Pallotti in Rome and for the establishment of the Archconfraternity of the Heart of Mary from Père Desgenettes in Paris. His catholic spirit led him to choose spiritual masters and guides from diverse schools (Jesuit, Carmelite, Franciscan, Oratorian) and different nationalities (Spain, Italy, France, Portugal, England, Germany, Austria). We have referred to this at greater length in *Mystic and Man of Action.*[68] This same sense of ecclesial communion also led him to lend his valiant support as royal confessor to a number of founders and foundresses and to bend every effort in the service of evangelization, especially by involving the laity in it and promoting ministries for women. We have already referred to the Apostolic Society of the Heart of Mary (1847), in which priests and laity, men and women, were meant to collaborate on a level of equality. He followed the same line of thought with regard to the Academy of St. Michael.

This sense of communion was manifested, too—and strikingly —in his obedience to the shepherds of the church. In his *Autobiography,* Claret dedicates a whole chapter to "The Care I Took to See That the Superior Sent Me to Preach."[69] In this chapter he has some very strong words on the subject.

> I had come to realize that a missionary must never thrust himself into an assignment. He should offer his services to the bishop, saying, "Here I am, send me." But he should not go until his bishop sends him, because when he is sent, it will be by God's sending. All the Old Testament prophets were sent by God. Jesus Christ himself was sent from God, and Jesus in turn sent his Apostles.[70]

He put his sense of total obedience into practice, even when one bishop, swayed by prejudice, showed his displeasure against one of the Saint's initiatives. We refer to the Apostolic Fraternity of the Heart of Mary, which he was unable to found because the archbishop of Tarragona did not want women to take active part in the apostolate. Anthony Claret destroyed all copies of the rules for this project, of which we would know nothing if his friend Caixal had not secretly kept a manuscript copy.

St. Anthony Claret had experienced a call to be a public and official preacher of the Gospel. This is something more than the common vocation to witness, which all Christians have in virtue of their baptism and confirmation. Because of it, Claret wished to be recognized as a preacher by the shepherds of the church and asked them to send him on canonical mission. This was also the reason why in the second *Constitutions,* immediately following the definition of the Congregation's apostolic mission, he wrote:

> Hence they shall manifest great reverence, love and obedience toward the Supreme Pontiff and the Holy Apostolic See, and shall be the steadfast helpers of the Prelates of the Church in the ministry of the Word.[71]

In translating the theme of obedience from the experience of the founder, who was an isolated missionary and not a member of a religious community, into the life of the Congregation, Claretian obedience assumes two aspects. On the one hand obedience, both of the individual and the group, relates to the shepherds of the church in what pertains to the pastoral office of the latter; on the other hand, obedience involves a continual search in communion with the saving will of God, a search which is realized in community. The first aspect is dealt with in the addition to Article 2 of the *Constitutions,* which we have just cited. The second aspect is dealt with in the paragraphs relating to obedience in both *Constitutions*[72] and in one talk during the 1865 retreat.[73] In both aspects obedience is an expression of ecclesial communion. In both aspects, too, obedience is decidedly apostolic in tone; that is to say, it develops around the concept of the ecclesial mission that the community has received and in which its members share.

Obedience means personal participation in the process whereby the community comes to discern the will of God in the here and now. It means detecting, in this concrete case, what is truly involved in being called to be instruments of saving grace. Far from diminishing personal responsibility, obedience broadens it into corresponsibility. It is not a question, either in the local church or in community, of being simple executors of official party lines or repeaters of messages from the top. Rather, in obeying and collaborating we do so actively, putting our own understanding of history and our own experience and energies at the service of the ecclesial community and its shepherds. This may well involve contrasting points of view and hence may be the source of some anguish. For this very reason, obedience must be practiced in dialogue inspired by love, a dialogue that should end with a prevailing sense of communion.

Prayer

Our examination of Claretian spirituality has touched upon its source (the Pentecost experience), its thrust (toward the service of God), its experiential object (Christ accompanied by the intercession of Mary), and its outreach (the church) and has shown us various typical traits of this spirit: faith, apostolic charity, celibacy, and obedience. Even so, we must still consider some other, equally important traits.

In the first place, there is the spirit of prayer. We have treated of the central importance of prayer in the religious experience of Anthony Claret in another work.[74] From 1859 on, he dedicated three consecutive hours in the early morning to prayer.[75] Still more significant is the fact of his sense of union with God, which he came to live in a habitual manner in the midst of his intense activity.

Speaking to his missionaries in the *Autobiography,* he lists prayer first among the means to be used in the apostolate:

The first means I have always employed and still do is *prayer.* In my opinion, this is the greatest means that can be used for the conversion of sinners, the perseverance of the just, and the relief of the souls in purgatory. . . . I not only prayed myself but asked others to pray—nuns, Sisters of Charity, Tertiaries, and all virtuous and zealous folk.[76]

He had written something similar in the "Letter to a Missionary," which served as a preface to the first volume of his *Missionary Sermons.* The "important counsels" in this letter begin:

You must be a great friend of prayer, in imitation of Jesus, who spent the night in prayer to God and strongly recommended prayer to his Apostles. All missionaries worthy of the name have been men of prayer. He who asks, receives.[77]

The figure of the apostle, then, is two-sided. On the one hand, there is the more obvious image of the man of action; on the other, there is the mediator, the man who intercedes with God on behalf of his people. In the last talk for the founding retreat, on prayer, Claret refers to this by citing the well-known text from Acts: "This will allow us to concentrate on prayer and the ministry of the word" (Acts 6:4). In developing the theme of apostolic intercession, the Saint cites a series of significant biblical figures and texts: Moses with his hands held up on behalf of his people while Joshua fights against the Amalekites (Exod. 17:9-13) or interceding to stave off the wrath of God from Israel (Exod. 32:12-14); the account in Numbers that represents Moses and Aaron praying to the Lord not to exterminate the whole people for the sins of a few (Num. 16:22); and, of course, Jeremiah, the prophet who so loved his brothers that he continually placed himself in intercession between the wrath of God and the sins of Israel (Jer. 7:16).[78]

He returned to this theme in the first talk of the retreats he preached successively to the missionaries at Vic and Gracia in 1865.

> All [Fathers, Students and Brothers] should pray for the Missionaries. You should do as Mary did—praying—and thus bringing about the conversion of many, even such a one as Saul. As Moses and so many Saints prayed.[79]

Here we have a clear expression of St. Anthony Claret's idea of the important role of prayer in his institute. It represents a conviction that progressively matured in the Saint's mind until its forceful appearance during his period in Madrid, but it had been clearly manifested during the first days of the new Congregation. His institute would have to be, like himself, entirely oriented toward apostolic action and preaching, but this would have no value unless it was backed up by a life of intense prayer and union with God. A few months after the founding, in a letter to Caixal, he puts prayer first on the list of the occupations of his missionaries.[80]

As to the forms of prayer, the Claretian Congregation, since its earliest days, has mainly developed two: liturgical prayer, celebrated in community, and mental prayer, in private. The founder and his first companions began by reciting the liturgy of the hours in common, but since this Office, influenced by the usage of monks and canons, was so very long, they soon realized that they would have to abandon that custom. After his coming to Santiago, Cuba, the Saint continued to recite vespers with his household.[81] As for private prayer, the founder in the *Constitutions* recommended mental prayer, daily examen of conscience, and spiritual reading.[82] These mental forms of prayer were aimed at interiorizing the missionaries' life and activity.

The Saint attached such great importance to liturgical piety and mental prayer that he never dispensed himself from them, no matter how exhausting his work might be, and he wanted his missionaries to imitate him in this. We know this from a letter of Fr. Xifré to Fr. Paul Vallier, the founder of the Province of Chile, concerning an interview Xifré held with the Saint shortly before the latter's death.

> Never omit the divine office or the meditation prescribed, no matter what the custom, authorization or need might be. These two things are spiritual nourishment without which we neither should nor can do in our Congregation. When our Founder was in the Canary Islands and later, in Cuba, he had as much and perhaps much more spiritual need than you do, but he never omitted these two things. He told me as much a few days ago, and charged me to write it to you.[83]

Apostolic Poverty

Poverty is one of the most outstanding characteristics of the life and spiritual teaching of St. Anthony Mary Claret. He comments on it several times in his *Autobiography,* but especially in the chapter on poverty in the ascetic section. He never took a stipend for his preaching or payment for his books. He would accept a change of clothing as an alms, but only if what he was wearing was beyond mending. Speaking of his ministry in the Canary Islands, he humorously remarks that the only thing he brought back to Spain were five rips the faithful had made in his old coat.[84] All of his goods—a Bible, a change of underwear, and a notebook—he carried about in a bandanna.[85] So as not to have to accept money, he went on foot from one town to the next.[86] Later, in Madrid as royal confessor, he lived most poorly, wearing simple vestments and a brass cross, with no servants or carriage, in a few apartments in a hospital. He so awed his visitors that one bishop, on returning home from a visit, decided to get rid of some of his own more luxurious furnishings.[87]

He not only practiced poverty but recommended it warmly in his writings. He frequently asked bishops,[88] priests,[89] and the Daughters of the Most Holy and Immaculate Heart of Mary,[90] to live in effective poverty. And he recommended to all Christians the spirit of poverty.[91]

Why was he so insistent on this subject? There was, above all, a personal and, so to speak, charismatic reason. The illuminations and movements whereby God had been moulding his apostolic soul during his seminary days had brought him to see that poverty forms part of the missionary vocation. Among the biblical texts that awakened his vocation and strongly shaped his spirituality were two on poverty. The first was the Lord's statement of His own poverty as a condition for those who were to follow Him: "The Son of Man has nowhere to lay his head," a text that he was to repeat all his life when explaining his own poverty or recommending it to others.[92] He stated it at the beginning of the chapter on poverty in the second *Constitutions.*[93] In the other text, which he read in the Vulgate edition, he heard the Lord saying: "I have chosen you in the furnace of poverty" (Isa. 48:10). That Saint Anthony Claret understood his earthly mission in this sense—a tireless apostolate and a poor life—is confirmed by some words he wrote a year before his death: "It seems to me that I have fulfilled my mission. I have preached the Law of God . . . I have observed holy poverty."[94]

The mere consideration of the poverty practiced by Claret and the motives that led him to practice it give us some insight into the importance and meaning of poverty in the spirit of his Congregation. The founder has dwelt on poverty repeatedly. Both *Constitutions* contain articles dedicated to this theme.[95] It appears again in the Saint's talks for the 1865 retreat,[96] and it is highly significant that in the *Autobiography,* written for the formation of his missionaries, he dealt with it so insistently and recommended it so forcefully.[97] The letters of Claret to Fr. Xifré likewise contain a number of considerations on poverty.[98]

As might be expected, St. Anthony Mary Claret explains the meaning and characteristics of poverty for his Congregation from the starting point of the missionary vocation. In a letter to his friend Caixal, he describes the tenor of life in the institute during its first weeks of existence: "In this college, we are living a truly poor and apostolic life"[99] and, we would add by way of commentary, a doubly apostolic life. In both *Constitutions,* in addition to the example of the Lord, the mainspring of his asceticism, he states the motive of imitating the Apostles,[100] citing a number of Gospel texts that describe the life they followed (e.g., Matthew 10:9, "Behold, we have left all things. . . ."). In the first *Constitutions,* altering a traditional description of poverty as the defensive wall of the religious life, he writes of poverty as the "wall of the Missionaries."[101]

If we analyze the various aspects of Claretian poverty, we discover in it those traits of poverty as professed by apostolic institutes. First of all, there is the matter of working for the poor. We have already seen the manner and meaning of the way the Saint felt called to evangelize the poor. Secondly, the first Claretian priests, even though they were not religious in the canonical sense, had to renounce those parishes or other ecclesiastical offices that the Canon Law of the day regarded as their due. This meant that they not only renounced their present stability for the life of itinerant missionaries but their future comfort and security as well. Thirdly, the personal example of the founder and the articles of the *Constitutions* recommended personal and collective austerity and simplicity. The primitive *Constitutions* forbid any "show of luxury."[102] The second *Constitutions* require that their meals, clothing, and furnishings be in accord with those of the poor.[103] Finally, the founder roundly forbade them to accept any stipend or salary for their ministries.[104] This prohibition led to many worries for the superior general, Fr. Xifré, so that the Saint was always writing him to trust in Divine Providence.[105] Toward the end of his life, in one of his notes, he added a further restriction to this rule, asking that his missionaries should not be maintained by the pastor or the town they were working in, so as to avoid complaints against them and to facilitate their being called to preach the Gospel; hence, they were to find a source of independent financing.[106] It should be noted, we might add, that the only ministries practiced by the Claretians at that time were those associated with missionary preaching, usually in poor towns. The Saint did not want the ministries of his missionaries to seem like a source of income at the expense of the poor.[107]

The multiplicity of concrete aspects characterizing Claretian poverty and the historic conditioning that surrounds some of its expression should not be allowed to make us lose sight of its fundamentally apostolic meaning and thrust. Poverty is nothing else than the attitude of a person who is not working for himself, for his own power, prestige, or security, but rather for the service of God in proclaiming the Gospel. One is poor when he recognizes the radical poverty of sinners before God, and comes down, like Christ, to the level of his brothers and sisters in misery, so as to share with them the grace that sets us all free. One is poor when he lives without moorings, without possessing even himself, his qualities, or education, but rather using all of these for the service of the church. One is poor when he lives in simplicity, practicing generosity.

The Cross and Glory

We bring this study of Claretian spirituality to a close by calling to mind the great love of the Cross that St. Anthony Claret lived and strove to inspire in his companions. The scriptural texts in which he discovered his missionary vocation spoke not only of the proclamation of God's Word but also of the conflicts and persecutions that he would meet on his path.[108] The portraits of the prophets that he left us in his *Autobiography* build up to their martyrdom as the culmination of their labors in the service of the living God.[109] Likewise, his picture of Jesus culminates in the cross.[110] The Apostles,[111] and especially St. Paul,[112] imitate him in this. The ideal pen-portrait of the Claretian ends with these words:

> Nothing daunts him; he delights in privations, welcomes work, embraces sacrifices, smiles at slander, and rejoices in suffering. His only concern is how he can best follow Jesus Christ and imitate him in working, suffering, and striving constantly and singlemindedly for the greater glory of God and the salvation of souls.[113]

This conviction of Claret's, that there was a close relationship between mission and suffering, came to him, then, by way of the Scriptures. He had occasion enough to experience it through-out his life in the harshness of his itinerant ministry in Catalo-nia, the Canary Islands, and Cuba, but above all in the fierce op-position that seemed to pursue him, from the attempt on his life at Holguín through all the defamation campaigns against him in Madrid to his hidden death in a Cistercian monastery. Although suffering is a fact of human life, anyone who lives a life totally committed to the Lord and His affairs is called to experience it to a particularly intense degree. In doing so, he not only collab-orates with Christ in the proclamation of the Kingdom, but also takes part in the mystery of the Cross. The missionary, then, must have that generosity and forcefulness that only come from love. Thus, too, it comes to us as no surprise that Anthony Clar-et dedicated two chapters to mortification, both in his *Autobi-ography*[114] and in the *Constitutions,*[115] and that he saw and lived this virtue as the very epitome of Christian life in its for-mative, ascetic aspect.[116] We must, on the other hand, bear in mind that in expounding various practical norms regarding mor-tification, especially mortification of the senses, he was acting under the influence of the ascetic theology of his day and age.[117] The most important thing to realize is that whoever is not dis-posed to renounce his own comfort cannot join Jesus and His disciples in proclaiming the Kingdom of God.

If the Cross and death are man's last word, then resurrection is God's last word: "This Jesus, whom you crucified, God has raised up" (Acts 2:23-24; 3:14-15). Thus, life in Christ ends in Easter glory.

IX

The Cofounders:
Fathers Xifré and Clotet

In the first generation of every religious institute there are usually a few relevant personalities who seem to have received a special mission from God to collaborate closely with the founder in the work of giving solid life and definitive shape to the institute. Among the disciples of the founder there are often those who have been surrounded by an aura of sanctity. A certain number of the first companions of St. Francis, for example, have been honored by their order with liturgical cult. Among the first Jesuits there is a whole squadron of canonized individuals. In every case this has to do with the first manifest fruits produced by the school of sanctity proper of the institute, while it is yet under the personal guidance of its founder. Hence, these saints or spiritual men or women are privileged witnesses of the spirit of the order or congregation. Moreover, it is evident that their spirituality has contributed to spread the heritage of their founders in the newborn organizations.

Sometimes it is possible to discover, alongside these personalities, one who has effectively collaborated with the founder or foundress in organizing and spreading the work. Alongside St. Francis, with his strong evangelical inspiration, Providence

placed Friar Elias, a man of government. The first Jesuits actively collaborated with St. Ignatius in the deliberations that gave
shape to the Company of Jesus, and some of them helped him
draw up his *Constitutions.*

Obviously, a positive study of the spirit of an institute can
always usefully bear in mind the contribution of these collaborators to the work of the founder, to understand how the
original inspiration came to take concrete shape. In some cases
such a study will be of historical interest only, and one that is
not decisive in the formulation of a doctrine, since the founder
sought this collaboration and it played a merely instrumental
role in his aims. The results of this collaboration form a single
whole, of which the responsibility and merit go to the founder
alone.

In other cases, however, one must pay greater attention to
the results of such an investigation. This is particularly so in the
case of those collaborators who have survived the founder for a
long time, continuing his work for many years after his death.
In such a case, it would prove particularly useful and even necessary to study the special contribution of these outstanding men,
judging it in the light of the spirit and mind of the founder. For
there can be no doubt—as we stated above, in keeping with the
teachings of the church—that it is the privilege of the Saint who
gave life to an institute to serve as a unique source of inspiration
for its tradition.

This is precisely the case with the Claretian Congregation. Its
founder had to give up living with his missionaries some fourteen months after the foundation, when he was appointed archbishop of Santiago de Cuba. During the following seven years
his relations with them were few, given the great distance that
separated them and the pressures of his ministry. When he returned to Madrid in May 1857, he took charge of the higher-
level direction of the institute, providing it with a revised edition
of the *Constitutions,* presiding over its General Chapters, and
widening its apostolic horizons. But its immediate guide was Fr.
Xifré. Hence, although the Saint intervened by way of counsels
and recommendations, the final decision was left to the father
general, and the Saint was the first to respect it, even on those
occasions when Fr. Xifré did not believe that the desires of the

founder could be put into effect immediately. When St. Anthony Claret died in 1870, Fr. Xifré was the absolute guide of the Congregation until his own death in 1899. Alongside him, from 1858 to 1888, Fr. James Clotet served as subdirector general.

Frs. Xifré and Clotet stand out among the group of St. Anthony Mary Claret's first companions. They deserve the title of cofounders in a special way, since they did not just share materially in the foundation, as did Frs. Fábregas and Vilaró, nor was their action limited to a short period of time, as was that of Fr. Stephen Sala. They always maintained special relations with the founder, and during their long lives both exercised a profound influence on the institute. Given the distinct characteristics of the services rendered by each of them, we will study their contributions separately.

Our study on the origin of the Claretian community would be somehow incomplete if we did not examine, at least in an appendix, the influence these two men had in shaping its life and spirit.

The Contribution of Fr. Joseph Xifré

Between these two collaborators of St. Anthony Claret, the primacy doubtless belongs to Fr. Joseph Xifré, since the title of cofounder fits him in a very special way. Divine Providence entrusted Fr. Xifré with the mission of giving life to the tiny seed planted by the Saint in 1849, of organizing the institute, of reinforcing its inner life, and of spreading it to other nations.[1]

Mosén Joseph Xifré, born in 1817 and ordained in 1840, had chosen to join the new Congregation, moved by a strong apostolic vocation. He, too, like St. Anthony Claret, had decided to renounce the care of souls in a parish to dedicate himself to missionary preaching. "I gave it up," he said later, "to go preaching in towns in the style of the apostles."[2]

These were his dispositions when the famous Catalán missionary invited him to join his first group of missionary preachers. From 1849 to 1858, although he had no special charge in the government of the newborn institute, he was one of the members most dedicated to its apostolic ideals and outstanding, even then, for his energy and the prestige that was his as a cofounder. On May 1, 1858, a few days after Fr. Sala's death, he was elect-

ed director general of the Congregation, a position he held until
his death in 1899.

We need only recall a few data to grasp all that the Congregation owes to Fr. Xifré. When he took charge, there was only one
house with sixteen members. When he died, there were sixty
communities, 1,368 professed members, and 108 novices.[3] In
1858 the Congregation was still only a simple association of
priests. In 1869 it was recognized as a Religious Congregation by
the Holy See, with its *Constitutions* approved perpetually. This
last fact was due especially to the interventions of the founder,
but Fr. Xifré has the merit of pushing him to do so by his constant requests.

A vigorous personality, with precise ideas that he strove to
accomplish despite all possible opposition, Fr. Joseph Xifré was
bound to leave a deep mark on the Congregation, above all if we
consider the extraordinary length of his tenure as general. His
influence was greatly heightened by the patriarchal way in which
he governed. Without his permission, the superior of any house
would not even entertain the least consideration of any action.
The extent of his pressure on the Congregation can be seen in
the fact that although the *Constitutions* had provided for provincial superiors in 1865, the first two provincials were not
elected until 1895. Fr. Xifré intervened throughout all this long
period as the immediate major superior of all the houses, and he
did so in accord with the tendencies of the times, even to the
extent of regulating the slightest details.[4] This is not the place
to formulate a complete historical judgment of his great merits
and the understandable limitations of his government. We are
interested here in two questions: (1) To what extent did his
long and omnipresent activity contribute to defining the spirit
of the institute? and (2) To what measure—the question must
be asked—did his points of view fit within the image that the
founder had of the Congregation?

Obedience and Responsibility

Obviously, such a long and incisive intervention would have
been very dangerous for the new institute's fidelity to its spirit,
if it had not taken place within the lines traced out by the founder. Fortunately, this providential man was deeply penetrated by

the idea of the unique worth of the spirit and ideals of the founder in regulating the life of the young Congregation. In 1862, writing to the Nuncio for the approval of our *Constitutions,* Fr. Xifré ascribes the vitality of the institute as deriving from its docility to its founder.

> This Congregation, Your Excellency, thanks to the Giver of all goods, continues to be animated by the same spirit which its Founder infused in it, and hence, its apostolic works have been highly blessed and fruitful.[5]

In the first chapter of *The Spirit of the Congregation,* written during the Saint's lifetime, Fr. Xifré writes that the Congregation "is the fruit of the burning zeal of Archbishop Claret, a new John of Avila," and therefore pursues the same object as he had in all of his apostolic labor.[6] In the second edition (1892), Fr. Xifré added some paragraphs on the founder's outstanding personality, virtues, and spirit. In 1886 he asked that his companions always be inspired and formed in all they did according to the pattern of their father. Fr. Xifré himself set an example in this, citing Saint Anthony Claret whenever he endeavored to establish some norm for the life and ministry of his Congregation.[7]

Nothing, then, could have been more foreign to the thinking of Fr. Xifré than to attribute to himself the definitive responsibility for the principles that were to regulate the Congregation, and nothing would have wounded him more deeply than to be suspected of straying from the paths marked out by his father. While the latter was alive, Fr. Xifré kept in constant contact with him, asking his advice on all serious matters. For his part, St. Anthony Claret held Xifré in high esteem. When Fr. Sala died, the Saint foresaw that Fr. Xifré would be elected to succeed him and expressed his satisfaction that this should be so.[8] Subsequently, whenever the Saint felt that it was his duty to manifest some desire concerning the management of his work, he addressed himself to Fr. Xifré and stood by his decision, even when the latter did not believe that what the Saint wanted was feasible at the time.[9] Whenever anyone approached the Saint regarding a foundation, he would promptly refer the matter to the father general. Since so many had direct recourse to the archbishop to obtain a community of missionaries, the latter felt obliged repeatedly to define his position with regard to the immediate government of the institute.

> I answered him [he writes to Fr. Xifré about a foundation in Chile] that the Congregation has its Superior General and that he is the one who assigns its personnel and hence, that he should address you.[10]
> I have told both His Lordship [the archbishop of Chile] and the Secretary of the Propaganda, that when they have anything to do with the Congregation, they should not address me, but You, the General, and I gave them a comparison. When a girl gets married, it is not her Father, but her husband, who governs her. I said the same to Señor de Tejada when he spoke to me of a foundation in Alfaro.[11]

Earlier, in 1867, he had given his motives for this prudent behavior in a response to a question by Fr. Xifré.

> As regards the foundation in Jaca, I do not know what to tell you. I am always fearful to advise you when you ask me about matters of the Congregation, because I always remember how cautiously St. Ignatius dealt with the Company, so as not to meddle with those who governed.[12]

Fr. Xifré's fidelity was met by the founder's extreme delicacy. The attitude of both prevented the Congregation from having to experience those ruptures between the father and his first sons that are not rare in the early years of religious orders and congregations.

But if Fr. Xifré's intention was to be totally faithful to the founder, a historical study cannot rest content with listening to these expressions of goodwill and indubitable sincerity. It must sift the measure to which these intentions were carried out throughout the long government of Fr. Xifré. We shall now investigate this matter in its overall features.

Father Xifré's Intervention During the Life of the Founder

In studying Fr. Xifré's intervention in the institute, we must distinguish two periods: (1) a constitutive period, during the life of St. Anthony Mary Claret, from 1858 to 1870; and (2) a purely developmental period, which runs from the death of Claret in 1870 to the death of Fr. Xifré in 1899.

During the first period, Fr. Xifré's government developed under the higher inspiration of the founder. The Saint called on

him to collaborate effectively with him or accepted his intervention in the process the institute was undergoing in developing its
definitive shape.

He also called on him to cooperate in drafting the second
Constitutions. In the 1864 chapter, the fathers had relinquished
any right to make decisions in this respect, entrusting the revision of the primitive text to the Saint. The latter, however,
wished to be advised by the two men in the Congregation who
were best informed and closest to his spirit. The intervention of
the first cannot be documented in detail, but there is no doubt
about the matter. Even before 1864, in his efforts at developing
the juridical section, Fr. Xifré kept up a correspondence with
the procurator in Rome, the Mercedarian, Fr. Reig, submitting
many questions to him.[13] Moreover, it is most probable that
Fr. Xifré was responsible for the first draft of the chapters on
the novices and novicemaster. Two data support this hypothesis:
first, there is no mention of these chapters in all of the correspondence of the founder or the fathers at Segovia with the
community at Vic, while it is certain that the Saint himself did
the chapters on the students and their prefect—we even have the
primitive draft of them; second, the biblical quotes, the vocabulary, and even the choice of virtues for the novitiate chapters
harmonize perfectly with the taste and style of Fr. Xifré. In addition, many of the disciplinary norms in Parts I and II faithfully echo the dispositions the general had been giving his communities at this time. It is clear that these norms, later introduced
into the *Constitutions,* were in response to an experience of domestic life that the founder had no share in.[14]

But Fr. Xifré's most decisive influence during this constitutive period of the Congregation was his increasing explication of
the evangelical life—which was always essential to the institute—
until he brought it to the public profession of vows. As we have
had occasion to see, when we expressly studied the process that
brought the Claretians to the religious life in the canonical sense
of the term, the initiative came from the missionaries at Vic,
and especially Fr. Xifré, both in 1862, with the taking of private
vows, and in 1869, with public profession. Fr. Xifré also took
the initiative with regard to the oath of perseverance, and his
impatience—the basic trait of his temperament—frequently

broke out in impulses to hasten the mechanics of getting the *Constitutions* approved.

Another aspect in which the influence of Fr. Xifré was felt was in promoting devotion to the Heart of Mary within the Congregation. The founder did not distinguish between love for the Blessed Virgin and devotion to the Heart of Mary because, on the one hand, his devotion to the Mother of God was centered on her charity and, on the other, all of his devotion was of a lively and personal character. Contrary to the tendencies of his times, which were so fond of devotions to different aspects or isolated mysteries, the Saint's attention focused on persons, on Christ and Mary. Fr. Xifré, in contrast, seems to have been the first to perceive the special devotion to the Heart of Mary—understood in its concrete expressions—that is entailed in the title. Hence, in the formula of consecration and profession where the Saint wrote: "I consecrate myself to the special service of God, of Jesus Christ and Mary Most Holy," Fr. Xifré corrected it to read: "I consecrate myself to the special service of God and of the Heart of Mary."[15] Likewise, it was the general who took the initiative in solemnly celebrating the feast of the Immaculate Heart, who prescribed that in all missions preached by Claretians the archconfraternity should be established (following the founder's example), and who commanded that an image of the Heart of Mary be placed on the high altars of Claretian churches.[16]

Although the initiative in all these things frequently came from Fr. Xifré, we must remember that the founder approved these decisions. With respect to religious profession, it was the Saint himself who petitioned the Holy See for it; as for concrete manifestations of devotion to the Heart of Mary, he approved the corrections introduced by Xifré in the formula of consecration.[17] It was he, also, who obtained from the Holy See the faculty of celebrating her liturgical feast.[18] On one point they disagreed, in both sensibility and taste: the spread of the institute. St. Anthony Mary Claret was always writing about founding new communities, both in Spain and abroad. He had spoken about this to Xifré, even when the latter was not general, in a letter dated October 1, 1857, telling him that a house should be founded in every diocese of Spain. He did so again in thirteen letters, plus two to Clotet. The Saint took the initiative in founding the house in Segovia, and his support made the foundation in Gracia possible. His efforts were responsible later for the foundations in Algeria and Chile. On August 12, 1859, he asked for a foundation at the Escorial.

> I see in history that all religious orders spread not only throughout the kingdom in which they were founded, but also in different parts of the world [he wrote to Clotet in mid-1861]. Well, then, why do not our members at least spread throughout this kingdom?[19]

It is clear that in this case, the Saint and the general disagreed not only in opinion but in basic sensibility. Claret was more preoccupied about the spread of the institute because his extensive travels throughout Spain had revealed to him the palpable needs of the church; Fr. Xifré, in contrast, was more preoccupied with internal organization. Judging from the Saint's responses to him, the general was always posing the same two objections: (1) the uncertainty of the times, aggravated by the fact that the government of Spain had not yet approved the institute; (2) lack of personnel, aggravated by the fact that their financial resources did not allow them to accept many new members. The archbishop frequently urged Xifré to accept more candidates, without waiting for the government's approval and without fearing for what this might do to the weak economic situation of the Congregation. On April 7, 1859, he writes:

> It seems to me that it would be a good thing to keep on accepting priests and coadjutors who show promise, and thus we shall see whether we spread.[20]

As things turned out, it took the Revolution of 1868, with the expulsion of the missionaries from Spain, to force their spread to Africa and South America.

Xifré's Government after 1870

The constitutive period of the history of the Claretian Congregation comes to a close in 1870, with the definitive approval of its *Constitutions,* the transformation of the priestly association into a Religious Congregation, and the death of the founder. For the next twenty-nine years Fr. Xifré, who had witnessed all this, was to promote its material growth and direct the life of

its communities. This fact alone, plus the absolutist and omnipresent character of his government, helps us understand that
the Congregation must needs have been marked by the influence
of such a vigorous personality.

Hence, any student of the history of the Congregation can do
no less than pay particular attention to this period, establishing
a system of comparisons between the principles that animated
Fr. Xifré's government and the mind of the founder. This is a
necessary step if we bear in mind, as Xifré himself frequently
insisted, that the Congregation must live and move and have its
being in the spirit of St. Anthony Mary Claret, the only man
God called to give it life and the only man who received from
the Lord that fullness of grace and light that must be spread
throughout his work. The singular value of the mind and spirit
of the Saint as a norm for the life of the Congregation has been
definitively stated by the church, which officially pronounced
on the holiness of the great missionary and proposed him as a
model for his sons to imitate.

It seems obvious to us that Fr. Xifré's notion of the Congregation was essentially the same as that of St. Anthony Mary
Claret. We need only compare Xifré's notion of the Congregation in both editions of his *Spirit of the Congregation* with that
in the first and second *Constitutions* to see that they essentially
coincide. For both Xifré and Claret the Congregation is, above
all, an institute of missionaries dedicated to the preaching of the
Word of God, and this is the central idea that presides over its
asceticism and its internal life. This conclusion is reinforced by
the fact that by the founder's own will, Xifré collaborated in
drawing up the definitive text of the *Constitutions* and wrote
the two chapters on the novices and the novicemaster. Moreover, we need only read through the *Circular Letters* of Xifré
to see how he remained faithful to these ideals throughout his
life.[21] Likewise, both the founder and his collaborator shared
the same high ideal of evangelical life, as demanded by the full
living out of a missionary vocation.[22]

Having affirmed the identity of Claret's and Xifré's viewpoints
on the two basic elements of the institute (its essentially missionary character and the high demands for evangelical life implicit in that missionary character), respect for historical truth

leads us to formulate a few reservations. We are not referring to
the government of Fr. Xifré—a matter that future historians will
have to deal with—but, rather, to two of his characteristic traits
that are closely related to the Claretian spirit.

In the first place, there is something in Xifré's writings that
has unfavorably impressed succeeding generations of Claretians,
namely, the narrowness and rigorism of his asceticism. The general lacked one element that St. Anthony Mary Claret possessed
in abundance, namely, the force of an extraordinary mystical
experience that centered the Saint's doctrine in the fundamental aspects of the mystery of Christ. This lack in Xifré, the man
of action, tied him down to some of the more regrettable tendencies of the spiritual milieu in which he was formed. We will
not dwell on this point here. We need only state that there is
no doubt that his teaching magisterium, which he exercised so
abundantly over a long period of time, left a strong mark on the
first generations of Claretians. We should not forget that until
1915, when Frs. Larraona and Postíus began to concentrate on
the study of the founder, the writings of Fr. Xifré were far better known by Claretians than were those of the founder.

In the second place—and this is perhaps more important—Fr.
Xifré had a narrower view than St. Anthony Claret with regard
to a matter of such importance as the means of apostolate that
were best suited to the Congregation. Fr. Xifré, like the rest of
the early missionaries, lacked the ampler experience that the
Saint had enjoyed in Cuba and in Madrid. Contact with the more
urgent needs of the church in his day had led the archbishop to
greatly broaden his apostolic horizons. Discreetly and delicately,
in his letters, in the chapters of 1862 and 1864, and in the new
drafting of the *Constitutions,* the Saint did his best to broaden
the apostolic horizons of his Congregation, as well.

It is clear that Fr. Xifré remained faithful to the primitive
missionary concept of the institute. But this led to a crisis in the
highest government of the Congregation from 1880 on, since its
subdirector general, Fr. James Clotet, defended broader points
of view. Fr. Mariano Aguilar, in his apologia for Fr. Xifré's position against Fr. Clotet and other members of the institute,
makes a number of claims that we would do well to consider.

Several Fathers, with the best of intentions, had striven to have our Congregation open colleges of secondary education, like those of other religious Institutes. Fr. Clotet figured among this group....

Aguilar goes on to relate that it was Fr. Clotet who promoted the foundation of the school in Segovia, and then adds:

In February of the following year, the Fr. General, who did not care for this new course our Congregation was taking, which involved such a large part of our personnel in education, took advantage of Montero Rios' abrogation of the privileges granted by Pidal for secondary teaching, to suppress that college.... There is nothing strange about our Most Reverend Father's having repeatedly opposed certain innovations attempted by some of our members, especially in these latter years. For these—although, doubtless, very well intended—would have greatly altered our way of life and led us somewhat astray from the spirit of our Venerable Founder, which should be the inheritance of all who boast of being his sons.[23]

There was, then, a clear dissent between the two most illustrious collaborators of St. Anthony Mary Claret, Frs. Xifré and Clotet, with regard to their distinct notions as to what means of the apostolate were proper to the Congregation. For the former, the Congregation must dedicate itself to missionary preaching. For the latter, it was within the spirit of the Congregation to dedicate itself to teaching, as well, and even to secondary education. Fr. Aguilar backs the position of Fr. Xifré, which he says is based on the spirit of the founder, and states that Fr. Clotet's criteria would have led astray from the mind of the Saint. But there is no doubt that Fr. Clotet based his claims on the spirit and, indeed, the express will of our founder. A careful collector of the handwritten documents of the Saint, Clotet was well aware that in 1869 the Saint had insistently recommended education as a ministry along with missionary preaching,[24] and that in a number of notes written at that time he had manifested the desire that one missionary in every one of the houses should be dedicated to teaching[25]—something that was far from being carried out, even in 1890. Moreover, the example of the founder's setting up a school in the Escorial led Fr. Clotet to realize that teaching ministry need not curtail the missionary ministry. What had happened, then? Simply, Fr. Xifré remained faithful to the

practice of the earliest days, without heed for the later development and enrichment intended by the founder. Xifré put the
same limitations on directing seminaries, despite the fact that
this was recommended as a preferred ministry in the *Constitutions* themselves. And when Fr. Clotet, following the example
of the founder, wanted to promote priestly associations, he was
forbidden to do so,[26] since Fr. Xifré considered such a project
to be unfeasible.[27]

Nevertheless, the express words of the founder and the insistence of the venerable Father Clotet must have influenced Fr.
Xifré. From 1883 on he began to permit the ministry of teaching (although with a number of misgivings), and later he allowed
teaching in seminaries and spiritual direction of seminarians.

The Servant of God, Father James Clotet

Having demonstrated the essential agreement between Fr. Xifré and the founder on the notion, aims, and religious life of the
Congregation, as well as their differing mentalities with regard
to the means of the apostolate, we must study the contribution
of Fr. James Clotet to the structure and life of the Congregation
during his long life in it.

Life and Mission

It seems that the main mission of James Clotet in the Claretian Congregation was to continue irradiating it with the holiness of the founder. Someone who knew him remarked that
Fr. Clotet was one of those saints God grants to new institutes
to reaffirm the heritage of their founders.[28] St. Anthony Mary
Claret must have intuited this when he called Fr. Clotet to join
his institute, despite the fact that the latter did not have the
ministerial qualities needed for missionary preaching, which was
their exclusive ministry at that time.

Born in 1822, he studied first with the Jesuits at Manresa, his
native town, and then in the seminaries of Barcelona and Vic.
He was ordained a priest in Rome on July 20, 1845. Sent to care
for a parish by his bishop, he soon sensed that this was not his
calling, although he could not tell just what the Lord wanted of
him. He told his bishop of his misgivings, and the latter told him
to put himself at the disposal of the celebrated missionary, Mosén Claret. Swallowing his misgivings about his lack of ability

for the preaching ministry, he decided to join the new institute and dedicate himself to an activity he had perhaps never dreamed of heretofore.[29]

Despite all this, Fr. Clotet joined his companions in preaching missions and giving retreats. Between 1849 and 1858 he preached a total of twenty-eight missions: six in the founding year; ten in the next missionary campaign; and two, five, and three in the succeeding campaigns. Meanwhile, Fr. Sala had entrusted him with the direction of the brothers and with preaching to various communities of sisters in the town. In 1858 Fr. Clotet was elected subdirector general, a post he occupied until 1888. In 1864 he was named local superior of the motherhouse. He was successively at the head of the seminaries of Prades, Thuir, Vic, Gracia, and again Thuir. As subdirector general, he had to take Fr. Xifré's place during the latter's long absences on trips to Equatorial Guinea in Africa and to South America.

Spiritual Profile of Fr. Clotet

Endowed by nature with a very simple and upright disposition and an affectionate and delicate soul, James Clotet found in the religious life an ideal ambient in which to grow in holiness. Heaven seemed to predestine him for this by granting him some notable graces. While he was a student he had a prophetic dream, involving the Blessed Virgin.[30] Throughout the year following his ordination he was favored by the experience of the habitual presence of the Lord.[31] Simple to the point of seeming naive,[32] James Clotet was a minute and introverted man, yet one who was so meek and humble that he won the hearts of those who lived with him. His whole life was spent on becoming holy himself and making it easy for his subjects to do so.

One of his most typical traits was his fidelity to the founder and the *Constitutions.* Clotet carefully collected the Saint's manuscripts, wrote his biography, and strove to put his recommendations into practice. In 1862 the archbishop had recommended that each of the missionaries privately read a chapter from Rodríguez each day.[33] Fr. Clotet must have put this exhortation into practice very early, since in his retreat resolutions for 1865 he proposed to follow this practice with greater fidelity.[34] On the same occasion, while he was making the Spiritual Exercises under the direction of the Saint, he imposed on himself a plan of mortifications imitating that of the founder.[35] This fidelity to his spiritual father was what motivated him later in insisting on opening colleges and on promoting associations for priests. The same motivation also is apparent in his careful observance of the *Constitutions* and in his use of them in his talks to the missionaries,[36] recalling to them the teaching and example of Archbishop Claret.

He resembled St. Anthony Mary Claret in his serenity, in the graciousness with which he presented virtue, in the intimacy of his union with Christ, and in the tender and filial love he had for his heavenly Mother. He also shared and, to some extent, surpassed the Saint in the habitual experience of the contemplation of Christ. This latter seems to have been his most fundamental spiritual trait and his most significant extraordinary gift. Prepared by the unexpected grace of remaining constantly in the presence of God for the entire year following his priestly ordination, the Servant of God felt a lifelong call to the interior life. In 1876 he felt the divine presence with great intensity, losing it only in brief moments of distraction.[37] This phenomenon continued until 1880.[38] In the following year, a brief note of a fault allows us to grasp the point he had reached in this. On June 12 he accuses himself of having glanced at the grass in the field while he was reciting the Lesser Hours, "and this," he states, "caused me a very brief distraction."[39] From this time on, he seems to have enjoyed the habitual imaginary vision of his guardian angel. His imaginary vision of Christ crucified lasted for months and years.[40] On October 15, 1886, he had a habitual intellectual vision of Christ present in the depths of his soul.[41] The Servant of God, Père Jean, abbot of Fontfroide, whom he had consulted on the supernatural value of this grace, calmed him and assured him that it was evidently of divine origin.[42]

From this point of view, his compenetration with the spirit of St. Anthony Mary Claret could not have been more complete. We find a difference from one fundamental aspect of the spirituality of the Saint, namely, in the different roles that apostolic zeal played in their respective spiritualities. A simple glance at the personal writings of Fr. Clotet reveals that we can hardly discover in them—and they are many—a single reference to his apostolic vocation. This corroborates the view that Fr. Clotet's spirituality was predominantly contemplative and centered on problems of his interior life and household living.

His Intervention During the Life of the Founder

St. Anthony Mary Claret always showed a predilection for the Servant of God, Fr. Clotet. Aware of his docility, the Saint let his confidences run freely in expressing his desires in letters to Clotet. In the early years of the Congregation he was entrusted with the care of the brothers, and published for them the *Directori dels Germans Ajudants.* Supplying for Fr. Xifré until 1864, and as superior of the House until 1868, he had also attended to the formation of the first novices and scholastics. He took part in the assembly of 1859 and in the chapters of 1862 and 1864, thus contributing to the definitive form of the *Constitutions.* In the last mentioned Chapter he took Claret's side, overcoming the opposition of some to accepting certain recommendations of the Roman Curia with regard to government.

Given his experience in governing the community, the Saint called him and Fr. Xifré to collaborate with him on the definitive drafting of the *Constitutions.* Fr. Clotet contributed part three, on the brothers, as well as certain norms in the chapter on the local superior and a few aspects of the discipline of the house. Sketches for eleven of these appear in his manuscripts.[43]

Attracted by the Congregation's opportunities for interior life and growth in holiness, Fr. James Clotet was one of the first Claretians who felt a desire to consecrate their apostolic vocation by taking private religious vows. His is the first formula of profession we have. He made his profession before the altar of the Blessed Virgin in Gracia, on Holy Thursday, April 18, 1861. In 1869 he was the first Claretian consulted by Fr. Xifré on the desirability of adopting the practice of obligatory profession and thus becoming a religious Congregation, and he was the first to give his consent.

His Influence in the Congregation from 1870 to 1898

After Claret's death, a good deal of the direction of the institute fell to Fr. Clotet, as the first collaborator of Fr. Xifré. Above all, he continued to watch over the formation of the students, since he was almost uninterruptedly superior of the novitiate and scholasticate in Vic, Thuir, and Santo Domingo. As superior of the general house and central college, he was able, throughout his long rule, to maintain a high level of spirituality and domestic discipline in the institute. The ordinary topics of his talks to the community were the virtues proper of religious.

His special mission during these years seems to have been that of keeping the memory of the founder alive. He soon began collecting testimonies on his sanctity and data on his life and undertakings, maintaining a rich and lively correspondence on the subject and traveling to gather firsthand reports from those who had dealt with Claret. The results of this research appeared in his *Résumé of the Life of . . . Claret,* which was published in 1882. He made a number of pilgrimages to the tomb of the founder and later, as a reward for his devotion, he was entrusted by Fr. Xifré with the task of transferring the Saint's remains to Vic.[44] As we have already seen, his docility to his spiritual father led him to defend a broader view of the apostolate of the institute, in contrast to Fr. Xifré's narrower view.

Nevertheless, it is understandable that since the Servant of God was so little inclined toward action and so fervently dedicated to promoting order and uniformity, his influence on the Congregation had mainly to do with setting a high value on the common elements of the religious life and on its domestic aspects. Except for the two or three years he spent at Vic when he was working on the cause of the Beatification of the Founder, Fr. Clotet did not live in a mission house from 1868 until his death nor did he exercise the preaching ministry, except in talks to the Claretians or to nuns in the vicinity. Since he ruled over a large community and was dedicated to the formation of young men, the prevailing tone of his writings stressed the domestic life that characterized the seminaries, and he treated of such matters with that peculiar minuteness that is so typical of him. A similar process appears in his teaching on the religious life as it appears in his talks to the community. While the talks he gave in 1864 are centered on the apostolic vocation,[45] his later talks, relating to professions, are limited to expositions on the common elements of religious perfection, on its value as a holocaust, on its sense of total consecration to God, without any allusion to the fundamental apostolic meaning of this consecration for the Claretians.[46] We do not mean that Fr. Clotet was totally lacking in awareness of the apostolic thrust of the Congregation.

He always attended to this, whenever his internal tasks permitted it and in accord with his own personal qualities and talents. The fervor with which he dedicated himself to catechesis[47] and his work for the deaf-mute are the result of his apostolic awareness. But it is evident to anyone who reads through his numerous manuscripts that his attention was centered—because of his own personal tendencies and because he was so deeply immersed in an almost purely domestic life—on the common elements and conventual expressions of the religious life. The significant absence of allusions to the apostolic vocation in his notes on his spiritual experiences and mystical gifts set him in sharp contrast to St. Anthony Claret.

Fr. Clotet promoted the transformation of Claretian piety in a community-oriented sense. Meditation in common, confession as a community act, the creation of a new community act by separating the Visit to the Blessed Sacrament from the Rosary, and certain annual devotions were all brought about by his initiative. And it is significant that in all these things, Fr. Clotet was expressly led by the usages of religious orders, especially the monastic orders.[48]

Conclusion

We believe that the instances we have cited suffice to set forth, at least in their essentials, the contributions made by the cofounders, Frs. Xifré and Clotet, to shaping the Claretian spirit. Speaking of each of them, we have arrived at the same conclusion: The fundamental elements of the Claretian spirit and mission in the church appear in each of them with sufficient clarity. On these fundamental issues, they are in complete accord with the founder.

There are some differences, nonetheless, in some important aspects, such as Fr. Xifré's strict conception of the means of the apostolate and Fr. Clotet's absorbing preoccupation with the generic elements of the religious life and with domestic life. In both of these aspects, the two cofounders exercised a profound influence on the Congregation, shaping it in a certain sense. Nevertheless, we judge that this influence was progressively limited, thanks to the General Chapters and to the teachings of the superiors general. The work of the General Chapter of 1922 and the teachings of Frs. García, Moroto, and Schweiger, which were so very attentive to the mind of St. Anthony M. Claret, have all contributed to put in ever-sharper relief the most vividly Claretian traits of the spirit of the Congregation. The Special Chapter held in 1968 completed this movement of return to the founder. It defined religious life in terms of the Claretian missionary goals, redirected the prayer of the Congregation from the devotional and conventual emphasis that was given after the founder's death, and combined a reaffirmation of the missionary calling of the Claretians with the acceptance of a broad spectrum of means to fulfill it.

On the other hand, if we were to set up a comparison between the mind of St. Anthony Mary Claret and that of the two cofounders, not from the point of view of their agreement or of their more or less marginal disagreements but, rather, from the point of view of their importance in an absolute scale of values, then no Claretian should be surprised that we could place the founder on a much higher level than either of his first companions. Both of them lack the Saint's geniality, the acute and lively sensitivity to the needs of the church, the sense of events (the "signs of the times"), and the prophetic understanding of history, which were so notable in Claret. There is nothing strange about this; figures as genial as Claret's rarely appear in the same milieu. The admiration that Frs. Xifré and Clotet felt for their founder was based not only in a feeling of loving sonship but upon their consciousness of the holy archbishop's superiority to them.

NOTES TO CHAPTER I

1. H. (Jerome) Nadal, S.J., "Exhortationes Colonienses, 1, 3," in *Commentarii de Instituto Sociatatis Iesu* (Rome, 1962), p. 779.

2. S. John of the Cross, "The Living Flame of Love," Stanza 2, nn. 12-13, in *The Collected Works of Saint John of the Cross,* trans. by K. Kavanaugh and O. Rodriguez (Garden City, N.Y.: Doubleday, 1964), p. 599.

3. J. M. Lozano, "Founder and Community: Inspiration and Charism," *Review for Religious* 37 (1978): 214-236. *El Fundador y su Familia Religiosa* (Madrid: Instituto Vida Religiosa), 1978.

4. *Lumen Gentium,* 42-43; *Perfectae Caritatis,* 12.

5. *Perfectae Caritatis,* 1 and 8.

6. *Evangelica Testificatio,* 11.

7. Paul III, *Regiminis militantis,* 2; Julius III, *Exposcit debitum,* 2. Pius VI, Encycl., *Quod Albiquantum,* March 10, 1791; Pius IX, Encycl. *Ubi Primum,* May 17, 1847; Pius XI, *Epistula Unigenitus: AAS* 16 (1924), 135.

8. *Perfectae Caritatis,* 2.

9. Saint Anthony M. Claret, *Autobiography* (*Autob.* hereafter) (Chicago: Claretian Publications, 1976), n. 113, p. 48.

10. Athanasius, "Life of Saint Anthony," 2, in *Early Christian Biographies,* ed. Roy J. Deferrari, *The Fathers of the Church* 15 (1952), p. 135.

11. *Autob.,* nn. 114, 118, pp. 48-49.

12. Ibid., nn. 681-682, p. 237.

13. It is even possible that the Greek *Huios*—Son—in the Synoptic accounts of the Baptism may correspond to an Aramaic *Abdhi*—my Servant. Cf. W. Zimmerli and J. Jeremias, *The Servant of God* (London, 1957), pp. 81-82, O. Cullmann, *The Christology of the New Testament* (London, 1959), p. 66.

14. "Luces y Gracias," 1859, in *Escritos Autobiográficos y Espirituales* (*Escritos* hereafter), pp. 636-637.

15. *Autob.,* n. 687, p. 239.

16. Ibid., nn. 117-118, p. 49.

17. S. Antonio M. Claret, *Constituciones y Textos sobre la Congregación de Misioneros* (*Constituciones y Textos* hereafter), ed. Juan M. Lozano (Barcelona: Editorial Claret, 1972), p. 564.

18. *Autob.,* nn. 215-224, pp. 78-80.

19. Ibid., nn. 9-15, pp. 6-7.

20. Ibid., n. 216, p. 79.

21. Cf. ibid., nn. 662-663, p. 232.

22. Ibid., n. 263, p. 93.

23. Ibid., n. 118, p. 49.

24. Ibid., n. 113, p. 48.

25. Ibid., n. 114, p. 48.

26. Ibid., n. 120, pp. 49-50.

27. Ibid., nn. 115-117, pp. 48-49.

28. J. M. Lozano, *Mystic and Man of Action,* trans. J. Daries (Chicago: Claretian Publications, 1977), pp. 161-162.

29. *Autob.,* nn. 357-358, p. 121.

30. Ibid., nn. 310-311, pp. 107-108.

31. Ibid., nn. 195-198, pp. 73-74.

32. Ibid., n. 466, pp. 148-149.

33. Ibid., n. 442, p. 142. *Pastoral Letter to the Cuban People,* Santiago, 1853, p. 5; Retreat of 1865 in *Constituciones y Textos,* p. 581.

34. *El Colegial o Seminarista Instruido* (Barcelona, 1961), II, pp. 269-270.

35. *Autob.,* nn. 340-353, pp. 116-118.

36. *Constituciones y Textos,* pp. 564-567, 584-585.

37. Ibid., pp. 193 ff., 469 ff.

38. *Autob.,* nn. 428-437, pp. 139-140.

39. Cf. X. Léon-Dufour, "Servant of God," in *Dictionary of Biblical Theology,* new rev. ed. (New York: Seabury Press, 1973), pp. 531-533. Also J. McKenzie, "Servant of the Lord," *Dictionary of the Bible* (Milwaukee: Pruce Publ., 1965), pp. 791-794.

40. *Autob.,* n. 120, pp. 49-50.

41. Ibid., n. 118, p. 49.

42. Cf. "Luces y Gracias," 1859, in *Escritos,* p. 637.

43. *Constituciones y Textos,* p. 359.

44. *Autob.,* nn. 193-198.

45. *El Colegial o Seminarista Instruido* (Barcelona, 1961), II, pp. 269-270.

46. *Autob.,* n. 118, p. 49.

47. Alfonso Maria de' Liguori, *Selva di materie predicabili* (Bassano, 1833).

48. Cf. *Constituciones y Textos,* p. 35. Geminiano Mislei, S.J. (1803-1867), author of several books of spirituality, elected Vicar of the General in 1963.

49. V. Juan de Avila (now Saint), *Obras* (Madrid, 1759), 9 vols. S. Francisco de Sales, *Obras* (Madrid: Ortega, 1768-1771).

50. P. Segneri, *El Cristiano Instruido* (Barcelona: Giralt, 1693), 4 vols.; *Panegíricos* (Barcelona: Giralt, 1720). P. Segneri Juniore, *Opere* (Bassano: Remondini, 1795), 3 vols.

51. L. Siniscalchi, *Quaresimale,* ed. 5 (Venice, 1773). F. Cuniliati, *El Catequista en el Púlpito,* ed. 2

(Madrid, 1797). M. de Santander, *Pláticas Doctrinales sobre el Sacramento de la Penitencia* (Bogotá, 1829). *Doctrinas y Sermones para Misión* (Madrid, 1802), 5 vols. A. Valsecchi, *Prediche Quaresimali* (Venice, 1837).

52. Cf. P. Hitz, C.SS.R., *To Preach the Gospel,* trans. R. Sheed (New York: Sheed and Ward, 1963), pp. 107-110.

53. *Autob.,* n. 118, p. 49.

54. Ibid., nn. 8-15, pp. 5-7.

55. Ibid., n. 311, p. 108.

56. Ibid., n. 310, pp. 107-108. *Memoir for the Academy of Saint Michel* (Madrid, 1854), p. 9.

57. *Autob.,* n. 545, pp. 200-201.

58. *Las Bibliotecas Populares* (Madrid, 1864), p. 18.

NOTES TO CHAPTER II

1. *Autob.,* n. 105, pp. 31-32.

2. *Processus Informativus Vicensis* (Informative Process for Claret's Beatification, Vich) (PIV hereafter), sess. 82, art. 97.

3. *Autob.,* n. 138, pp. 56-57.

4. Documents Apostolic Fraternity; I and II: *Constituciones y Textos,* pp. 35-59. Letter to Soler, November 25, 1842, *Epistolario Claretiano* (*EC* hereafter), I, p. 114.

5. *Autob.,* n. 167, p. 66.

6. Ibid., n. 193, p. 72.

7. Letter to Soler, November 25, 1842, *EC* I, pp. 112-116.

8. F. Aguilar, *Vida del Excmo. e Ilmo. Sr. D. Antonio M. Claret, Misioneros Apostólico, Arzobispo de Cuba y después de Trajanópolis* (*Vida del Excmo.* hereafter) (Madrid, 1871).

9. Letter of Soler to Masmitjá, December 17, 1844; copy in Studium Claretianum, Rome.

10. *Constituciones y Textos,* p. 79.

11. Ibid., p. 32.

12. Claret's letters to Caixal, March 26 and May 28, 1847, *EC* I, pp. 205, 220.

13. F. Aguilar, *Vida del Excmo.,* pp. 80-81.

14. *Liber defunctorum,* p. 1; Archives of the Claretian Generalate, Rome.

15. Quoted by E. Fort Cogull, *El Beato Claret y el Arzobispado de Tarragona* (Tarragona, 1949), p. 126. Cf. E. Fort i Cogull, *Fra Ignasi Carbó i Florensa, fill de la Riba, Monjo de Poblet i Missioner Claretiá* (Tarragona, 1935).

16. Claret's letter to Casadevall, February 4, 1847, *EC* I, pp. 198-199.

17. *Constituciones y Textos* (Document IV), pp. 84-87.

18. Cf. V. Porta y Villalta, *Biografía del Excmo. e Ilmo. Sr.*

Dr. D. José Caixal Estradé, obispo de Urgel (Barcelona, 1898).

19. *Constituciones y Textos* (Document V), pp. 88-91.

20. The manuscript of the notes taken by Benet during this retreat has been preserved: "Algunas breus apuntacions que féu José Benet para son us privat de las Meditacions y Platicas dels Exercisis espirituals que donaba al Clero de la ciutat de Vich lo R. A. Claret en lo any 1844," Ms in 4°, cf. S. Vela, *Ensayo de una Biblioteca Ibero-Americana de la Orden de S. Agustín* (Madrid, 1913), I, pp. 367-368.

21. *Constituciones y Textos,* p. 91.

22. Ibid. (Document VII), pp. 100-101.

23. Claret's letter to Caixal, May 28, 1847, *EC* I, p. 221.

24. *Autob.,* n. 592, p. 212.

25. Claret's letters to Casadevall, February 4 and 22, 1847, *EC* I, pp. 199, 201.

26. *EC* I, p. 186.

27. Cf. "Apuntes doctrinales sobre el Decálogo al ús de Fr. José Benet fets per la Quaresma predicada en Solsona any 1848," Mss in 4°, cf. S. Vela, pp. 367-368.

28. *Revista Católica* (Barcelona) 13, (1848/2) 57.

29. Claret's letter to Caixal, June 19, 1847, *EC* I, pp. 224-225.

30. Letter to Caixal, July 3, 1847, *EC* I, p. 227.

31. Letter to Caixal, July 22, 1847, *EC* I, p. 213.

32. Letters to Cruells, April 3, 1847, *EC* I, p. 223.

33. To Caixal, May 28, 1847, *EC* I, p. 231.

34. To Caixal, March 26, 1847, *EC* I, p. 207.

35. To Caixal, May 28 and August 12, 1847, *EC* I, pp. 221-222, 237.

36. *EC* I, pp. 243-244.

37. Ibid., p. 237.

38. *Constituciones y Textos* (Document III), p. 79.

39. Claret's letter to Caixal, December 11, 1848, *EC* I, pp. 284-287.

40. *Autob.,* n. 477, p. 152.

41. *EC* I, pp. 273-276.

42. Ibid., pp. 277-280.

43. Ibid., p. 283.

44. The rights of Don Carlos were based on the provisions of the Salic Law, promulgated by Philip V, excluding women from succession to the throne of Spain. Partisans of the absolute power of the king, opposed to the liberal Constitution, gathered about Don Carlos. The Spanish bishops accepted the succession of Isabel II, despite the Vatican's reluctance to her recognition. But a number of the clergy, and among them some bishops, had strong sympathies for the "Catholic monarchy," of which Don Carlos seemed the very incarnation.

45. Cf. J. M. Lozano, *Con mi Iglesia te desposaré, Estudio sobre la experiencia religiosa de la Sierva de Dios M. Antonia París* (Madrid,

1974), pp. 137-151. Later, when Sor Antonia was called to Cuba by Claret, she founded, together with him, the Congregation of Claretian Missionary Sisters, the Teaching Sisters of the Immaculate Conception, in 1855.

46. Claret to Caixal, December 11, 1848, *EC* I, pp. 284-287.

47. Cf. *Revista Católica* (Barcelona) 13 (1848/2), 57.

48. *Autob.*, n. 488, p. 155.

49. *Processus Apostolicus Vicensis* (Apostolic Process for Claret's Beatification, Vich) (PAV hereafter), sess. 43 ad 25.

50. *EC* I, p. 283.

51. *Constituciones y Textos* (Document III), p. 79.

52. J. Xifré, *Espíritu de la Congregación*, ed. 2 (Madrid, 1892), pp. 12-13.

53. Ibid., p. 13.

54. J. Clotet, *Notas para los Anales.*

55. C. Fernández, *La Congregación de los Misioneros Hijos del Inmaculado Corazón de María*, I (Madrid, 1967), p. 101.

NOTES TO CHAPTER III

1. Claret to Caixal, May 29, 1849, *EC* I, pp. 291-292.

2. Claret to Barjau, January 8, 1858, *EC* I, pp. 1488-1489.

3. Cf. Document V: *Constituciones y Textos*, p. 89.

4. Ibid., p. 89.

5. Claret to Caixal, May 20, 1850, *EC* I, p. 381; June 13, 1850, *EC* I, p. 394.

6. *Autob.*, n. 489, pp. 155-156.

7. Claret to Pius IX, April 3, 1859, *EC* I, p. 1740.

8. Claret to Nuntius Barilli, July 29, 1859, *EC* I, p. 1835.

9. *El Colegial Instruido* (Barcelona, 1861), II, p. 263.

10. Ibid., p. 269.

11. Cf. *Constituciones y Textos*, p. 566, n. 5; p. 563, n. 3; p. 570, n. 4.

12. *Perfectae Caritatis*, 2 b.

13. *Constitutions*, 1857, n. 2; *Constituciones y Textos*, pp. 167-169.

14. *Constitutions*, 1865, n. 2; *Constituciones y Textos*, p. 359.

15. *Constituciones y Textos*, p. 87.

16. Ibid., p. 103.

17. Ibid., p. 107.

18. Ibid., p. 629.

19. Claret to Nuntius Barilli, February 2, 1864, *EC* II, p. 761. For the *Breve Noticia*, cf. *Annales Congregationis C.M.F.* (*Annales* hereafter) 35 (1939): 165-166.

20. Claret to Xifré, July 16, 1869, *EC* II, p. 1406.

21. IIa-IIae q 26 aa 1-4.

22. *Constitutions,* 1857, ch. 1; *Constituciones y Textos,* pp. 165-169.

23. *Constitutions,* 1857, ch. 2-8; *Constituciones y Textos,* pp. 170-191.

24. *Constitutions,* 1857, ch. 9; *Constituciones y Textos,* pp. 192-231.

25. *Constitutions,* 1857, ch. 10; *Constituciones y Textos,* pp. 231-237.

26. *Examen S.J.,* 1.2.

27. IIa-IIae q 188 a 2 ad 1.

28. *Contra Impugn.,* 1.

29. C. Fernández, *El Beato Padre Claret* (Madrid: Coculsa, 1949), I, p. 425.

30. *Constituciones y Textos,* p. 117.

31. *Conferencias de S. Vicente de Paul* (Barcelona, 1857), p. 20.

32. *Plan for the Academy of St. Michael* (Barcelona, 1859), p. 4.

33. *Apuntes de un Plan* (Madrid, 1865), p. 127.

34. Claret to Brunelli, August 12, 1849, *EC* I, pp. 304 ff.

35. Claret to Pius IX, April 3, 1859, *EC* I, pp. 1740-1741.

36. Claret to Gregory XVI, August 1845, *EC* I, pp. 147-150.

37. Claret to Nuntius Barilli, February 4, 1864, *EC* II, p. 761.

38. *Annales* 15 (1915): 304.

39. J. Xifré, *Espíritu de la Congregación* (Vich, 1867), p. 1.

40. *Revista Católica* 47 (Barcelona, 1962): 426.

41. Circular Letter, November 22, 1890: *Circulares* (Madrid: Coculsa, 1941), p. 25.

42. *Annales* 15 (1915): 190-191.

43. J. Clotet, *Notas para los Anales,* p. 1.

44. PIV, sess. 82. Cf. F. de A. Aguilar, *Vida del Excmo.,* p. 43.

45. PIV, sess. 82.

46. Claret to Barilli, February 2, 1864, *EC* II, p. 761; Claret to Xifré, July 16, 1869, *EC* II, pp. 1405-1408.

47. Claret to Nuntius Barilli, February 2, 1864, *EC* II, p. 761.

48. *Autob.,* n. 199, p. 74.

49. Ibid., nn. 200-213, pp. 74-78.

50. Cf. *Cartas Pastorales...del Excmo. Sr. D. Felipe Beltrán* (Madrid, 1783), I, pp. 3-58.

51. *Constitutions,* 1865, I, 2; *Constituciones y Textos,* p. 359.

52. *Constitutions,* 1857, n. 2; *Constituciones y Textos,* pp. 167-169.

53. *Avisos a un Sacerdote* (Barcelona: Pla, 1846), p. 48.

54. *Reglas Clérigos* (1864), pp. 7-8.

55. Claret to Nuntius Brunelli, August 12, 1849, *EC* I, pp. 304 ff.

56. Claret to Ramonet, June 26, 1861, *EC* II, pp. 316-317; Claret to Nuntius Barilli, February 2, 1864, *EC* II, p. 761. Retreat of 1865, second talk, *Constituciones y Textos,* pp. 583-585.

NOTES TO CHAPTER IV

1. PIV, sess. 82.

2. J. Clotet, *Notas para los Anales,* p. 1. Cf. also J. Clotet, *Resumen de la admirable vida,* p. 48.

3. J. Xifré, "Crónica de la Congregación," in *Annales* 15 (1915): 304.

4. *Constituciones y Textos* (Document VIII), p. 103.

5. Ibid. (Document I), p. 33.

6. Ibid. (Document IX), pp. 107-108.

7. Claret to Nuntius Brunelli, August 12, 1849, *EC* I, p. 305.

8. *Constitutions,* 1857, nn. 87-91; *Constituciones y Textos,* pp. 231-235.

9. *Constitutions,* 1857, n. 17; *Constituciones y Textos,* p. 177.

10. *Constitutions,* 1857, nn. 114-125; *Constituciones y Textos,* pp. 245-247.

11. *Constitutions,* 1857, nn. 66, 70, 71, etc.; *Constituciones y Textos,* pp. 209, 213.

12. *Revista Católica* 48 (Barcelona, 1962): 218-224.

13. Ibid., 47 (Barcelona, 1962): 426.

14. Claret to Ramonet, April 20, 1861, *EC* II, p. 270.

15. *Positio Prima super Constitutionibus C.M.F.* I, pp. 107-108; II, p. 257.

16. J. Clotet, *Notas para los Anales,* p. 1.

17. *Constituciones y Textos,* pp. 107 ff.

18. Ibid., p. 103.

19. *Constitutions,* 1857, n. 87; *Constituciones y Textos,* p. 231.

20. Claret to Gregory XVI, August 1845, *EC* I, p. 147.

21. Claret to Caixal, September 5, 1849, *EC* I, pp. 314 ff.

22. Claret to Caixal, June 13, 1850, *EC* I, pp. 393-394.

23. Claret to Caixal, July 12, 1850, *EC* I, p. 410.

24. Cf. *Autob.,* n. 476, pp. 151-152 (the Librería Religiosa); nn. 555-556, p. 203 (the seminary in Cuba); n. 560, p. 204 (the Confraternity of Christian Doctrine); nn. 563-567, pp. 204-205 (the model ranch and school for needy girls and boys); n. 568, pp. 205-206 (social writings and works, such as licensed credit unions); n. 581, p. 209 (the Academy of Saint Michael); n. 799, pp. 279-280 (clergy living in community and parish lending libraries).

25. Claret to Xifré, March 6, May 1, November 18, 1863; November 8, 1864; February 16, 1866, *EC* II, pp. 635 ff., 721-722, 828-829, 986-987. Claret to Clotet, December 19, 1863, *EC* II, pp. 734-735.

26. Claret to Xifré, May 1, 1863, *EC* II, pp. 650 ff.

27. *Posito super Constitutionibus C.M.F.* II, p. 739.

28. *Constitutions,* 1857, n. 87; *Constituciones y Textos,* p. 231.

29. *Constitutions,* 1865, II, n. 63;

Constituciones y Textos, pp. 421-423.

30. Claret to Xifré, July 16, 1869; *EC* II, pp. 1405 ff.

31. "Notas sobre la Congregación VIII"; *Constituciones y Textos,* p. 633.

32. Cf. *Constituciones y Textos,* p. 632.

33. Claret to Xifré, July 16, 1869; *EC* II, p. 1406.

34. Claret to Xifré, August 20, 1861; *EC* II, pp. 349-352. Claret to Mother A. París, February 23, 1863, *EC* II, pp. 626 ff.

35. *Autob.,* n. 678, p. 237; cf. "Luces y Gracias," in *Escritos,* p. 632.

36. "Retreat Resolutions for 1858," in *Escritos,* p. 555.

37. *Autob.,* nn. 646, 763, pp. 228, 271.

38. *Constitutions,* 1865, n. 2; *Constituciones y Textos,* p. 359.

39. *Apuntes de un Plan* (Madrid, 1865), p. 41.

40. *Constitutions,* 1865, I, n. 95; *Constituciones y Textos,* p. 453.

41. *Constitutions,* 1865, II, nn. 82, 85; *Constituciones y Textos,* pp. 441, 442.

42. *Constituciones y Textos,* pp. 275-277.

43. Cited in C. Fernández, *Compendio Histórico de la Congregación,* p. 760.

44. General Chapter 1904, Acts, p. 42 (Archives of the Claretian Generalate).

45. *Codex Iuzis Addititii,* n. 544. Cf. General Chapter 1922, sess. 51.

46. *Constitutions,* 1865, II, n. 63; *Constituciones y Textos,* p. 521.

47. *EC* II, pp. 635, 650, 721, 734, 828, 986.

48. Claret to Xifré, July 16, 1869, *EC* II, pp. 1405 ff.

NOTES TO CHAPTER V

1. *Constitutions,* 1857, nn. 48, 57-59, 64-66, 70, 73, 77, 81, 85-88, etc.; *Constituciones y Textos,* pp. 193, 199-201, 205-209, 213, 215, 221, 225, 229-231.

2. *Constitutions,* 1857, n. 17, p. 177.

3. Ibid., n. 44, pp. 187-189.

4. Ibid., n. 47, pp. 189-191.

5. *Constitutions,* 1865, I, 58, 60; *Constituciones y Textos,* pp. 417, 419.

6. *Constitutions,* 1865, I, 62, p. 421.

7. J. Xifré, *Instructio pro examine personali eorum qui in*

Congregationem missionariorum Imm. Cordis B.M.V. admitti postulant (Barcelona, 1864), pp. 3-5; *Constituciones y Textos,* pp. 654-656.

8. *Constitutions,* 1857, n. 43, p. 187.

9. *Constitutions,* 1865, I, 82, p. 441.

10. Ibid., I, 82, p. 441.

11. Ibid., I, 83, p. 441.

12. Ibid., I, 85, p. 443.

13. Ibid., I, 104, p. 457.

14. *Constitutions,* 1857, n. 60, p. 201.

15. Ibid., nn. 64 ff., pp. 205 ff.

16. Ibid., nn. 71, 73-74, 77, pp. 213-217, 221.

17. *Constitutions,* 1865, II, 6, p. 477.

18. Ibid., II, 14, p. 485.

19. Ibid., II, 12, p. 483.

20. Ibid., II, 11, p. 481.

21. *Constituciones y Textos,* p. 564.

22. Ibid., pp. 567-578.

23. Ibid., p. 581.

24. Ibid., p. 583.

25. Ibid., pp. 585-604.

26. Ibid., pp. 585 ff.

27. Ibid., p. 588.

28. *Autob.,* n. 340, p. 116.

29. Cf. J. M. Lozano, *Mystic and Man of Action,* pp. 184-201, 269-272.

30. *Autob.,* n. 491, p. 156.

31. *Reglas para Clérigos* (Barcelona, 1864), pp. 5-6; *Constituciones y Textos,* pp. 628-630.

32. *Apuntes de un Plan* (Madrid, 1865), pp. 40-41.

33. *L'Egoismo vinto* (Rome, 1869), pp. 51-52.

34. Claret to Xifré, October 1, 1857; August 4, November 4, 1858; August 12, 1859; in *EC* I, pp. 1419-1450, 1623-1626, 1657-1658, and II, pp. 16-20.

35. Claret to Xifré, October 30, 1862; March 6, May 1, 1863; July 16, 1869; *EC* II, pp. 558-564, 635-638, 650-653, 1405-1408.

36. Mss. Clotet I, pp. 355 ff.

37. Cf. *Constituciones y Textos,* pp. 617-625.

38. *Miscelánea Interesante* (Barcelona, 1865), pp. 323 ff.

39. *Revista Católica* 48 (Barcelona, 1862): 220. Cf. *Constituciones y Textos,* p. 619.

40. *Revista Católica* 48 (Barcelona, 1862): 220-221. Cf. *Constituciones y Textos,* p. 620.

41. *Revista Católica* 48 (Barcelona, 1862): 620.

42. *Espíritu de la Congregación* (Vich, 1867), foreword.

43. Ibid., pp. 17 ff.

44. *Autob.,* n. 494, p. 157.

45. Ibid., n. 223, p. 80.

46. Ibid., n. 224, p. 80.

47. Claret to Caixal, September 5, 1849, *EC* I, pp. 314-317.

48. *Annales* 15 (1915): 207.

49. *Autob.,* n. 491, p. 156.

50. *Constitutions,* 1857, nn. 64-67; *Constituciones y Textos,* pp. 205-209. Cf. *Autob.,* nn. 192-198, pp. 72-74.

51. *Constitutions,* 1865, II, 44, p. 507 and *Autob.,* nn. 484-485, p. 154.

52. *Constitutions,* 1857, ch. XI, XII, pp. 237-247.

53. Ibid., n. 49, p. 193.

54. *Revista Católica* 54 (1864): 26.

55. Ibid., 48 (1862): 298; 52 (1863): 485.

56. *EC* I, pp. 310-313. Concerning the life of the community at Segovia in its earliest days, see "Crónica de la Casa de Segovia," by Fr. Clement Serrat, in *Crónica de la Provincia Claretiana de Castilla,* 1951-1952, pp. 369-373; 1953-1954, pp. 15-21; 1955-1956, pp. 110, 116.

57. *Constitutions,* 1857, nn. 114-125, pp. 245-247.

58. Ibid., n. 114, p. 245.

59. Ibid., n. 117, p. 245.

60. Acta of the General Chapter of 1862, in *Positio super Constitutionibus C.M.F.* II, p. 128.

61. *Constitutions,* 1865, II, 41, pp. 505-507.

62. *Constitutions,* 1857, nn. 100, 104-105, pp. 239-241.

63. *Constitutions,* 1865, II, 50-51, p. 511.

64. Mss. Claret X, p. 35; Claret to Xifré, August 4, 1958, *EC* I, pp. 1623-1626.

65. Claret to Caixal, September 5, 1849, *EC* I, pp. 314-317.

66. Claret to Sala, February 27, 1850, *EC* I, pp. 359-363: "My plan is to put a house in each diocese."

67. Claret to Xifré, August 4, 1858, *EC* I, pp. 1623-1626.

68. Claret to Xifré, August 12, 1859, *EC* II, pp. 16-20.

69. Claret to Xifré, November 3 and 30, 1858, *EC* I, pp. 1657-1658, 1678 ff.

70. Claret to Xifré, September 7 and 9, 1861, *EC* II, pp. 375 ff., 378-379.

71. Claret to Xifré, May 20, 1866, *EC* II, pp. 1007-1008.

72. Claret to Xifré, February 28 and July 4, 1869, *EC* II, pp. 1243 ff., 1399-1400.

73. Claret to Xifré, March 14 and April 27, 1868, *EC* II, pp. 1247-1250, 1260-1261.

74. Claret to Xifré, July 4, September 12, October 27, and November 16, 1869, *EC* II, pp. 1399-1400, 1417-1418, 1427-1428, 1429 ff.

75. Claret to Xifré, November 16, 1869, *EC* II, p. 1317.

76. *EC* I, pp. 1625-1626.

77. *EC* II, p. 19.

78. Letter to Clotet, *EC* II, p. 321.

79. *EC* II, pp. 1007-1008.

80. Claret to Xifré, October 1, 1857, *EC* I, pp. 1419-1420.

81. Ibid.

82. Claret to Xifré, November 30, 1858, *EC* I, p. 1680. See also *Apuntes de un Plan* (Madrid, 1865), pp. 40-41.

83. Cf. Claret to Xifré, August 4, November 3 and 30, 1858, *EC* I, pp. 1624, 1658, 1680.

84. *EC* I, p. 1419.

85. *Constitutions*, 1865, I, 2, p. 359.

86. Claret to Xifré, November 21, 1862, *EC* II, p. 568.

87. *Apuntes de un Plan* (Madrid, 1865), p. 41.

88. On retreats at Vich, cf. C. Fernández, *El Beato Claret*, I, p. 551. In the Archives of Vich, there is a copy of the book of retreatants, opened by the founder. On retreats at Segovia, cf. *Crónica de la Provincia Claretiana de Castilla*, VII (1953-1954), pp. 119-120. See also J. Clotet, *Directori dels Hermanos Ajudants* (Vich, 1858), pp. 46 ff.

89. Claret to Xifré, September 17, 1867, *EC* II, pp. 1199-1200.

90. *Positio super Constitutionibus*, I, pp. 64-65.

91. *Constitutions*, 1865, I.4, p. 361.

92. Cf. J. Clotet, *Directori dels Hermanos Ajudants* (Vich, 1858), pp. 69-71.

93. Claret to Xifré, September 17, 1867, *EC* II, pp. 1199-1200.

94. *Reglas para Clérigos* (Barcelona, 1864), pp. 7-8; *Constituciones y Textos*, pp. 629-630.

95. M. Aguilar, *Historia de la*

Congregación (Madrid, 1910), I, p. 43.

96. M. Aguilar, *Biografía de . . . P. Esteban Sala* (Barcelona, 1901), pp. 33, 41; *Biografía del S. de D. P. Jaime Clotet* (Barcelona, 1907), p. 54.

97. C. Fernández, *La Congregación*, p. 162.

98. Ibid., p. 143. Cf. C. Fernández, *El Beato Claret*, I, p. 547.

99. J. Clotet, *Notas para los Anales*, p. 4.

100. Cf. C. Fernández, *La Congregación*, I, p. 140.

101. J. Clotet, *Notas para los Anales*, p. 6.

102. *Constitutions*, 1857, pp. 75-76 (in the original edition).

103. Ibid., nn. 141-165, pp. 253-265.

104. *Positio super Constitutionibus*, II, p. 124.

105. Cf. C. Fernández, *La Congregación*, pp. 481-482.

106. *Reglas para Clérigos* (Barcelona, 1864), pp. 5-6; *Constituciones y Textos*, p. 629.

107. *Constitutions*, 1857, n. 5; *Constituciones y Textos*, p. 171.

108. *Constitutions*, 1857, nn. 141-165, pp. 253-265.

109. Ibid., p. 257.

110. *Constitutions*, 1865, I, 5, 61; II, 1, 4, pp. 361, 419, 527, 529.

111. *Reglas para Clérigos*, pp. 5-6; *Constituciones y Textos*, p. 629.

112. *Directori del Hermanos Ajudants* (Vich, 1858), pp. 48-68.

113. *Autob.*, n. 491, p. 156.

114. *L'Egoismo Vinto* (Rome, 1869), p. 52. We might also note here that the 1865 *Constitutions* speak of the "sacred ministry" in Article 84 of the chapter on novices, written by Fr. Xifré. In this case, we might wonder whether Fr. Xifré lost sight of the brother novices while drafting this chapter or whether he understood "sacred ministry" in a rather broad sense. As to Fr. Xifré's authorship of the chapter in question, see *Constituciones y Textos*, p. 275.

115. *Positio super Constitutionibus,* II, p. 124. Cf. *Constituciones y Textos*, p. 361.

116. *Constitutions,* 1857, n. 88, p. 231; *Constitutions,* 1865, II, 63, p. 521.

117. Cf. "Constituciones de la Hermandad del Smo. e Ido. Corazón de María," n. 19, in *Constituciones y Textos*, p. 121. See also *Religiosas en sus Casas* (Barcelona, 1850).

118. Claret to Xifré, July 16, 1869, *EC* II, pp. 1905-1906.

119. *Constitutions,* 1857, n. 91, pp. 233-235; *Autob.*, nn. 310-322, pp. 107-111.

NOTES TO CHAPTER VI

1. *Autob.*, n. 340, p. 116; *Constitutions,* 1857, n. 60; *Constituciones y Textos*, p. 201.

2. *Autob.*, n. 438, p. 141.

3. Ibid., nn. 390-413, pp. 130-136.

4. Ibid., nn. 357-371, pp. 121-124.

5. *Escritos,* B.A.C., pp. 434-437.

6. Claret to Caixal, September 5, 1849, *EC* I, pp. 314-317.

7. Cf. Claret to Xifré, December 6, 10 and 13, 1862, and November 22, 1863, *EC* II, pp. 572, 573, 574-575, 723.

8. *EC* II, pp. 279 ff.

9. *Constituciones y Textos*, p. 632. Written in 1869 or 1870.

10. *L'Egoismo Vinto* (Rome, 1869), p. 51.

11. Ibid., pp. 47-62.

12. Ibid., pp. 51-52.

13. Cf. *La Congregación de los Misioneros Hijos del Ido. Corazón de María* (Madrid, 1967), pp. 479-500.

14. Concordat of 1851, Art. 29. Cf. E. Piñuela, *El Concordato de 1851* (Madrid, 1921), p. 234.

15. *Autob.*, n. 488, p. 155.

16. J. Clotet, *Notas para los Anales,* p. 1; *Resumen de la Vida admirable,* p. 138.

17. Ms. Claret X, 23, Cf. *Constituciones y Textos*, p. 563.

18. Claret to Ramonet, June 26, 1861, *EC* II, pp. 316-317.

19. *Reglas para Clérigos* (Barcelona, 1864), pp. 5-8. Cf. *Constituciones y Textos,* pp. 628-630; *Avisos a un sacerdote* (Barcelona: Pla, 1846), pp. 47-48.

20. *Constitutions,* 1865, I, nn. 76, 78, 80; *Constituciones y Textos,* pp. 437, 439. The reference to *defectus spiritus religiosi* in n. 88 of the Claretian *Constitutions* was added in 1922, based on a 1869 text of Fr. Xifré.

21. *Apuntes de un Plan* (Madrid, 1865), pp. 40-41.

22. *Guía para la dirección de las Hermanas de enseñanza de la Purísima Concepción* (Barcelona, 1851).

23. Cited in C. Fernández, *La Congregación . . . , p. 178.*

24. Ms. Clotet I, p. 361. Archives of the Claretian Generalate.

25. J. M. Lozano, *Con mi Iglesia te desposaré. Estudio sobre la experiencia religiosa de la Sierva de Dios M. Antonia París* (Madrid, 1974), pp. 137-157.

26. M. Aguilar, *Historia de la Congregación,* I, p. 111.

27. Claret to Xifré, April 20, 1861, *EC* II, pp. 266-269.

28. Cf. C. Fernández, *La Congregación . . . , p. 482.*

29. Ibid., pp. 481-482.

30. *EC* II, pp. 460-461.

31. *Positio super Constitutionibus C.M.F.* II, p. 124.

32. Ibid.

33. Claret to Xifré, August 22, 1862, *EC* II, pp. 519-520.

34. Cf. *Boletín de la Provincia Claretiana de Castilla* 13 (1948): 276-277; *Constituciones y Textos,* pp. 312-314.

35. *Constituciones y Textos,* p. 312.

36. Ibid., pp. 312-313.

37. M. Aguilar, *Historia de la Congregación,* I, p. 11.

38. *Constituciones y Textos,* pp. 308 ff. For further details, cf. C. Fernández, *La Congregación . . . ,* pp. 484-485.

39. Claret to Xifré, January 15, 1863, *EC* II, pp. 612-615.

40. *Positio super Constitutionibus,* II, p. 257.

41. *Annales* 15 (1915): 328-329.

42. Xifré to Claret, November 14, 1869, *Positio super Constitutionibus,* III, p. 339.

43. Claret to Xifré, December 16, 1869, *EC* II, pp. 1437-1440.

44. *Positio super Constitutionibus,* III, p. 406.

45. Ibid., III, pp. 392-393.

46. Ms. Clotet X, p. 77.

47. *Positio super Constitutionibus,* III, p. 339.

48. Ms. Clotet III, p. 356.

49. Xifré to Batlló, December 26, 1890.

50. *Autob.,* nn. 192-198, pp. 72-74; *Constitutions,* 1857, nn. 64-67; 1865, II, nn. 19-20; *Constituciones y Textos,* pp. 205-209, 491.

51. *Autob.,* nn. 192-198, pp. 72-74;

Constitutions, 1857, nn. 68-73; 1865, II, nn. 14-16; *Constituciones y Textos,* pp. 211-215, 485-487.

52. *Constitutions,* 1865, II, nn. 61-62; *Constituciones y Textos,* p. 519.

53. *Espíritu de la Congregación* (Madrid, 1892), pp. 25, 50 ff.

54. *Annales* 38 (1946): 242 ff.

55. Ibid., 19 (1923): 212.

56. Cf. Ibid., 24 (1928): 385-390; 37 (1943): 216 ff., 219 ff.

57. Ibid., 38 (1946): 243-244.

58. Ibid., 33 (1937): 158.

59. Ibid., 46 (1963): 294.

60. Fr. M. Alsina in *Annales* 17 (1920). Fr. N. García in *Annales* 18 (1922): 888-889; 27 (1931): 209; 36 (1940): 103. Fr. P. Schweiger in *Annales* 48 (1965): 236.

61. *Annales* 48 (1965): 236.

NOTES TO CHAPTER VII

1. *Apuntes de un Plan* (Madrid, 1865), p. 6. The entire paragraph was inspired by Bossuet, *Lettre a una demoiselle de Metz.* Cf. *Ouevres Completes,* vol. IX (Paris, 1885), pp. 159-163.

2. Reloj de la Pasión, *Escritos* (Madrid: BAC, 1959), p. 721.

3. *Apuntes de un Plan,* pp. 6-7; *Dos Banderas* (Barcelona, 1870), pp. 22-27.

4. *Autob.,* n. 694, p. 240.

5. Ibid., n. 695, p. 240.

6. Cf. *Escritos,* pp. 497-502.

7. Claret to Gregory XVI, August, 1845, *EC* I, pp. 147-148.

8. Claret to Brunelli, August 12, 1849, *EC* I, pp. 304 ff.

9. Cf. J. M. Cuenca, *La Iglesia Española ante la Revolución Liberal* (Madrid: Rialp, 1971), p. 73.

10. Cf. V. de la Fuente, *Historia Eclesiástica de España* (Barcelona: Librería Religiosa, 1855), III, p. 500 n.

11. *Apuntes de un Plan,* p. 54.

12. *Autob.,* nn. 516-517, 525-528, 535-536, 538-545, pp. 190-201.

13. *Apuntes de un Plan,* pp. 168-169.

14. *Constitutions,* 1857, n. 2; *Constituciones y Textos,* pp. 167-169.

15. *Constitutions,* 1865, I, 2; *Constituciones y Textos,* p. 359.

16. *Positio super Constitutionibus C.M.F.* I, p. 90; II, pp. 221-222.

17. Claret to Nuntius Barilli, February 1, 1864, *EC* II, p. 761, cf. footnote.

18. Claret to Xifré, November 16, 1869, *EC* II, pp. 1429-1432.

19. Claret to Nuntius Brunelli, August 12, 1849, *EC* I, pp. 304 ff.

20. *Reglas para Clérigos* (Barcelona, 1864), pp. 7-8; *Stimulus Episcoporum* (Madrid, 1934), p. 208.

21. *Annales* 38 (1965): 223.

22. Claret to Xifré, October 1, 1857, *EC* I, pp. 1419-1420.

23. *Apuntes de un Plan*, p. 41.

24. *Constitutions,* 1865, I, 2; *Constituciones y Textos,* p. 359.

25. Claret to Xifré, September 17, 1867, *EC* II, pp. 1198 ff.

26. *Constitutions,* 1865, II, 21; *Constituciones y Textos,* p. 493.

27. Cf. *Constituciones y Textos,* p. 493.

28. *L'Egoismo Vinto* (Rome, 1869), pp. 47-52.

29. Claret to Nuntius Brunelli, August 12, 1849, *EC* I, pp. 304 ff.

30. Ms. Claret X, 75-76; *Constituciones y Textos,* p. 602.

31. *Autob.,* n. 695, p. 240.

32. Cf. *Un segle de vida catalana* (Barcelona, 1961), I, pp. 165-166.

33. Cf. the testimony of his sister, María Claret, in PIV, sess. 37.

34. *Autob.,* nn. 66-76, pp. 20-23.

35. Ibid., nn. 563-569, pp. 204-206.

36. Ibid., nn. 717-735, pp. 260-266.

37. J. M. Cuenca, *La Iglesia Española ante la Revolución Liberal* (Madrid: Rialp, 1971), pp. 104-105.

38. *Autob.,* n. 685, p. 238.

39. Ibid., n. 695, p. 240.

40. Claret to Xifré, August 27, 1861, *EC* II, pp. 358-359. Cf. Claret to M. París, August 27, 1861, *EC* II, pp. 360-361.

41. *Autob.,* nn. 563-569, pp. 204-206.

42. Ibid., nn. 729-733, pp. 264-265.

43. Ibid., n. 357, p. 121.

44. Cf. *Constituciones y Textos,* pp. 116-123.

45. Claret to Caixal, September 5, 1849, *EC* I, pp. 314-317.

46. *Reglas para Clérigos* (Barcelona, 1864), pp. 5-6.

NOTES TO CHAPTER VIII

1. *Autob.,* nn. 686-687, p. 239.

2. Ibid., nn. 439-440, p. 141.

3. *Constituciones y Textos,* p. 581.

4. *Autob.,* n. 494, p. 157.

5. *Retreat Resolutions 1862,* n. 8, in *Escritos,* p. 566.

6. *Autob.,* nn. 13-14, p. 7.

7. *Constitutions,* 1865, I, 83-84; *Constituciones y Textos,* p. 441.

8. *Retreat 1849; Constituciones y Textos,* p. 564.

9. *Autob.,* n. 224, p. 80.

10. Ibid., n. 494, p. 157.

11. J. M. Lozano, *Mystic and Man of Action* (Chicago: Claretian Publications, 1977), pp. 119-132, 224-225, 276-278.

12. "Luces y Gracias" 1859, in *Escritos,* pp. 636-637, *Autob.,* nn. 686-687, pp. 238-239.

13. *Constituciones y Textos,* p. 564.

14. *Sermones de Misión,* I, p. 6.

15. Ibid., I, p. 6.

16. *Autob.,* n. 195, p. 73; *Constituciones y Textos,* p. 564.

17. *Revista Católica* 48 (1962 III): 220.

18. *Autob.,* n. 494, p. 157.

19. *Colegial Instruido* (Barcelona, 1861), II, p. 269.

20. *Sermones de Misión,* I, p. 24.

21. Ibid., p. 25.

22. Ibid., p. 25.

23. *Constitutions,* 1857, nn. 54, 69, 71, 83; *Constituciones y Textos,* pp. 197, 211, 213, 227.

24. *Constituciones y Textos,* pp. 205-207.

25. Ibid., pp. 211, 215, 221-223.

26. Ibid., pp. 197, 199, 225.

27. *Constitutions,* 1865, I, 86; *Constituciones y Textos,* p. 443.

28. *Constitutions,* 1865, II, 14, p. 485.

29. Ibid., II, 10, p. 481.

30. Ibid., II, 19, p. 491.

31. Ibid., II, 11, p. 481.

32. Ibid., II, 21, p. 493.

33. *Autob.,* nn. 393-398, pp. 130-132.

34. *Constituciones y Textos,* pp. 563-578.

35. Ibid., pp. 581-606.

36. *Sermones de Misión* (Barcelona, 1858), I, p. 10.

37. Ibid., p. 11.

38. Ibid., p. 12.

39. Cf. Lozano, *Mystic and Man of Action,* p. 279.

40. Ibid., pp. 284-286.

41. Ibid., pp. 224-225.

42. *Autob.,* n. 694, p. 240.

43. *Constitutions,* 1857, nn. 102, 104, 106; *Constitutions,* 1865, I, 94 and II, 33; *Constituciones y Textos,* pp. 241, 451, 503.

44. Appendix 1862; *Constitutions,* 1865, I, 94; *Constituciones y Textos,* pp. 289, 451. Cf. *Constitutions,* 1865, II, 69, p. 523.

45. *Autob.,* nn. 95-98, pp. 28-29. Cf. *Mystic and Man of Action,* pp. 73-81.

46. J. Clotet, *Notas para los Anales,* p. 179.

47. *L'Egoismo vinto* (Rome, 1869), pp. 47 ff.

48. *Constituciones y Textos,* p. 602. We have already dealt with this and the preceding text in Chapter VII.

49. *Escritos,* p. 652. Cf. *Autob.,* p. 328.

50. *Constitutions*, 1865, I, 1, p. 359.

51. *Constitutions*, 1857, n. 1, p. 165.

52. *Annales Congregationis* 15 (1915):191.

53. Document I, n. 2, in *Constituciones y Textos*, p. 33.

54. Collected in *Constituciones y Textos*, pp. 32-123.

55. Ibid., p. 93.

56. Ibid., p. 103.

57. J. M. Lozano, *El Corazón de María en San Antonio M. Claret* (Madrid: Coculsa, 1963), pp. 17-45.

58. Cf. *EC* I, p. 825 n. Also the testimony of Palladius Curríus at Informative Process for Claret's beatification, Tarragona (IPT hereafter), sess. 6.

59. *EC* I, p. 188.

60. Ibid., p. 240.

61. *Anales de la Archicofradía del Smo. e Ido. Corazón de María* (Bilbao, 1845-46), I, pp. 50 and 112; II, pp. 152 and 203. The Saint used this issue in compiling his *Brief Notice* in 1847.

62. *Breu Noticia*, pp. 47-48; Claret to Caixal, August 2, 1847, and January 1, 1848, *EC* I, pp. 234, 261.

63. "Carto a un devoto," in *Escritos*, pp. 766-772.

64. *Religiosas en sus Casas* (Barcelona: Librería Religiosa, 1850), p. 3.

65. *Autob.*, n. 357, p. 121.

66. Ibid., n. 315, p. 109.

67. Cf. *Autob.*, nn. 674-700, pp. 236-241; *Escritos*, pp. 628-651.

68. J. M. Lozano, *Mystic and Man of Action*, pp. 55-69.

69. *Autob.*, nn. 192-198, pp. 72-74.

70. Ibid., n. 195, p. 73.

71. *Constitutions*, 1865, I, 2, p. 359.

72. *Constitutions*, 1857, nn. 64-67; *Constitutions*, 1865, II, 19-20; *Constituciones y Textos*, pp. 205-209, 491.

73. *Constituciones y Textos*, pp. 599-601.

74. J. M. Lozano, *Mystic and Man of Action*, pp. 167-183.

75. "Retreat Resolutions," 1859, n. 5, in *Escritos*, p. 556.

76. *Autob.*, nn. 264-265, p. 94.

77. *Sermones de Misión*, I, p. 10.

78. *Constituciones y Textos*, p. 578.

79. Ibid., p. 583.

80. Claret to Caixal, September 5, 1849, *EC* I, p. 316.

81. C. Fernández, *El Beato Padre Claret* (Madrid: Coculsa, 1949), I, pp. 337, 382, 1000.

82. *Constitutions*, 1857, nn. 99, 101; *Constitutions*, 1865, II, 31; *Constituciones y Textos*, pp. 239, 501.

83. Xifré to Vallier, October 5, 1870, Gen. Archives C.M.F., Rome.

84. *Autob.*, n. 486, pp. 154-155.

85. Ibid., n. 359, pp. 121-122.

86. Ibid., nn. 360-361, p. 122.

87. Testimony of Don Carmelo Sala, IPT, sess. 6.

88. *Apuntes de un Plan,* 1865, pp. 83, 181.

89. *Avisos a un sacerdote,* 1844, p. 7; *Autob.,* n. 133, p. 55; *Colegial Instruido,* 1861, II, p. 112; *Apuntes de un Plan,* 1865, p. 45; "Notas del Concilio," in *Escritos,* p. 474.

90. *Religiosas en sus Casas,* 1850, p. 121.

91. *Santa Mónica,* 1883, p. 16; *Dos Banderas,* 1871, p. 62.

92. *Autob.,* n. 431; p. 140; *Colegial Instruido,* 1861, II, p. 486; *Constitutions,* 1865, II, 14, p. 485; *Vocación de Niños,* 1864, p. 70.

93. *Constitutions,* 1865, II, 14, p. 485.

94. Claret to Curríus, October 2, 1869, *EC* II, p. 1423.

95. *Constitutions,* 1857, nn. 68-73, p. 125; *Constitutions,* 1865, II, 14-16, pp. 211-217, 247, 485-487.

96. *Constituciones y Textos,* pp. 596-598.

97. *Autob.,* nn. 357-371.

98. Claret to Xifré, October 1, 1857; May 7, 1858; November 30, 1858; September 17, 1867; January 24, 1869; *EC* I, pp. 1419, 1572, 1679; II, pp. 1198, 1346-1347.

99. Claret to Caixal, September 5, 1849, *EC* I, p. 316.

100. *Constitutions,* 1857, n. 68; *Constitutions,* 1865, II, 14; *Constituciones y Textos,* pp. 211, 485.

101. *Constitutions,* 1857, n. 68, p. 211.

102. Ibid., n. 73, p. 215.

103. *Constitutions,* 1865, II, 15, p. 485.

104. *Constitutions,* 1857, nn. 67-70; 1865, II, 16, pp. 211-213, 487.

105. Claret to Xifré, November 30, 1858, *EC* I, pp. 1079-1080.

106. "Notas sobre la Congregación," VII, in *Constituciones y Textos,* pp. 631-632.

107. After the founder's death, the General Chapter of 1876, in view of the fact that they were unable to create a fund for independent financing apart from the ministry, declared that the missionaries might accept what was spontaneously offered them for their services. Cf. Acta of the General Chapter of 1876, sess. 5, p. 8.

108. *Autob.,* nn. 116-117, pp. 48-49.

109. Ibid., nn. 215-219, pp. 78-79.

110. Ibid., n. 222, p. 80.

111. Ibid., n. 223, p. 80.

112. Ibid., n. 224, p. 80.

113. Ibid., n. 494, p. 157.

114. Ibid., nn. 390-427, pp. 130-139.

115. *Constitutions,* 1865, II, 3-5, 10-11, pp. 473-475, 481.

116. J. M. Lozano, *Mystic and Man of Action,* pp. 156-157.

117. Claret derived these norms from J. Petitdidier's *Exercitia Spiritualia* (Prague, 1775), p. 89. They had already been generalized, around 1660, by the French Oratorian Tronson, in his *Examens Particuliers,* cf. 1811, ed. p. 100, which had a great influence on priestly spirituality.

NOTES TO CHAPTER IX

1. Unfortunately, a critical biography of Fr. Xifré has not yet been written. M. Aguilar, his enthusiastic admirer, began to write one, in the same style as the one he had dedicated to Fr. Clotet, but he had to interrupt it after completing Chapter VII, up to the 1868 revolution. Cf. *Biografía del Revmo. P. José Xifré y Musach...:* Archives of the Claretian Generalate, Rome, B.A. 3.13.

2. Testimony of Fr. Armengol Coll in P. Luna, *Vida del P. Xifré,* p. 26.

3. Catalogue C.M.F., 1900, p. 110.

4. Cf. Acts of the canonical visitation by Fr. Xifré to the house of Segovia, Arch. C.M.F. F.B. 1.4.

5. Xifré to the Nuntius in Madrid, September 1862, Arch. C.M.F. B.A. 2.5.

6. *Espíritu de la Congregación* (Vich, 1867), p. 1.

7. Circular Letters, January 30, 1880 (six mentions); April 11, 1887; November 5, 1890; October 23, 1891.

8. Claret to Xifré, May 7, 1858, *EC* I, p. 1571.

9. Cf. Claret to Xifré, August 4, 1858, and October 15, 1858, *EC* II, pp. 1625-1626, 1653.

10. Claret to Xifré, September 12, 1869, *EC* II, p. 1417.

11. Claret to Xifré, May 14, 1870, *EC* II, p. 1467.

12. Claret to Xifré, July 11, 1867, *EC* II, p. 1172.

13. Cf. Letters, Fr. Reig, O.M. Arch. Gral. C.M.F. B.M. 9.4.

14. Cf. Acts visitation Segovia, April 15, 1864, Arch. C.M.F. F.B. 1.4(7).

15. *Constituciones y Textos,* p. 310.

16. Acts visitation Segovia, April 15, 1864, pp. 6 and 9, Arch. C.M.F. 1.4.

17. Claret to Xifré, August 22, 1862; January 15, 1863; *EC* II, pp. 520, 612.

18. Claret to Xifré, January 30, 1862; July 20, 1862; *EC* II, pp. 435, 494-495. Concerning the celebration of the feast of the Heart of Mary in the Claretian Congregation, cf. Claret to Xifré, October 15, 1858, *EC* I, p. 1655; September 2, 1863, *EC* II, p. 696.

19. Claret to Clotet, July 1, 1861, *EC* II, p. 321.

20. Claret to Xifré, April 7, 1859, *EC* I, p. 1746.

21. Circular Letters, October 23, 1891; September 27, 1891; *Circulares* 1892, pp. 117, 141-142. *Espíritu de la Congregación,* ed. 2 (Madrid, 1892), pp. 9 ff., 22, 35.

22. Circular Letters, October 10, 1886; April 11, 1887; September 26, 1888; September 27, 1881; *Circulares,* pp. 31-33, 34-37, 37-38, 141-142. *Espíritu de la Congregación,* pp. 25-26.

23. M. Aguilar, *Historia de la Congregación,* I, pp. 656-657.

24. Claret to Xifré, July 16, 1869, *EC* II, pp. 1406-1408.

25. *Constituciones y Textos*, p. 633.

26. Entry of July 12, 1882, Ms. Clotet V, 660.

27. Cf. M. Aguilar, *Biografía del S. de D.P. Jaime Clotet* (Barcelona: Montserrat, 1907), pp. 276-277.

28. Testimony of Bro. Mariano Hernansanz in PIV, *Summarium*, p. 18.

29. Cf. J. Clotet, *Notas para los Anales*, pp. 1 ff. *Summarium*, p. 43, M. Aguilar, *Biografía*, pp. 46-47.

30. Ms. Clotet X, 130. Cf. J. M. Lozano, *Un Hombre en la Presencia de Dios, Estudio sobre la experiencia espiritual del S. de D.P. Jaime Clotet* (Rome, 1971), pp. 227, 240.

31. Ibid., pp. 227, 240.

32. Cf. Fr. Xifré's judgment on this in C. Fernández, *La Congregación ...*, p. 113.

33. Claret to Clotet, July 1, 1861, *EC* II, p. 320.

34. Cf. Clotet's resolutions, September 1, 1865, in *Un Hombre en la Presencia de Dios*, p. 253.

35. Ibid., p. 253.

36. Cf. Cause of Beatification, *Summarium*, pp. 9, 19, 26, 77. The testimonies of the process are abundantly confirmed by the sketches of Clotet's conferences kept in his manuscripts.

37. *Un Hombre en la Presencia de Dios*, p. 229.

38. Ibid., p. 230.

39. Ibid., pp. 326-327.

40. Ibid., p. 238.

41. Ibid., pp. 237-238.

42. Ibid., pp. 239, 243.

43. *Constituciones y Textos*, pp. 663-690.

44. M. Aguilar, *Biografía del P. Jaime Clotet*, p. 301. *Summarium*, p. 14.

45. Ms. Clotet III, 190-191.

46. Ms. Clotet IV, 208; V, 80-81, 124, 148, 194.

47. M. Aguilar, *Biografía*, pp. 302-323.

48. Ms. Clotet III, 340.

Bibliography

Sources

Annales Congregationis C.M.F. I (1889). Published as *Boletín Religioso de la Congregación* in 1885-1888.

Circular Letters of the Superiors General.

Colección de las Circulares publicadas por el R. P. José Xifré...desde 1885 hasta 1892. Madrid: Sales, 1892. 195 pp.

Colección de Circulares. Madrid: Coculsa, 1941. 866 pp.

Para formar apóstoles. Published by Fr. Nicolas García. Edited by José M. Mesa, C.M.F. Madrid: Coculsa, 1964. 427 pp.

Claret, Saint Anthony M. *Autobiography.* Edited by José M. Viñas, C.M.F. Translated by Joseph Daries, C.M.F. Chicago: Claretian Publications, 1976.

————. *Constituciones y Textos sobre la Congregación de Misioneros.* Edited by Juan M. Lozano, C.M.F. Barcelona: Editorial Claret, 1972.

————. *Epistolario Claretiano.* 2 vols. Edited by José M. Gil, C.M.F. Madrid: Coculsa, 1970.

————. *Escritos Autobiográficos y Espirituales.* Madrid: BAC, 1959.

Clotet, James, C.M.F. *Anales de la Congregación.* General Archives C.M.F., Rome.

A series of notes on the origin and early history of the Claretian Congregation, disseminated throughout his manuscripts and partially collected in a volume.

————. *Directori dels Hermanos Ajudants.* Vich, Spain: Ll. Anglada, 1858. 95 pp.

————. *Resumen de la admirable vida del Excmo. e Ilmo. Sr. Don Antonio M. Claret y Clará.* Barcelona: Librería Religiosa, 1882. French translation: *Abrégé de la vie admirable de M. D. Antoine-M. Claret et Clará.* Amiens: Delattre-Denoël, 1884.

————. *Vida edificante y admirable del Excmo. e Ilmo. Sr. D. Antonio M. Claret.* Manuscript, 7 vols.

General Chapters C.M.F. Acta, General Archives C.M.F. Rome.

Lozano, Juan M. *Ensayo de Bibliografía Crítica Claretiana.* Rome: Studium Claretianum, 1962.

Positio super Constitutionibus C.M.F. (Dossier regarding the approval of the Congregation and its Constitutions.) Archives S. Congregation for the Religious. The Vatican.

Processus (Informativus et Apostolicus) Beatificationis et Canonizationis S. D. Antonii M. Claret, Archiepiscopi. Acta. in Archives of the S. Congregation for the Causes of the Saints. The Vatican.

Processus (Informativus et Apostolicus) Beatificationis et Canonizationis S. D. Iacobi Clotet. Acta, in Archives of the S. Congregation for the Causes of the Saints. The Vatican.

Xifré, José, C.M.F. *Colección de las Circulares publicadas por el R. P. José Xifré...desde 1885 hasta 1892.* Madrid: Sales, 1982. 195 pp.

———. "Crónica de la Congregación." In *Annales Congregationis C.M.F.* 15 (1915).

———. *Espíritu de la Congregación.* 1st ed., Vich, 1867; 2d ed., Madrid, 1892.

———. Several minor documents, included in *Constituciones y Textos,* are cited in the Notes to Chapters.

Studies

Aguilar, Mariano, C.M.F. *Biografía del S. de D. P. Jaime Clotet y Fabrés.* Barcelona: Montserrat, 1907. 491 pp.

———. *Biografía del Revmo. P. José Xifré y Musach.* Mss. General Archives C.M.F. Rome B.A. 3.13.

———. *Historia de la Congregación de Misioneros.* Barcelona, 1901. Vol. 1, 718 pp. Vol. 2, 438 pp.

Fernández, Cristóbal, C.M.F. *La Congregación de Misioneros Hijos del Inmaculado Corazón de María.* Vol. 1 (1849-1970). Madrid, 1967. 780 pp.

Lozano, Juan M. *Con mi Iglesia te desposaré. Estudio sobre la experiencia religiosa de la M. Antonia París.* Madrid, 1974. 320 pp.

———. *El Corazón de María en San Antonio M. Claret.* Madrid: Coculsa, 1963. 286 pp.

———. *Un hombre en la presencia de Dios. Estudio sobre la experiencia espiritual de Siervo de Dios, P. Jaime Clotet.* Rome, 1971. 341 pp.

———. *Misión y Espíritu del Claretiano en la Iglesia.* Rome, 1967. 470 pp.

———. *Mystic and Man of Action.* Translated by Joseph Daries. Chicago: Claretian Publications, 1977. Cf. *Un Místico de la Acción.* Madrid: Coculsa, 1964.